THE STATE OF HEALTH ATLAS

THE
STATE OF HEALTH
ATLAS

Judith Mackay

A PLUTO PROJECT

SIMON & SCHUSTER

LONDON·SYDNEY·NEW YORK·TOKYO·SINGAPORE·TORONTO

First published in Great Britain by
Simon and Schuster Ltd in 1993
A Paramount Communications Company

Text copyright © 1993 Judith Mackay
Maps and graphics copyright © 1993 Swanston Publishing Limited

Simon & Schuster Ltd
West Garden Place
Kendal Street
London W2 2AQ

Simon & Schuster of Australia Pty Ltd
Sydney

Published in USA by
Simon & Schuster Inc.
Simon & Schuster Building
Rockefeller Center
1230 Avenue of the Americas
New York, NY 10020

Coordinated by Anne Benewick for
Swanston Publishing Limited, Derby and London

Editorial Consultant: Michael Kidron

Edited by Anne Benewick and Philip Boys
with Cathy Jones
Production: Alex de Berry

Maps created by Swanston Graphics Limited, Derby, England
Artwork and design by Isabelle Lewis, Andrew Bright,
Andrea Fairbrass, Jeanne Radford and Malcolm Swanston

Printed and bound in Hong Kong
Produced by Mandarin Offset Ltd.

10 9 8 7 6 5 4 3 2 1
10 9 8 7 6 5 4 3 2 1 Pbk

A CIP catalogue record for this book is available from the British Library
ISBN 0-671-71151-2 pbk
ISBN 0-671-71147-4 hbk

CONTENTS

INTRODUCTION

'A state of complete physical, mental and social well-being, not merely the absence of disease or infirmity' is the way that health is defined by the World Health Organization, which also states that the enjoyment of the highest attainable standard of health is one of the fundamental rights of every human without distinction of race, religion, political belief or economic or social condition. This book illustrates that these ideals are a long way from fulfilment.

It is difficult to measure health and well-being and only ill-defined and subjective parameters are available. The very word 'health' is often confused with sickness; for example, 'health services' usually refer to the provision of curative medical care.

Nor is it always easy to measure sickness even by using self-determined feelings of being unwell. Scientific advances make it more and more difficult to define sickness. If someone is carrying potentially harmful bacteria like tuberculosis or a virus like AIDS but has not yet developed any symptoms, is that person 'healthy' or 'sick'? Likewise, should an apparently well person be considered unhealthy if they carry a potentially damaging gene or have a medical condition that makes them predisposed to a later illness? Will the growing science of genetics create a whole new range of people to be classified as 'unhealthy'?

Global health has little to do with doctors and hospitals. The basic determinants of health are nutritious food, adequate shelter, clean water, elementary education (especially of women), being a non-smoker, and having access to low-cost, low-tech primary and preventive health services, which include immunization and family planning. Almost one third of the world's population live in poverty and their health is correspondingly poor: people living in poor countries (especially in Africa) have the shortest life expectancy, the highest infant and child mortality, the least adequate nutrition, the least education, the least immunization and the highest fertility.

The common modalities to all health systems are few: a belief in that particular health system, rest, and the feeling of being cared for. These are the fundamentals of health care throughout the world. Voltaire once said that the art of medicine consists of amusing the patient while nature cures the disease.

Most people in the world have no regular access to 'Western' medicine. In general, traditional health systems are local, largely unrecorded, and are tested by time. Not surprisingly, there are no reliable data available for traditional health systems.

Although the data derived from demographic surveys, for example, life expectancy and population size, are comprehensive and readily available from the UN agencies, health statistics are much more difficult to obtain. Even when they are available, they are only as good as the quality and coverage achieved by a country's own health information system. Poor countries with poor health systems provide the least reliable data. This is not necessarily a criticism. Many are grappling with other serious problems. However, on some maps, rich countries with good data collection may erroneously appear to have comparatively more severe health problems. Readers must interpret data with caution, particularly from countries in sub-

Saharan Africa. The World Health Organization has made a plea for all countries to use the WHO criteria and collect standardized data.

It was also difficult to obtain data for the newly emergent states in Europe, but in some cases the absence of data means there is no perceived problem and therefore action is thought unnecessary. Violence, tobacco-related deaths and motor vehicle accidents are still not regarded as public health problems in many countries and data are not collected.

The international agencies have a special responsibility to support efforts of many countries to develop robust, simple, sustainable and affordable health information systems. Even when statistics are available, they are often not comparable between countries – the population sample may be different, for example, diverse age groups may be used; and exposure definitions, for example in relation to smoking and alcohol, vary from country to country. Some of the shortcomings of health statistics may have been redressed before the next edition of this atlas. Meanwhile, readers' contributions would be welcome.

Health takes a back seat to poverty, famine or war. But success stories emerge: life expectancy in the world has steadily increased from an average of 47 years in 1950 to 66 years today; even in poor countries it has improved from 42 years to 63 years (see **6. Three Score Years and Ten**). The immunization programme (see **35. Catching Them Young**) has saved the lives and improved the well-being of millions of children in the world. China's success in only 40 years in making health care available to over one billion people (increasing life expectancy from 41 years to 71 years in the process) is a model for poor countries (see **29. A Stitch in Time**).

But the health of the world, with its concomitant improvement in economic advancement, education and family size, will only improve when two things happen: governments deem health a priority and they focus that priority on prevention rather than cure. With political commitment, global health can improve.

Dr Judith Longstaff Mackay
October 1992

ACKNOWLEDGEMENTS

Particular thanks are due to four colleagues. Dr Alan Lopez, medical statistician with the World Health Organization, was wholeheartedly enthusiastic and encouraging. He directed me towards data sources and kept the book firmly on track with the use of these data. Professor Richard Peto of the University of Oxford added penetrating and pertinent comments, and gave welcome assistance on many of the early drafts. Dr Rory Collins, Clinical Trial Service Unit, University of Oxford, helped and advised on data sources, especially in relation to mortality and morbidity data, and was generous with his time in reviewing the final draft. Dr Derek Yach of the Medical Research Council in South Africa added very helpful advice and assistance, principally on data quality.

I would especially like to thank three people who helped on the editorial side. Anne Benewick acted as editor, guide, adviser and friend. Her experience and sound judgement were truly invaluable. Philip Boys added creative input and made many constructive suggestions. Michael Kidron gave freely of his expertise as an established author of other books in the series, and added humour and perceptive comments during the writing.

Another sincere acknowledgement is to my husband John, whose comments proved invaluable and who gave me total, unremitting support for this project. I am also grateful to Andrew and Richard Mackay, Mrs Margaret Longstaff and Lucy Abenoja for assisting in the checking and rechecking of the 20,000 statistics involved.

CONTRIBUTORS
I am very grateful to several people, listed below, who provided the data for individual maps:

Philip Boys, London: 8. The Elements
Lesley Doyal, University of the West Country, Bath, UK: 10. Personal Violence
Lelia Duley, National Perinatal Epidemiology Unit, Radcliffe Infirmary, Oxford: 3. The Perils of Pregnancy
John Jackson and Anthony Webster, Monitoring and Assessment Research Centre, King's College, University of London: 14. Air and Water
Penny Kane, Family Planning Federation of Australia : 2. Birth Counts
Michael Kidron, London: 5. A Picture of Health?
Barrie Lambert, Department of Radiobiology, St Bartholomew's Hospital, London: 32. Contrasting Fortunes
Alison Macfarlane, National Perinatal Epidemiology Unit, Radcliffe Infirmary, Oxford: 4. The First Year Milestone
Harriet Muir Moxham and Lesley A. Rogers, Policy Research in Science and Medicine, The Wellcome Trust, London: 34. Training and Research
Dan Smith, Transnational Institute, Amsterdam and International Peace Research Institute, Oslo: 9. The Costs of War

Many others who provided data or helped with individual maps are acknowledged on page 88 or within the Notes to the Maps, starting on page 89.

Final thanks go to Alex de Berry and Cathy Jones of Swanston Publishing, who assisted with the maps and book production; and to designers Isabelle Lewis and Andrew Bright of Swanston Graphics.

J.M.

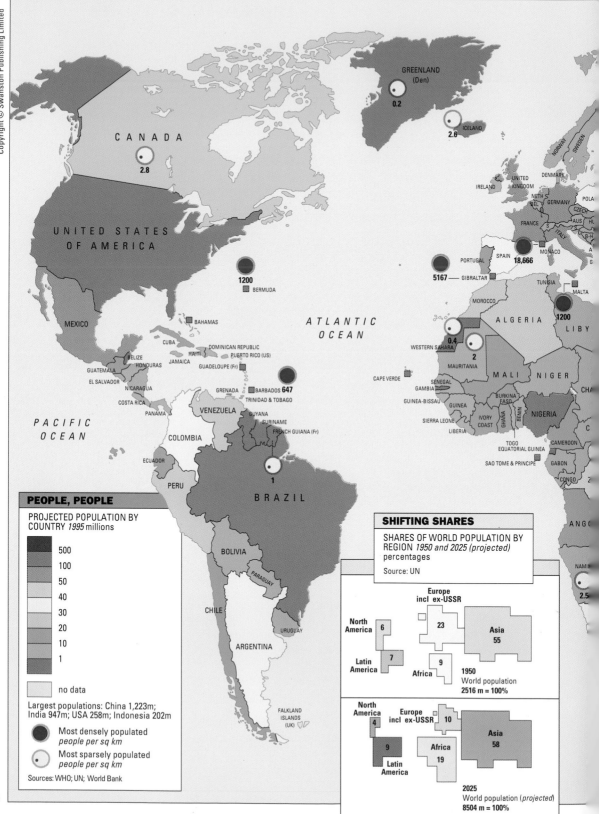

GREENLAND
(Den)
0.2

ICELAND
2.6

C A N A D A
2.8

UNITED STATES
OF AMERICA

NORWAY
SWEDEN
IRELAND
UNITED KINGDOM
DENMARK
NETH
BEL
GERMANY
POLA
CZECH
AUS
HL
FRANCE
S
ITALY
MONACO
G
B-H
PORTUGAL
SPAIN
18,666
5167
GIBRALTAR
TUNISIA
MALTA
1200
MOROCCO
ALGERIA
LIBY

1200
BERMUDA

MEXICO

BAHAMAS

CUBA
DOMINICAN REPUBLIC
HAITI
PUERTO RICO (US)
BELIZE
JAMAICA
GUADELOUPE (Fr)
GUATEMALA
HONDURAS
EL SALVADOR
NICARAGUA
GRENADA
BARBADOS 647
COSTA RICA
TRINIDAD & TOBAGO
PANAMA

A T L A N T I C
O C E A N

WESTERN SAHARA
0.4
2
MAURITANIA
CAPE VERDE
SENEGAL
GAMBIA
GUINEA-BISSAU
GUINEA
SIERRA LEONE
IVORY COAST
GHANA
BENIN
LIBERIA
TOGO
EQUATORIAL GUINEA
SAO TOME & PRINCIPE
GABON
CONGO
MALI
NIGER
CHA
BURKINA FASO
NIGERIA
CAMEROON
C

VENEZUELA
GUYANA
SURINAME
FRENCH GUIANA (Fr)

COLOMBIA

ECUADOR

PERU

P A C I F I C
O C E A N

B R A Z I L
1

BOLIVIA

PARAGUAY

CHILE

URUGUAY

ARGENTINA

FALKLAND
ISLANDS
(UK)

A N G O

NAMI
2.5

PEOPLE, PEOPLE

PROJECTED POPULATION BY
COUNTRY *1995* millions

500
100
50
40
30
20
10
1

no data

Largest populations: China 1,223m;
India 947m; USA 258m; Indonesia 202m

Most densely populated
people per sq km

Most sparsely populated
people per sq km

Sources: WHO; UN; World Bank

SHIFTING SHARES

SHARES OF WORLD POPULATION BY
REGION *1950 and 2025 (projected)*
percentages

Source: UN

Europe
incl ex-USSR

North
America
6

23

Asia
55

Latin
America
7

Africa
9

1950
World population
2516 m = 100%

North
America
4

Europe
incl ex-USSR
10

Asia
58

Latin
America
9

Africa
19

2025
World population (*projected*)
8504 m = 100%

There are over 5 billion people in the world. In 30 years there will be another 3 billion. 95 percent of this increase will be in poor countries. Where on earth are they going to live?

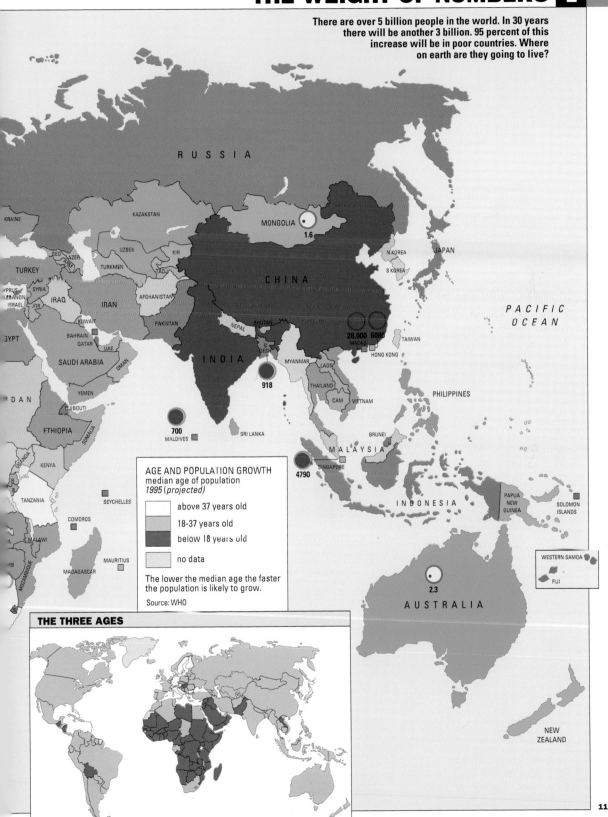

AGE AND POPULATION GROWTH
median age of population
1995 (projected)

- above 37 years old
- 18-37 years old
- below 18 years old
- no data

The lower the median age the faster the population is likely to grow.

Source: WHO

THE THREE AGES

GREENLAND
(Den)

ICELAND

C A N A D A

NORWAY

SWEDEN

DENMARK

IRELAND

UNITED
KINGDOM

NETH
BEL

GERMANY

CZECH

POL

UNITED STATES
OF AMERICA

FRANCE

S

AUS

ITALY

H

Form

PORTUGAL

SPAIN

TUNISIA

MEXICO

BAHAMAS

ATLANTIC
OCEAN

MOROCCO

ALGERIA

LIBY

CUBA

WESTERN SAHARA

DOMINICAN REPUBLIC

HAITI

PUERTO RICO (US)

BELIZE

JAMAICA

GUADELOUPE (Fr)

CAPE VERDE

MAURITANIA

MALI

NIGER

GUATEMALA

HONDURAS

SENEGAL

EL SALVADOR

GAMBIA

NICARAGUA

BARBADOS

GUINEA-BISSAU

GUINEA

BURKINA
FASO

BENIN

NIGERIA

COSTA RICA

TRINIDAD & TOBAGO

SIERRA LEONE

IVORY
COAST

GHANA

CH

PANAMA

VENEZUELA

GUYANA

LIBERIA

TOGO

C A

PACIFIC
OCEAN

COLOMBIA

SURINAME

FRENCH GUIANA (Fr)

CAMEROON

EQUATORIAL GUINEA

ECUADOR

SAO TOME & PRINCIPE

GABON

CONGO

PERU

BRAZIL

ANG

BOLIVIA

PARAGUAY

NAMI

CHILE

URUGUAY

ARGENTINA

FALKLAND ISLANDS
(UK)

FERTILITY

AVERAGE NUMBER OF BIRTHS
DURING A WOMAN'S LIFETIME
Women of childbearing age *1990*

7
6
5
4
3
2

no data

Highest: Rwanda 8.1; Yemen 7.7;
Malawi 7.6

Lowest: Hong Kong, Italy 1.4; Austria,
Denmark, Germany, Switzerland 1.5

Source: UNICEF

CONTRACEPTION

ACCESS TO CONTRACEPTIVES *1990*

none or limited range
of methods available

a quarter or more of couples
practising contraception use
traditional methods

Sources: PRB; IPPF

Data compiled by Penny Kane

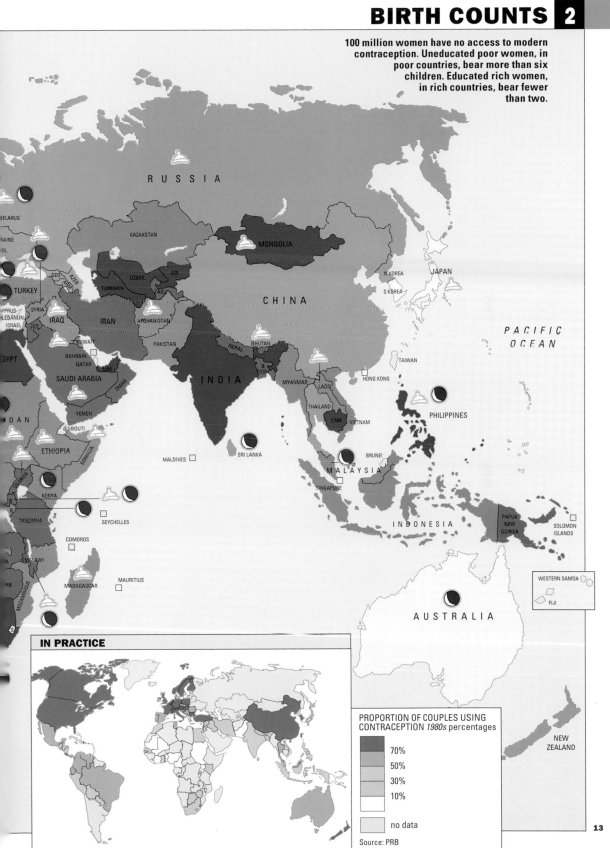

100 million women have no access to modern contraception. Uneducated poor women, in poor countries, bear more than six children. Educated rich women, in rich countries, bear fewer than two.

RUSSIA

BELARUS

RAINE
OL

TURKEY

KAZAKSTAN

MONGOLIA

JAPAN

N.KOREA

S.KOREA

PACIFIC
OCEAN

GEO
AZER

UZBEK
KIR

TURKMEN
TAJ

CYPRUS
LEBANON
ISRAEL
JOD

SYRIA

IRAQ

IRAN

AFGHANISTAN

CHINA

GYPT

KUWAIT
BAHRAIN
QATAR
UAE

SAUDI ARABIA

OMAN

YEMEN

DJIBOUTI

DAN

ETHIOPIA

SOMALIA

PAKISTAN

NEPAL
BHUTAN

B
DESH

INDIA

MYANMAR

LAOS

THAILAND

CAM
VIETNAM

MALDIVES

SRI LANKA

BRUNEI

MALAYSIA

SINGAPORE

TAIWAN

HONG KONG

PHILIPPINES

KENYA

TANZANIA

SEYCHELLES

COMOROS

MALAWI

MB

MOZAMBIQUE

MADAGASCAR

MAURITIUS

INDONESIA

PAPUA
NEW
GUINEA

SOLOMON
ISLANDS

AUSTRALIA

WESTERN SAMOA

FIJI

NEW
ZEALAND

IN PRACTICE

PROPORTION OF COUPLES USING
CONTRACEPTION *1980s* percentages

70%
50%
30%
10%

no data

Source: PRB

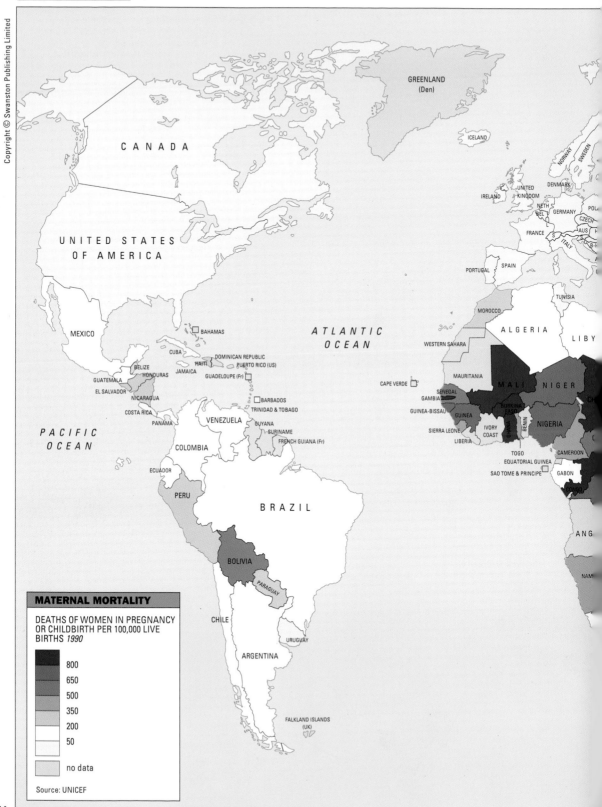

GREENLAND
(Den)

ICELAND

C A N A D A

NORWAY   SWEDEN

IRELAND   UNITED
KINGDOM   DENMARK

U N I T E D   S T A T E S
O F   A M E R I C A

NETH
BEL   GERMANY   POL

CZECH
FRANCE   S   AUS   H

ITALY

PORTUGAL   SPAIN

MEXICO

BAHAMAS

ATLANTIC
OCEAN

MOROCCO

TUNISIA

A L G E R I A   L I B Y

WESTERN SAHARA

CUBA

DOMINICAN REPUBLIC
PUERTO RICO (US)

BELIZE
HONDURAS
GUATEMALA
EL SALVADOR
NICARAGUA

HAITI
JAMAICA   GUADELOUPE (Fr)

MAURITANIA

CAPE VERDE

M A L I   N I G E R   CH

SENEGAL
GAMBIA

GUINEA-BISSAU

BARBADOS
TRINIDAD & TOBAGO

GUINEA

BURKINA
FASO
GHANA
BENIN
NIGERIA

COSTA RICA
PANAMA

VENEZUELA

GUYANA
SURINAME
FRENCH GUIANA (Fr)

SIERRA LEONE
LIBERIA

IVORY
COAST

TOGO
CAMEROON

PACIFIC
OCEAN

COLOMBIA

EQUATORIAL GUINEA
SAO TOME & PRINCIPE   GABON

ECUADOR

CONGO

PERU

B R A Z I L

A N G

NAM

BOLIVIA

PARAGUAY

MATERNAL MORTALITY

CHILE

URUGUAY

DEATHS OF WOMEN IN PREGNANCY
OR CHILDBIRTH PER 100,000 LIVE
BIRTHS *1990*

ARGENTINA

800

650

500

350

200

50

FALKLAND ISLANDS
(UK)

no data

Source: UNICEF

Data compiled by Lelia Duley

In rich countries, deaths in pregnancy and childbirth are now rare. Elsewhere they can rise to as much as a third of all deaths among women during their reproductive years.

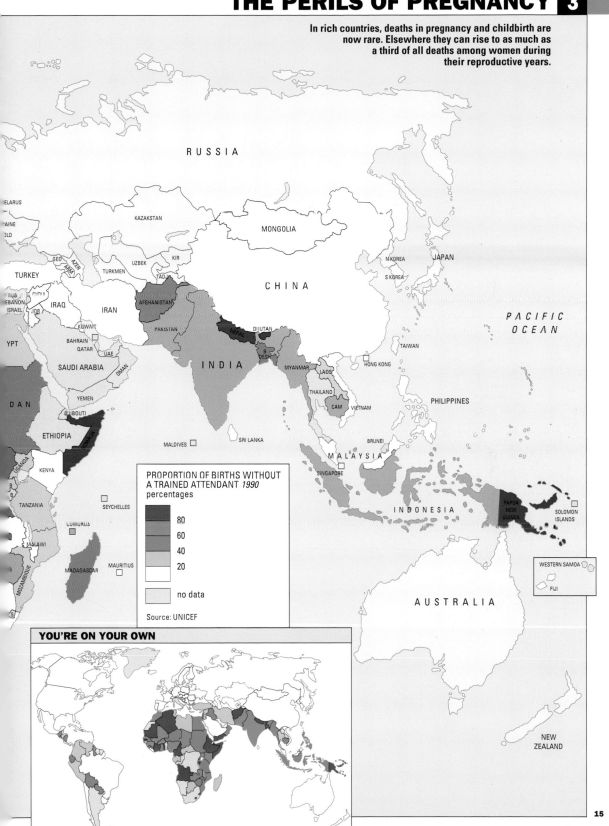

RUSSIA

BELARUS
UKRAINE
MOLD
KAZAKSTAN
MONGOLIA
GEO
AZER
ARM
UZBEK
TURKMEN
KIR
TADJ
TURKEY
SYRIA
LEBANON
ISRAEL
IRAQ
JOR
KUWAIT
BAHRAIN
QATAR
UAE
EGYPT
SAUDI ARABIA
OMAN
YEMEN
DJIBOUTI
SUDAN
ETHIOPIA
SOMALIA
UGANDA
KENYA
TANZANIA
MALAWI
MOZAMBIQUE
MADAGASCAR
COMOROS
SEYCHELLES
MAURITIUS

IRAN
AFGHANISTAN
PAKISTAN
NEPAL
BHUTAN
B DESH
INDIA
MYANMAR
MALDIVES
SRI LANKA

CHINA
N KOREA
S KOREA
JAPAN
TAIWAN
HONG KONG
LAOS
THAILAND
CAM
VIETNAM
PHILIPPINES

PACIFIC OCEAN

MALAYSIA
SINGAPORE
BRUNEI
INDONESIA
PAPUA NEW GUINEA
SOLOMON ISLANDS
WESTERN SAMOA
FIJI
AUSTRALIA
NEW ZEALAND

PROPORTION OF BIRTHS WITHOUT A TRAINED ATTENDANT *1990*
percentages

- 80
- 60
- 40
- 20

no data

Source: UNICEF

YOU'RE ON YOUR OWN

GREENLAND
(Den)

CANADA

UNITED STATES
OF AMERICA

ICELAND

NORWAY SWEDEN

IRELAND UNITED
KINGDOM

DENMARK

NETH GERMANY POL
BEL
CZECH
FRANCE AUS
S
ITALY Port

PORTUGAL SPAIN

MEXICO

BAHAMAS

CUBA

BELIZE
GUATEMALA HONDURAS
EL SALVADOR
NICARAGUA
COSTA RICA
PANAMA

DOMINICAN REPUBLIC
HAITI PUERTO RICO (US)
JAMAICA
GUADELOUPE (Fr)

BARBADOS
TRINIDAD & TOBAGO

VENEZUELA GUYANA
SURINAME
FRENCH GUIANA (Fr)
COLOMBIA

ECUADOR

PERU

BOLIVIA

BRAZIL

PARAGUAY

CHILE

URUGUAY

ARGENTINA

FALKLAND ISLANDS
(UK)

ATLANTIC
OCEAN

PACIFIC
OCEAN

TUNISIA

MOROCCO

WESTERN SAHARA

ALGERIA

LIBY

CAPE VERDE

MAURITANIA

MALI NIGER

SENEGAL
GAMBIA
GUINEA-BISSAU GUINEA
SIERRA LEONE
LIBERIA
IVORY
COAST

BURKINA
FASO

CH

GHANA

NIGERIA

TOGO

CA

CAMEROON

EQUATORIAL GUINEA

SAO TOME & PRINCIPE

GABON

CONGO

AN

NAI

INFANT MORTALITY 1990

DEATHS IN THE FIRST YEAR OF LIFE
PER 1000 LIVE BIRTHS *1990*

- 10
- 25
- 50
- 75
- 150

no data

Sources: UNICEF, UNDP

DANGER

LOW BIRTHWEIGHT
1980s where known

1 in 5 or more babies born
with seriously low weight

Sources: UNICEF, UNDP

Data compiled by: Alison Macfarlane

Babies are particularly vulnerable at birth and during their first year. In rich countries up to one in a hundred babies dies in the first year of life. In most African and some Asian countries, as many as one in ten do so.

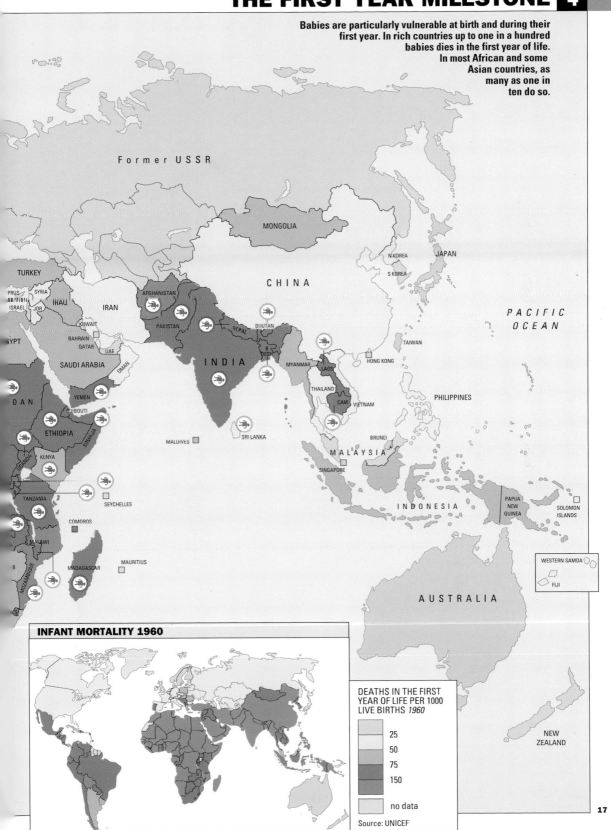

Former USSR

MONGOLIA

TURKEY

PRUS
SYRIA
ISRAEL
JOR
IRAU
EYPT
KUWAIT
BAHRAIN
QATAR
UAE
OMAN
SAUDI ARABIA
D A N
YEMEN
DJIBOUTI
ETHIOPIA
SOMALIA
UGANDA
KENYA
TANZANIA
COMOROS
MALAWI
MOZAMBIQUE
MADAGASCAR
MAURITIUS
SEYCHELLES

IRAN

AFGHANISTAN

PAKISTAN

I N D I A

NEPAL
BHUTAN
B DESH
MYANMAR

SRI LANKA

MALDIVES

C H I N A

N KOREA
S KOREA

JAPAN

TAIWAN

HONG KONG

THAILAND
LAOS
CAM
VIETNAM

MALAYSIA

SINGAPORE

BRUNEI

PHILIPPINES

PACIFIC
OCEAN

I N D O N E S I A

PAPUA
NEW
GUINEA

SOLOMON
ISLANDS

WESTERN SAMOA

FIJI

A U S T R A L I A

NEW
ZEALAND

INFANT MORTALITY 1960

DEATHS IN THE FIRST YEAR OF LIFE PER 1000 LIVE BIRTHS *1960*

- 25
- 50
- 75
- 150
- no data

Source: UNICEF

THE QUALITY OF LIFE

RELATIVE HUMAN DEVELOPMENT
early 1992 an index

- highest
- high
- high medium
- low medium
- low
- lowest
- no data

The Human Development Index is based on three key components: longevity, knowledge, and income

Top 10: Canada .982; Japan .981; Norway .978; Switzerland .977; Sweden, USA .976; Australia .969; Netherlands .968; UK .962

Bottom 10: Guinea .052; Sierra Leone .062; Afghanistan .065; Burkina Faso .074; Niger .078; Mali .081; Gambia .083; Djibouti .084; Guinea-Bissau, Somalia .088; India .297; China .612

Source: UNDP

SORRY, I CAN'T MAKE IT

DAILY ABSENCES FROM WORK FOR REASONS OF ILLNESS OR INJURY
19 rich countries *1988, 1989 or 1990* percentages

- more than 5 percent of employees
- 4 - 4.9%
- 3 - 3.9%
- 2 - 2.9%
- 1 - 1.9%
- less than 1 percent

Source: OECD

Data compiled by Michael Kidron

Health and the feeling of well-being are difficult to measure. It is easier to measure sickness by statistics on specific disorders or, more broadly, by the amount of time taken off work.

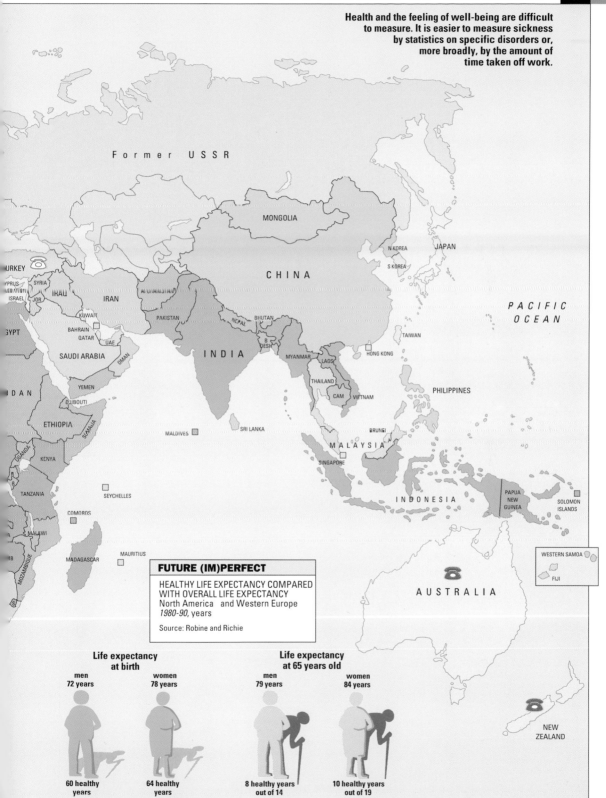

Former U S S R

MONGOLIA

N-KOREA   JAPAN

S KOREA

CHINA

PACIFIC
OCEAN

URKEY

YPRUS
ICO   TION
ISRAEL   JOR

SYRIA
IRAQ
IRAN

AFGHANISTAN

KUWAIT
BAHRAIN
QATAR
UAE

PAKISTAN

NEPAL   BHUTAN

B
DESH

TAIWAN

HONG KONG

GYPT

SAUDI ARABIA

OMAN

INDIA

MYANMAR

LAOS

THAILAND

CAM   VIETNAM

PHILIPPINES

DAN

YEMEN

DJIBOUTI

ETHIOPIA

SOMALIA

MALDIVES

SRI LANKA

BRUNEI

MALAYSIA

SINGAPORE

INDONESIA

PAPUA
NEW
GUINEA

SOLOMON
ISLANDS

UGANDA

KENYA

TANZANIA

SEYCHELLES

COMOROS

MALAWI

B

MADAGASCAR

MAURITIUS

MOZAMBIQUE

WESTERN SAMOA

FIJI

AUSTRALIA

FUTURE (IM)PERFECT

HEALTHY LIFE EXPECTANCY COMPARED
WITH OVERALL LIFE EXPECTANCY
North America   and Western Europe
1980-90, years

Source: Robine and Richie

NEW
ZEALAND

**Life expectancy
at birth**

men
72 years

women
78 years

**Life expectancy
at 65 years old**

men
79 years

women
84 years

60 healthy
years

64 healthy
years

8 healthy years
out of 14

10 healthy years
out of 19

Copyright © Swanston Publishing Limited

ICELAND

NORWAY **80** SWEDEN **80** FINLA

IRELAND

UNITED
KINGDOM **80** DENMARK

NETH
BEL GERMANY POLAND

CZECHOSLOVAKIA

FRANCE
SWITZ AUSTRIA HUNGARY

80 **80** ITALY ROMANIA

Form YUG

BULGARIA

SPAIN **80** ALBANIA

PORTUGAL

GREECE

MALTA

C A N A D A **80**

UNITED STATES
OF AMERICA

MEXICO

BAHAMAS

CUBA

BELIZE JAMAICA HAITI
GUATEMALA HONDURAS
EL SALVADOR
NICARAGUA
COSTA RICA
PANAMA

DOMINICAN REPUBLIC
PUERTO RICO (US)
GUADELOUPE (Fr)
MARTINIQUE (Fr)
BARBADOS
TRINIDAD & TOBAGO

A T L A N T I C
O C E A N

CAPE VERDE

TUNISIA

MOROCCO

ALGERIA LIBY

WESTERN SAHARA

MAURITANIA MALI NIGER CH

SENEGAL
GAMBIA BURKINA
GUINEA-BISSAU GUINEA FASO
SIERRA LEONE IVORY GHANA NIGERIA
LIBERIA COAST BENIN

TOGO CAMEROON
EQUATORIAL GUINEA C
SAO TOME & PRINCIPE GABON
CONGO

VENEZUELA
GUYANA
SURINAME
FRENCH GUIANA (Fr)

COLOMBIA

P A C I F I C
O C E A N

ECUADOR

PERU

B R A Z I L

BOLIVIA

PARAGUAY

ANG

NAMI

LIFE EXPECTANCY 1990s

AVERAGE PREDICTED LIFE SPAN AT
BIRTH FOR CHILD BORN *1990-95*

- 70
- 60
- 50
- no data

People live on average
more than 75 years

80 Women live on average
more than 80 years

Men outlive women

Longest life expectancy:
Japan: women 82, men 79

Shortest life expectancy:
Sierra Leone: women 45, men 43

Source: UN

CHILE ARGENTINA

URUGUAY

early
1950s

early
1960s

late
1960s

early
1970s

early
1980s

early
1990s

79

77 78
Sweden

Japan 64 69 71 73

61
Hong Kong

69 70 72
USSR USA Australia

JAPAN IN THE FAST LANE

PREDICTED AVERAGE LIFE SPAN AT
BIRTH IN JAPAN COMPARED TO
SELECTED COUNTRIES *1950s-90s*
→ Japan

Source: UN; World Bank

20

Worldwide, people can expect to live longer, especially women. In more than 40 countries both men and women can now aspire to the Biblical three score years and ten. In Sierra Leone, they can expect to reach no more than 45, but this is 15 years longer than in 1950.

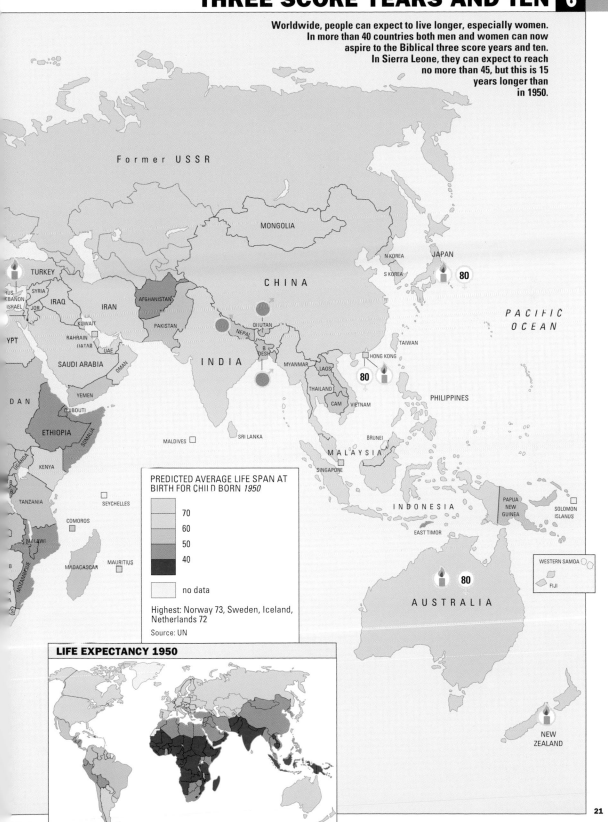

Former USSR

MONGOLIA

CHINA

N KOREA

JAPAN

80

S KOREA

TURKEY

RUS

SYRIA

IRAQ

IRAN

AFGHANISTAN

LEBANON

ISRAEL

JOR

KUWAIT

PAKISTAN

BHUTAN

NEPAL

B DESH

MYANMAR

LAOS

TAIWAN

HONG KONG

80

BAHRAIN

QATAR

UAE

SAUDI ARABIA

OMAN

INDIA

THAILAND

CAM

VIETNAM

PHILIPPINES

YPT

YEMEN

DJIBOUTI

ETHIOPIA

SOMALIA

MALDIVES

SRI LANKA

BRUNEI

MALAYSIA

SINGAPORE

UGANDA

KENYA

SEYCHELLES

INDONESIA

PAPUA NEW GUINEA

SOLOMON ISLANDS

COMOROS

TANZANIA

EAST TIMOR

MALAWI

MADAGASCAR

MAURITIUS

MOZAMBIQUE

PACIFIC OCEAN

WESTERN SAMOA

FIJI

80

AUSTRALIA

PREDICTED AVERAGE LIFE SPAN AT BIRTH FOR CHILD BORN *1950*

- 70
- 60
- 50
- 40

no data

Highest: Norway 73, Sweden, Iceland, Netherlands 72

Source: UN

NEW ZEALAND

LIFE EXPECTANCY 1950

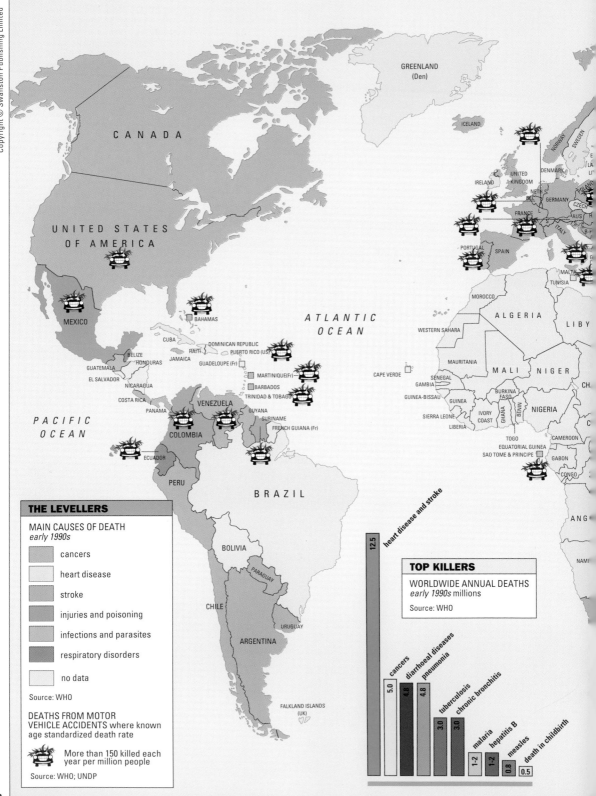

GREENLAND
(Den)

ICELAND

CANADA

NORWAY SWEDEN

IRELAND UNITED
KINGDOM DENMARK

NETH
BEL
GERMANY CZECH
FRANCE AUS

UNITED STATES
OF AMERICA

PORTUGAL SPAIN ITALY

MALTA
TUNISIA

MEXICO

BAHAMAS

ATLANTIC
OCEAN

MOROCCO

WESTERN SAHARA

ALGERIA LIBY

CUBA
DOMINICAN REPUBLIC
HAITI PUERTO RICO (US)
JAMAICA
BELIZE
HONDURAS GUADELOUPE (Fr)
GUATEMALA
EL SALVADOR MARTINIQUE(Fr)
NICARAGUA BARBADOS
COSTA RICA TRINIDAD & TOBAGO
PANAMA VENEZUELA
GUYANA
SURINAME
COLOMBIA FRENCH GUIANA (Fr)
ECUADOR

CAPE VERDE

MAURITANIA MALI NIGER

SENEGAL
GAMBIA BURKINA
GUINEA-BISSAU FASO
GUINEA NIGERIA
SIERRA LEONE IVORY
LIBERIA COAST GHANA BENIN

TOGO CAMEROON
EQUATORIAL GUINEA
SAO TOME & PRINCIPE GABON
CONGO

PACIFIC
OCEAN

PERU

BRAZIL

ANG

BOLIVIA

PARAGUAY

NAMI

CHILE

URUGUAY

ARGENTINA

FALKLAND ISLANDS
(UK)

THE LEVELLERS

MAIN CAUSES OF DEATH
early 1990s

- cancers
- heart disease
- stroke
- injuries and poisoning
- infections and parasites
- respiratory disorders
- no data

Source: WHO

**DEATHS FROM MOTOR
VEHICLE ACCIDENTS** where known
age standardized death rate

More than 150 killed each
year per million people

Source: WHO; UNDP

TOP KILLERS

WORLDWIDE ANNUAL DEATHS
early 1990s millions

Source: WHO

heart disease and stroke — 12.5
cancers — 5.0
diarrhoeal diseases — 4.8
pneumonia — 4.8
tuberculosis — 3.0
chronic bronchitis — 3.0
malaria — 1-2
hepatitis B — 1-2
measles — 0.8
death in childbirth — 0.5

In rich countries most people die from heart disease, stroke or cancers. In poor countries, infectious diseases remain the major cause of death.

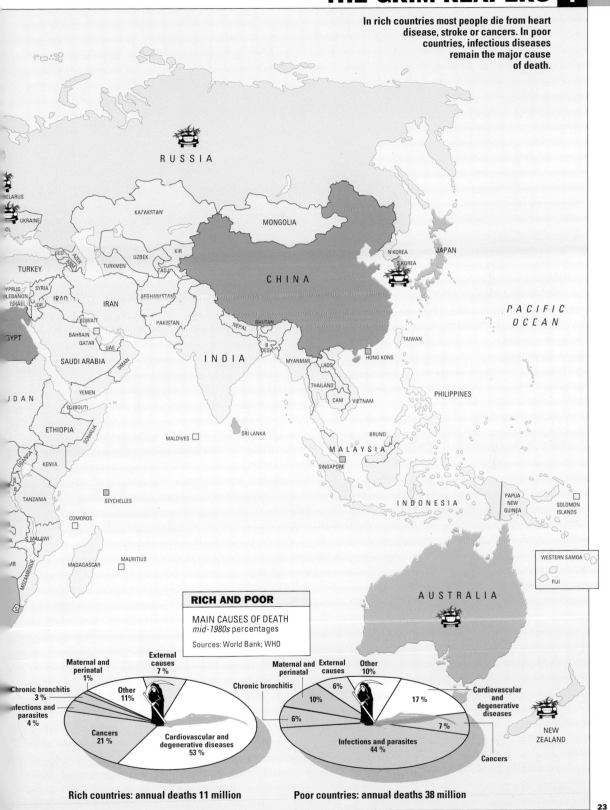

RUSSIA

BELARUS

UKRAINE

KAZAKSTAN

MONGOLIA

TURKEY

GEO AZER

UZBEK KIR

TURKMEN

TADJ

N KOREA JAPAN

S KOREA

CHINA

CYPRUS SYRIA
LEBANON
ISRAEL JOR IRAQ

IRAN

AFGHANISTAN

KUWAIT

BAHRAIN
QATAR
UAE

PAKISTAN

NEPAL BHUTAN

B
DESH

TAIWAN

PACIFIC
OCEAN

EGYPT

SAUDI ARABIA

OMAN

INDIA

MYANMAR

HONG KONG

LAOS

SUDAN

YEMEN

DJIBOUTI

THAILAND

CAM VIETNAM

PHILIPPINES

ETHIOPIA

SOMALIA

MALDIVES

SRI LANKA

BRUNEI

UGANDA

KENYA

MALAYSIA

SINGAPORE

R
B

TANZANIA

SEYCHELLES

INDONESIA

PAPUA
NEW
GUINEA

SOLOMON
ISLANDS

COMOROS

MALAWI

MAURITIUS

MADAGASCAR

WESTERN SAMOA

FIJI

MOZAMBIQUE

AUSTRALIA

RICH AND POOR

MAIN CAUSES OF DEATH
mid-1980s percentages

Sources: World Bank; WHO

**Maternal and
perinatal
1%**

**External
causes
7 %**

**Chronic bronchitis
3 %**

**Other
11%**

**Infections and
parasites
4 %**

**Cancers
21 %**

**Cardiovascular and
degenerative diseases
53 %**

**Maternal and
perinatal**

**External
causes
6%**

**Other
10%**

Chronic bronchitis

**Cardiovascular
and
degenerative
diseases**

10%

17 %

6%

7 %

**Infections and parasites
44 %**

Cancers

NEW
ZEALAND

Rich countries: annual deaths 11 million

Poor countries: annual deaths 38 million

GREENLAND
(Den)

ICELAND

C A N A D A

UNITED STATES
OF AMERICA

MEXICO

ATLANTIC
OCEAN

BAHAMAS

CUBA

DOMINICAN REPUBLIC
HAITI
PUERTO RICO (US)
BELIZE
HONDURAS
JAMAICA
GUADELOUPE (Fr)
GUATEMALA
EL SALVADOR
NICARAGUA
BARBADOS
COSTA RICA
TRINIDAD & TOBAGO
PANAMA
VENEZUELA
GUYANA
SURINAME
FRENCH GUIANA (Fr)
COLOMBIA
ECUADOR
PERU
BRAZIL

PACIFIC
OCEAN

BOLIVIA

PARAGUAY

CHILE

URUGUAY

ARGENTINA

FALKLAND ISLANDS
(UK)

NORWAY
SWEDEN
DENMARK
IRELAND
UNITED
KINGDOM
NETH
BEL
GERMANY
POLA
CZECH
AUS H
FRANCE
S
ITALY
For
SPAIN
PORTUGAL

TUNISIA
MOROCCO
ALGERIA
LIBY
WESTERN SAHARA
MALI
NIGER
CH
MAURITANIA
CAPE VERDE
SENEGAL
GAMBIA
BURKINA
FASO
GUINEA-BISSAU
GUINEA
NIGERIA
SIERRA LEONE
IVORY
COAST
GHANA
BENIN
LIBERIA
TOGO
CAMEROON
EQUATORIAL GUINEA
SAO TOME & PRINCIPE
GABON
CONGO

A N G

NAM

WINDSTORMS AND FLOODS

RECORDED DEATHS DURING
DISASTERS RESULTING FROM
WINDSTORMS AND FLOODS
January 1980 - August 1990

Windstorms include tropical cyclones,
hurricanes, typhoons, monsoons,
thunderstorms and tornadoes

	5
	50
	500
	5000
	15,000
	no data
	drought caused serious food shortage

Sources: AID/OFDA; UNEP

MAJOR DISASTERS

DEATH TOLLS IN MAJOR
DISASTERS *millions*

- famine
- floods
- earthquake

Source: WHO

Ireland	China	China	Bangladesh	China	Bangladesh
1.5	9.5	3.7	0.3	0.24	0.13
1846-51	1877	1931	1970	1976	1991

Data compiled by Philip Boys

The rich world accounts for only 3 percent of all 'natural' disasters, and less than 1 percent of resulting deaths. Far more people are profoundly affected by disasters than die from them. Most are poor.

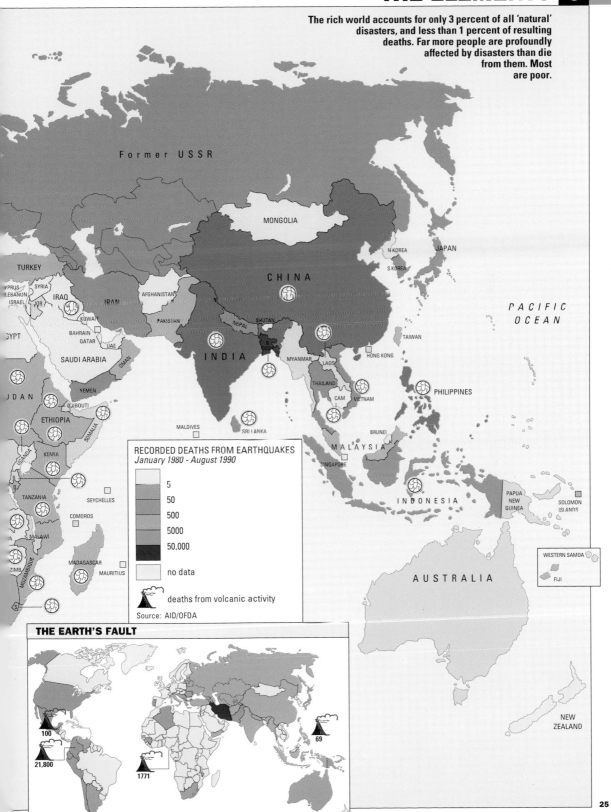

RECORDED DEATHS FROM EARTHQUAKES
January 1980 - August 1990

- 5
- 50
- 500
- 5000
- 50,000
- no data

deaths from volcanic activity

Source: AID/OFDA

THE EARTH'S FAULT

100

69

21,800

1771

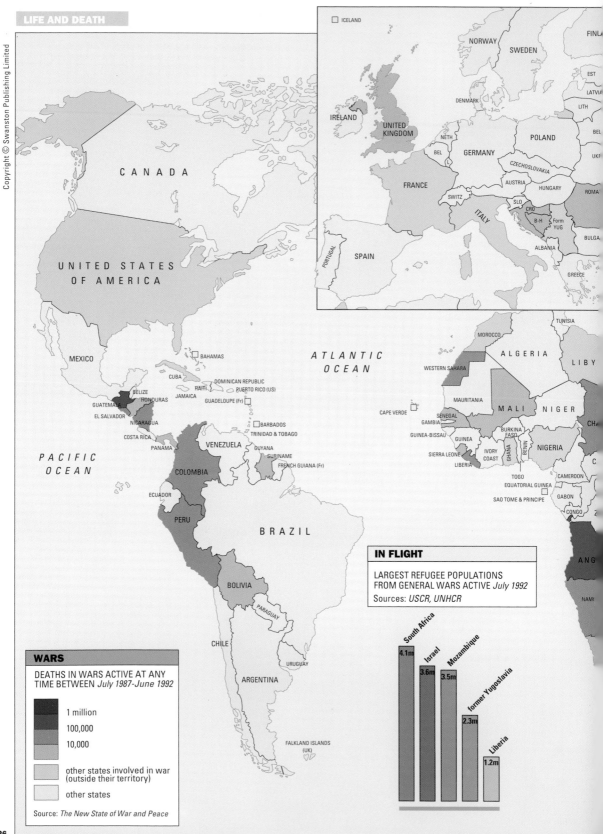

ICELAND

NORWAY   SWEDEN   FINLA

DENMARK

EST

LATVIA

LITH

IRELAND

UNITED
KINGDOM

NETH

BEL

GERMANY

POLAND

BEL

UKR

CZECHOSLOVAKIA

FRANCE

SWITZ

AUSTRIA

HUNGARY

ROMA

PORTUGAL

SPAIN

ITALY

SLO

CRO

B-H

Form
YUG

BULGA

ALBANIA

GREECE

C A N A D A

UNITED STATES
OF AMERICA

MEXICO

BAHAMAS

CUBA

DOMINICAN REPUBLIC

BELIZE

HAITI

PUERTO RICO (US)

GUATEMALA

HONDURAS

JAMAICA

GUADELOUPE (Fr)

EL SALVADOR

NICARAGUA

COSTA RICA

PANAMA

COLOMBIA

ECUADOR

PERU

BOLIVIA

PARAGUAY

VENEZUELA

GUYANA

SURINAME

FRENCH GUIANA (Fr)

BARBADOS

TRINIDAD & TOBAGO

CAPE VERDE

A T L A N T I C
O C E A N

P A C I F I C
O C E A N

B R A Z I L

CHILE

URUGUAY

ARGENTINA

FALKLAND ISLANDS
(UK)

TUNISIA

MOROCCO

ALGERIA

LIBY

WESTERN SAHARA

MAURITANIA

MALI

NIGER

CH

SENEGAL

GAMBIA

GUINEA-BISSAU

GUINEA

SIERRA LEONE

LIBERIA

IVORY
COAST

BURKINA
FASO

GHANA

BENIN

TOGO

NIGERIA

EQUATORIAL GUINEA

SAO TOME & PRINCIPE

CAMEROON

GABON

CONGO

C

Z

ANG

NAMI

IN FLIGHT

LARGEST REFUGEE POPULATIONS
FROM GENERAL WARS ACTIVE *July 1992*

Sources: *USCR, UNHCR*

South Africa 4.1m

Israel 3.6m

Mozambique 3.5m

former Yugoslavia 2.3m

Liberia 1.2m

WARS

DEATHS IN WARS ACTIVE AT ANY
TIME BETWEEN *July 1987-June 1992*

1 million

100,000

10,000

other states involved in war
(outside their territory)

other states

Source: *The New State of War and Peace*

Data compiled by Dan Smith

In modern wars, 75 percent of those killed and 90 percent of those wounded are civilians. The effects of war on the wounded, the bereaved, on fugitive refugees, last long after the war is over. Of the world's 43 million refugees many live in squalid, unhealthy conditions.

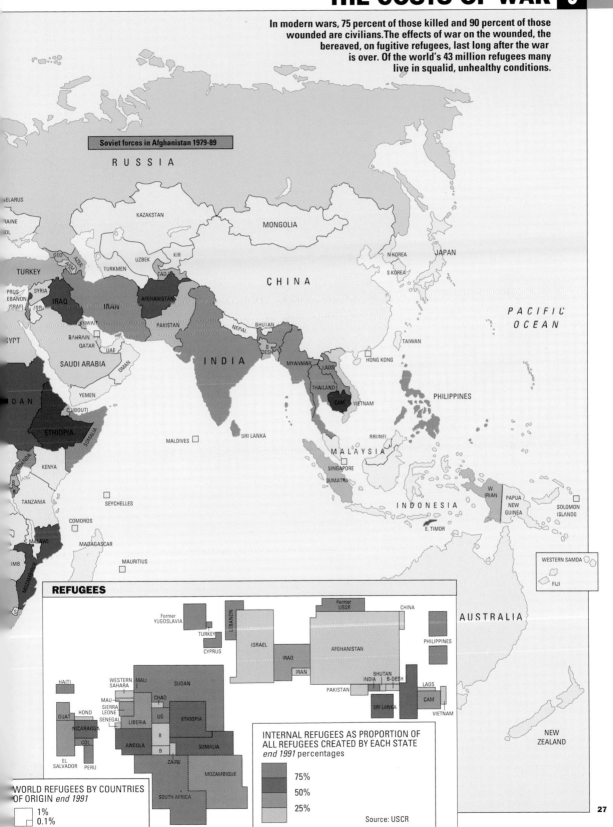

Soviet forces in Afghanistan 1979-89

REFUGEES

INTERNAL REFUGEES AS PROPORTION OF ALL REFUGEES CREATED BY EACH STATE
end 1991 percentages

- 75%
- 50%
- 25%

Source: USCR

WORLD REFUGEES BY COUNTRIES OF ORIGIN *end 1991*

- 1%
- 0.1%

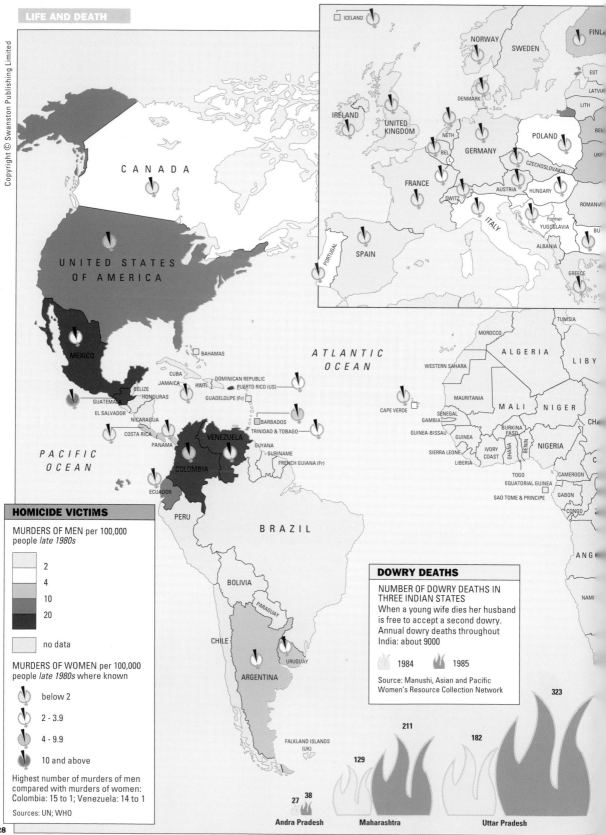

HOMICIDE VICTIMS

MURDERS OF MEN per 100,000
people *late 1980s*

	2
	4
	10
	20
	no data

MURDERS OF WOMEN per 100,000
people *late 1980s* where known

below 2

2 - 3.9

4 - 9.9

10 and above

Highest number of murders of men
compared with murders of women:
Colombia: 15 to 1; Venezuela: 14 to 1

Sources: UN; WHO

DOWRY DEATHS

NUMBER OF DOWRY DEATHS IN
THREE INDIAN STATES
When a young wife dies her husband
is free to accept a second dowry.
Annual dowry deaths throughout
India: about 9000

1984   1985

Source: Manushi, Asian and Pacific
Women's Resource Collection Network

38
27

Andra Pradesh

129   **211**

Maharashtra

182   **323**

Uttar Pradesh

28

Data compiled by Lesley Doyal

Men are more likely than women to be murdered, but they are also more likely to be murderers. Most women victims are killed by their 'nearest and dearest'. Their deaths are symbolic of a vast but largely unrecorded seam of domestic violence, including rape and sexual abuse.

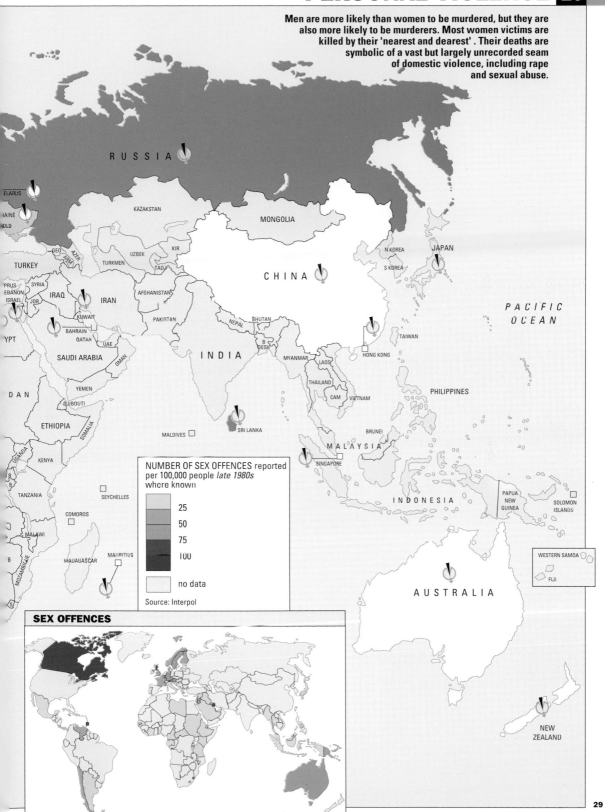

NUMBER OF SEX OFFENCES reported per 100,000 people *late 1980s* where known

25
50
75
100

no data

Source: Interpol

SEX OFFENCES

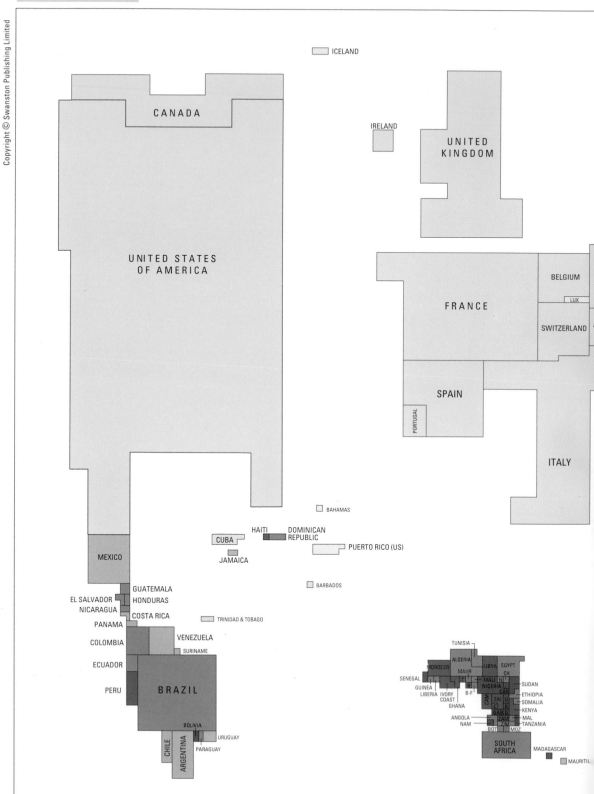

The health of poor countries is worse than
that of rich countries. The health of the
poor within a country is worse
than that of the rich.

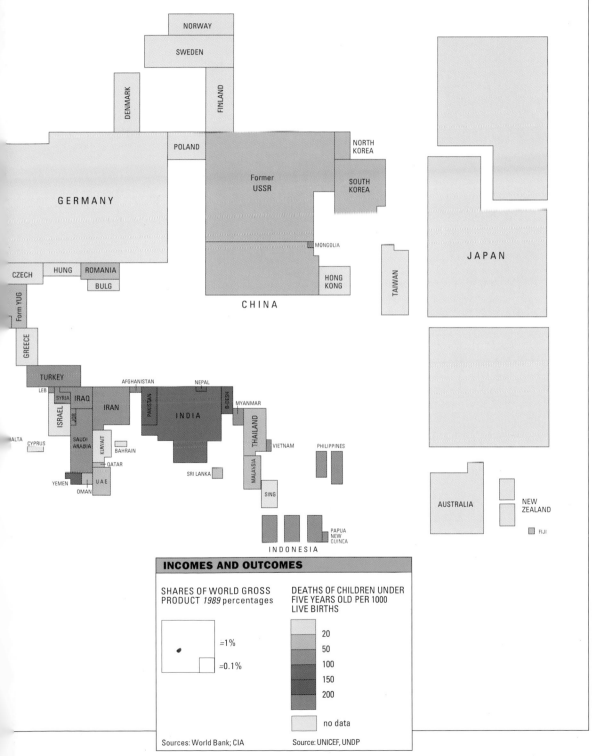

INCOMES AND OUTCOMES

SHARES OF WORLD GROSS
PRODUCT *1989* percentages

=1%

=0.1%

DEATHS OF CHILDREN UNDER
FIVE YEARS OLD PER 1000
LIVE BIRTHS

20
50
100
150
200

no data

Sources: World Bank; CIA

Source: UNICEF, UNDP

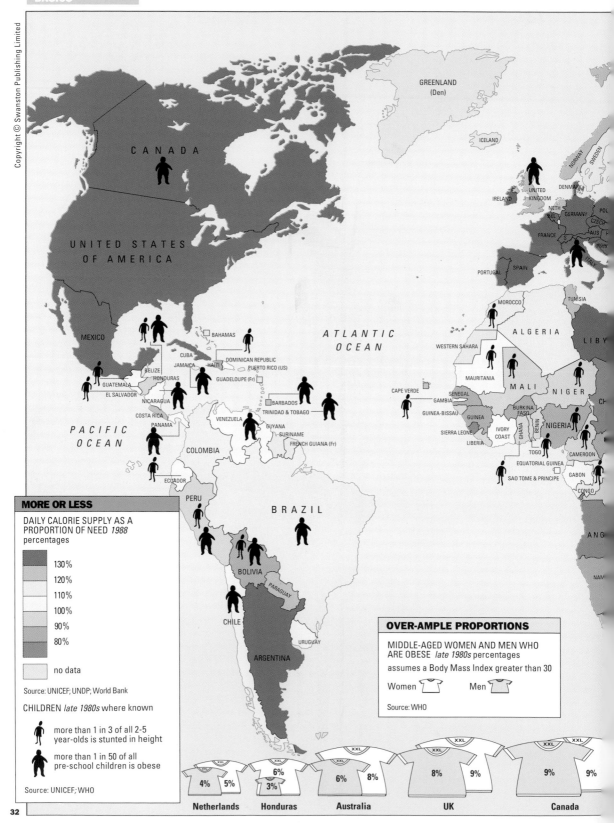

Copyright © Swanston Publishing Limited

MORE OR LESS

DAILY CALORIE SUPPLY AS A
PROPORTION OF NEED *1988*
percentages

- 130%
- 120%
- 110%
- 100%
- 90%
- 80%

no data

Source: UNICEF; UNDP; World Bank

CHILDREN *late 1980s* where known

more than 1 in 3 of all 2-5
year-olds is stunted in height

more than 1 in 50 of all
pre-school children is obese

Source: UNICEF; WHO

OVER-AMPLE PROPORTIONS

MIDDLE-AGED WOMEN AND MEN WHO
ARE OBESE *late 1980s* percentages

assumes a Body Mass Index greater than 30

Women   Men

Source: WHO

Netherlands	Honduras	Australia	UK	Canada
4% 5%	6% 3%	6% 8%	8% 9%	9% 9%

There is enough food to go round.
But while many get too little,
others get too much.

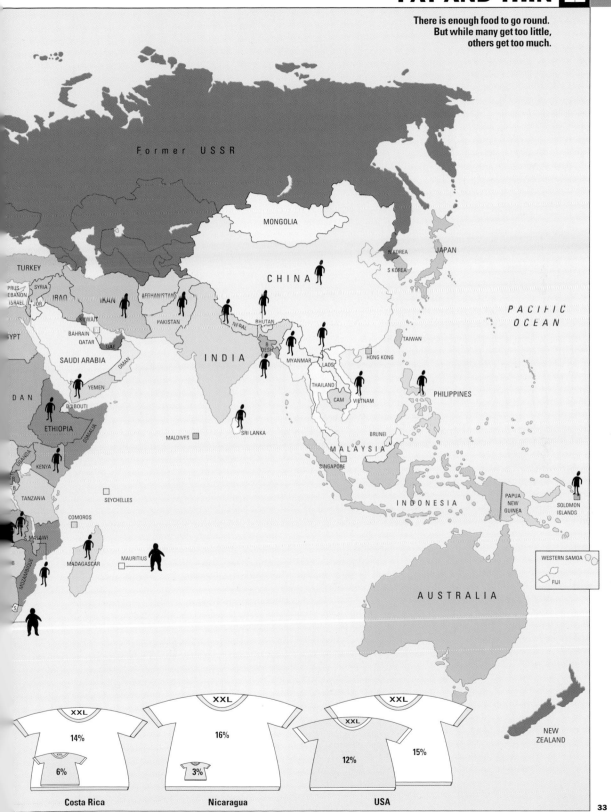

Former USSR

MONGOLIA

TURKEY

PRUS
LEBANON
ISRAEL
JOR
IRAQ
IRAN
SYRIA
KUWAIT
BAHRAIN
QATAR
UAE
OMAN
SAUDI ARABIA
AFGHANISTAN
PAKISTAN
YEMEN
DJIBOUTI
D A N
ETHIOPIA
SOMALIA
YPT

N.KOREA
S KOREA
JAPAN

C H I N A

TAIWAN

HONG KONG

NEPAL
BHUTAN
B
DESH
INDIA
MYANMAR
LAOS
THAILAND
CAM
VIETNAM
PHILIPPINES

SRI LANKA
MALDIVES

BRUNEI
M A L A Y S I A
SINGAPORE

PACIFIC
OCEAN

UGANDA
KENYA
TANZANIA
B
MALAWI
MOZAMBIQUE
S

SEYCHELLES

COMOROS

MADAGASCAR
MAURITIUS

I N D O N E S I A

PAPUA
NEW
GUINEA

SOLOMON
ISLANDS

WESTERN SAMOA

FIJI

A U S T R A L I A

NEW
ZEALAND

Costa Rica

XXL
14%

XXL
6%

Nicaragua

XXL
16%

XXL
3%

USA

XXL
XXL
12%

XXL
15%

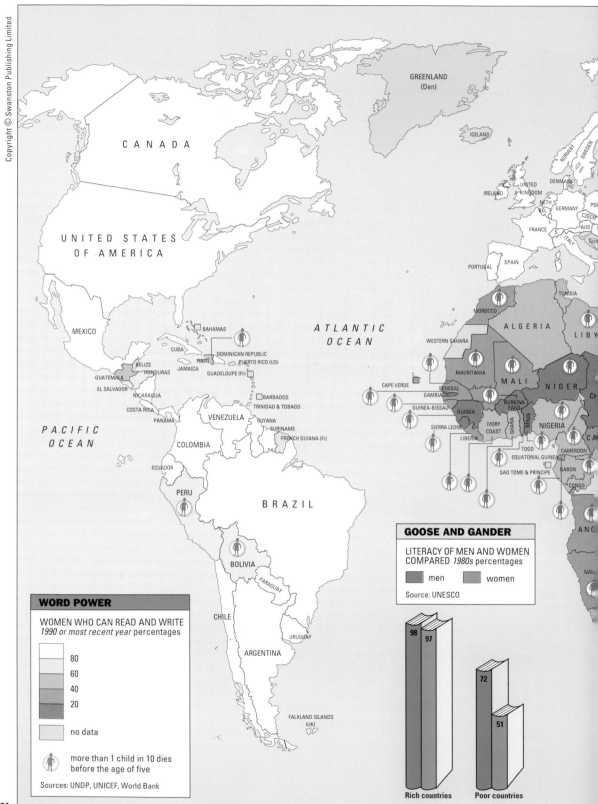

GREENLAND
(Den)

ICELAND

CANADA

UNITED STATES
OF AMERICA

NORWAY
SWEDEN

IRELAND
UNITED
KINGDOM
DENMARK
NETH'S
BEL
GERMANY
POL
CZECH
AUS
FRANCE
S
ITALY
Rom

MEXICO

BAHAMAS
CUBA
HAITI
BELIZE
HONDURAS
JAMAICA
GUATEMALA
EL SALVADOR
NICARAGUA
COSTA RICA
PANAMA

DOMINICAN REPUBLIC
PUERTO RICO (US)
GUADELOUPE (Fr)

BARBADOS
TRINIDAD & TOBAGO

ATLANTIC
OCEAN

PORTUGAL
SPAIN

TUNISIA
MOROCCO
ALGERIA
LIBY
WESTERN SAHARA
MAURITANIA
MALI
NIGER
CH

CAPE VERDE
SENEGAL
GAMBIA
GUINEA-BISSAU
GUINEA
SIERRA LEONE
LIBERIA
IVORY
COAST
GHANA
BURKINA
FASO
BENIN
NIGERIA
TOGO
EQUATORIAL GUINEA
SAO TOME & PRINCIPE
CAMEROON
GABON
CONGO
CA

ANG

PACIFIC
OCEAN

VENEZUELA
COLOMBIA
GUYANA
SURINAME
FRENCH GUIANA (Fr)

ECUADOR

PERU

BRAZIL

BOLIVIA

PARAGUAY

CHILE

URUGUAY

ARGENTINA

NAM

FALKLAND ISLANDS
(UK)

GOOSE AND GANDER

LITERACY OF MEN AND WOMEN
COMPARED *1980s* percentages

▮ men   ▮ women

Source: UNESCO

98 97

72

51

Rich countries   Poor countries

WORD POWER

WOMEN WHO CAN READ AND WRITE
1990 or most recent year percentages

80
60
40
20

no data

more than 1 child in 10 dies
before the age of five

Sources: UNDP, UNICEF, World Bank

34

When literacy lifts women out of poverty, child mortality declines, family planning is more accepted, children are more likely to be literate, and families are likely to be better fed.

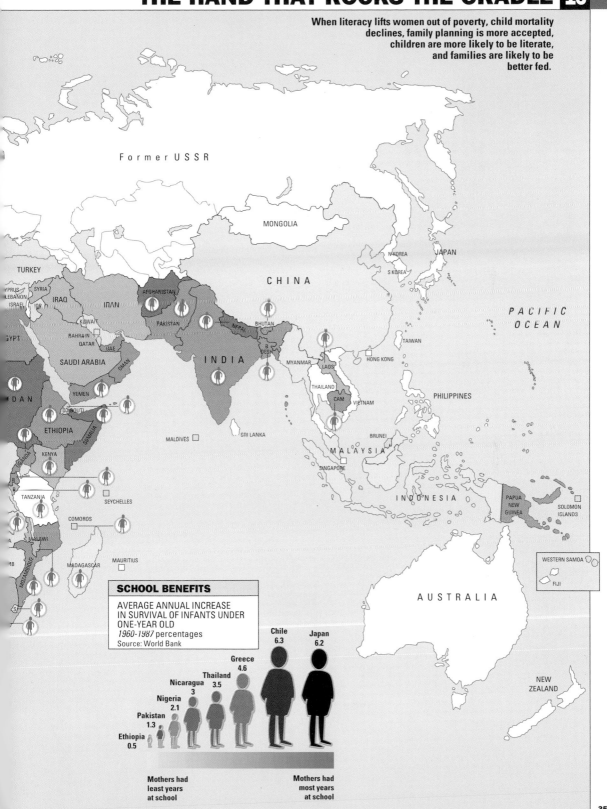

SCHOOL BENEFITS

AVERAGE ANNUAL INCREASE IN SURVIVAL OF INFANTS UNDER ONE-YEAR OLD
1960-1987 percentages
Source: World Bank

Ethiopia
0.5

Pakistan
1.3

Nigeria
2.1

Nicaragua
3

Thailand
3.5

Greece
4.6

Chile
6.3

Japan
6.2

Mothers had least years at school

Mothers had most years at school

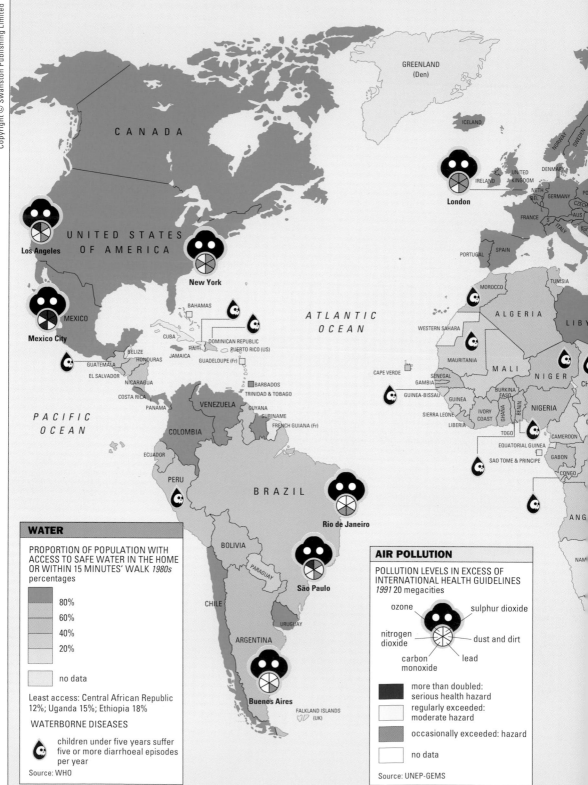

GREENLAND
(Den)

ICELAND

NORWAY SWEDEN

IRELAND UNITED
KINGDOM

DENMARK

NETH S
BEL GERMANY POL

London

CZECH
FRANCE AUS

ITALY

C A N A D A

U N I T E D   S T A T E S
O F   A M E R I C A

Los Angeles

New York

MEXICO

Mexico City

BAHAMAS

CUBA
BELIZE
HAITI
GUATEMALA HONDURAS JAMAICA
EL SALVADOR
NICARAGUA
COSTA RICA
PANAMA

DOMINICAN REPUBLIC
PUERTO RICO (US)
GUADELOUPE (Fr)

BARBADOS
TRINIDAD & TOBAGO

A T L A N T I C
O C E A N

PORTUGAL SPAIN

MOROCCO

TUNISIA

ALGERIA LIBY

WESTERN SAHARA

MAURITANIA

CAPE VERDE

SENEGAL
GAMBIA
GUINEA-BISSAU

MALI

NIGER CH

BURKINA
FASO

GUINEA

SIERRA LEONE IVORY
COAST

LIBERIA

GHANA BENIN
TOGO

NIGERIA

CAMEROON

EQUATORIAL GUINEA
SAO TOME & PRINCIPE

GABON

CONGO

ANG

P A C I F I C
O C E A N

VENEZUELA

COLOMBIA
ECUADOR

PERU

GUYANA
SURINAME
FRENCH GUIANA (Fr)

B R A Z I L

Rio de Janeiro

São Paulo

BOLIVIA

PARAGUAY

CHILE

URUGUAY

ARGENTINA

Buenos Aires

FALKLAND ISLANDS
(UK)

NAM

WATER

PROPORTION OF POPULATION WITH
ACCESS TO SAFE WATER IN THE HOME
OR WITHIN 15 MINUTES' WALK *1980s*
percentages

- 80%
- 60%
- 40%
- 20%

- no data

Least access: Central African Republic
12%; Uganda 15%; Ethiopia 18%

WATERBORNE DISEASES

children under five years suffer
five or more diarrhoeal episodes
per year

Source: WHO

AIR POLLUTION

POLLUTION LEVELS IN EXCESS OF
INTERNATIONAL HEALTH GUIDELINES
1991 20 megacities

ozone — sulphur dioxide
nitrogen
dioxide — dust and dirt
carbon — lead
monoxide

- more than doubled:
  serious health hazard
- regularly exceeded:
  moderate hazard
- occasionally exceeded: hazard
- no data

Source: UNEP-GEMS

Data compiled by: John Jackson and Anthony Webster, Monitoring and Assessment Research Centre, London

People who live in the countryside may have limited access to safe drinking water and adequate sanitation. In many of the world's cities, however, air is harmful to health and pollution is getting worse.

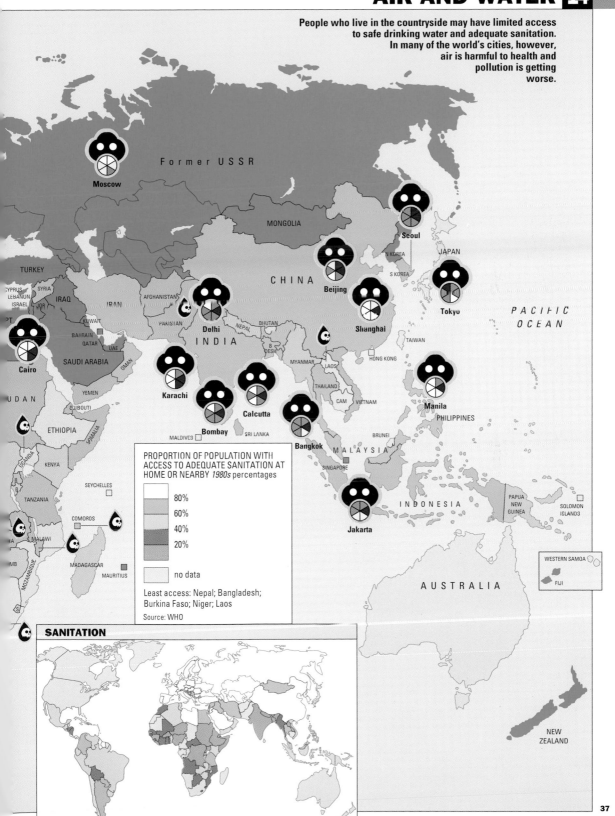

PROPORTION OF POPULATION WITH ACCESS TO ADEQUATE SANITATION AT HOME OR NEARBY *1980s* percentages

- 80%
- 60%
- 40%
- 20%
- no data

Least access: Nepal; Bangladesh; Burkina Faso; Niger; Laos

Source: WHO

SANITATION

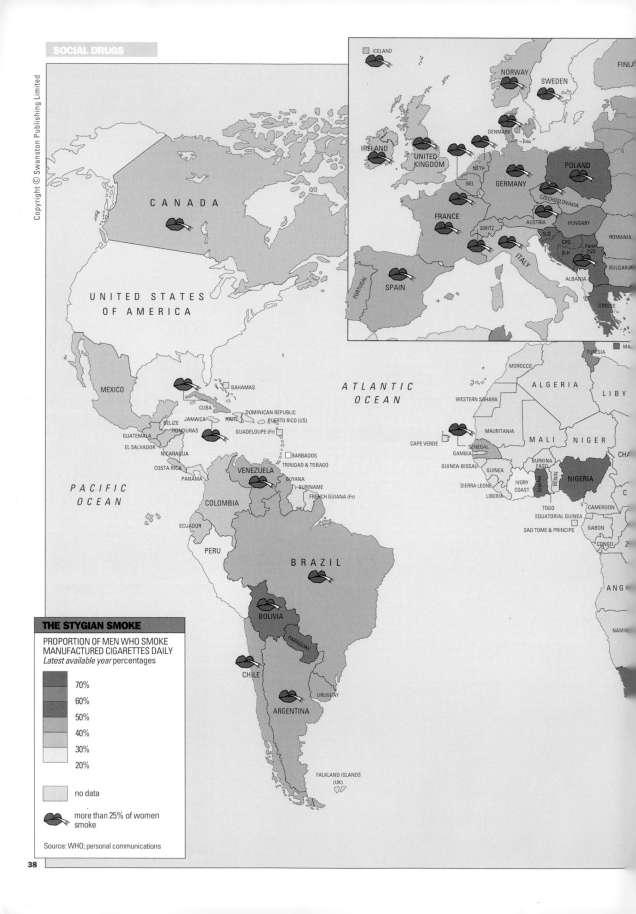

ICELAND

NORWAY   SWEDEN   FINLA

DENMARK

IRELAND   UNITED   POLAND
KINGDOM
NETH   GERMANY
BEL
L   CZECHOSLOVAKIA
FRANCE   AUSTRIA   HUNGARY   ROMANIA
SWITZ   SLO
CRO   Form
B-H   YUG   BULGARIA
PORTUGAL   ITALY
SPAIN   ALBANIA
GREECE

CANADA

UNITED STATES
OF AMERICA

MEXICO   BAHAMAS   ATLANTIC
OCEAN   TUNISIA   MA

CUBA   MOROCCO
DOMINICAN REPUBLIC   ALGERIA   LIBY
BELIZE   HAITI   PUERTO RICO (US)   WESTERN SAHARA
JAMAICA
GUADELOUPE (Fr)
HONDURAS   MAURITANIA   MALI   NIGER   CHA
GUATEMALA
EL SALVADOR   BARBADOS   CAPE VERDE   SENEGAL
NICARAGUA   TRINIDAD & TOBAGO   GAMBIA   BURKINA
COSTA RICA   VENEZUELA   GUYANA   GUINEA-BISSAU   FASO   NIGERIA
PANAMA   GUINEA   BENIN
PACIFIC   SURINAME   SIERRA LEONE   IVORY   GHANA   C
OCEAN   COLOMBIA   FRENCH GUIANA (Fr)   LIBERIA   COAST
TOGO   CAMEROON
EQUATORIAL GUINEA
ECUADOR   SAO TOME & PRINCIPE   GABON
CONGO   Z
PERU   BRAZIL
ANG
BOLIVIA
NAMIB
PARAGUAY

CHILE

URUGUAY
ARGENTINA

FALKLAND ISLANDS
(UK)

THE STYGIAN SMOKE

PROPORTION OF MEN WHO SMOKE
MANUFACTURED CIGARETTES DAILY
Latest available year percentages

- 70%
- 60%
- 50%
- 40%
- 30%
- 20%

no data

more than 25% of women
smoke

Source: WHO; personal communications

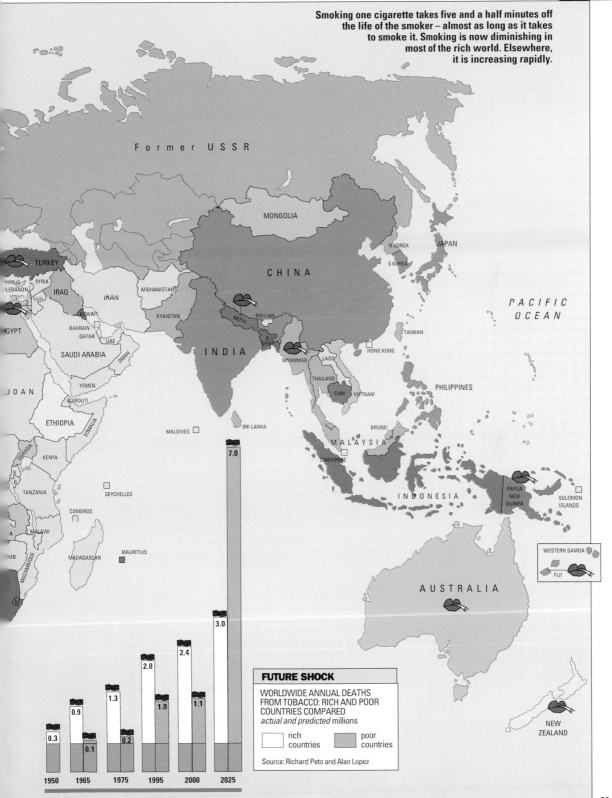

Smoking one cigarette takes five and a half minutes off
the life of the smoker – almost as long as it takes
to smoke it. Smoking is now diminishing in
most of the rich world. Elsewhere,
it is increasing rapidly.

FUTURE SHOCK

WORLDWIDE ANNUAL DEATHS
FROM TOBACCO: RICH AND POOR
COUNTRIES COMPARED
actual and predicted millions

☐ rich countries   ▨ poor countries

Source: Richard Peto and Alan Lopez

1950	1965	1975	1995	2000	2025
0.3	0.9 / 0.1	1.3 / 0.2	2.0 / 1.0	2.4 / 1.1	7.0 / 3.0

ICELAND

NORWAY

SWEDEN

FINLA

IRELAND

UNITED KINGDOM

DENMARK

NETH

BEL

GERMANY

POLAND

CZECHOSLOVAKIA

FRANCE

SWITZ

AUSTRIA

HUNGARY

ROMANIA

PORTUGAL

SPAIN

ITALY

Former YUG

BULGARIA

ALBANIA

GREECE

GIBRALTAR

MALTA

C A N A D A

U N I T E D   S T A T E S
O F   A M E R I C A

MEXICO

CUBA

BELIZE

JAMAICA

HAITI

BAHAMAS

DOMINICAN REPUBLIC

PUERTO RICO (US)

GUADELOUPE (Fr)

ST. LUCIA

BARBADOS

TRINIDAD & TOBAGO

BERMUDA

A T L A N T I C
O C E A N

TUNISIA

MOROCCO

ALGERIA

LIBY

WESTERN SAHARA

CAPE VERDE

MAURITANIA

MALI

NIGER

CHA

GUATEMALA

EL SALVADOR

HONDURAS

NICARAGUA

COSTA RICA

PANAMA

VENEZUELA

GUYANA

SURINAME

FRENCH GUIANA (Fr)

SENEGAL

GAMBIA

GUINEA-BISSAU

GUINEA

SIERRA LEONE

LIBERIA

IVORY
COAST

BURKINA
FASO

GHANA

BENIN

TOGO

NIGERIA

CAMEROON

EQUATORIAL GUINEA

SAO TOME & PRINCIPE

GABON

CONGO

C

Z

P A C I F I C
O C E A N

COLOMBIA

ECUADOR

PERU

B R Á Z I L

A N G O

BOLIVIA

PARAGUAY

CHILE

ARGENTINA

URUGUAY

NAMIE

FALKLAND ISLANDS
(UK)

ALCOHOL

ALCOHOL CONSUMPTION PER
ADULT PER YEAR *1992* litres

15

10

5

1

no data

existing group of
Alcoholics Anonymous

Source: Addiction Research Foundation,
Toronto

'Bacchus has drowned more men
than Neptune.'

Thomas Fuller

Alcohol is associated with traffic accidents, cirrhosis and alcoholism. In small quantities it may protect against heart disease.

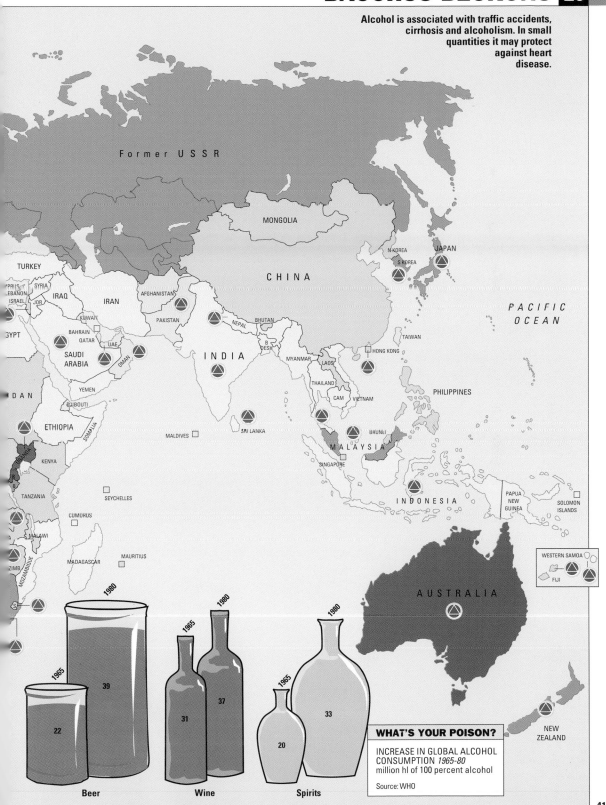

Former U S S R

MONGOLIA

N·KOREA

S KOREA

JAPAN

CHINA

TURKEY

CYPRUS
LEBANON
ISRAEL
SYRIA
JOR
IRAQ
IRAN
AFGHANISTAN
KUWAIT
PAKISTAN
NEPAL
BHUTAN
B DESH
TAIWAN
HONG KONG

BAHRAIN
QATAR
UAE
OMAN
SAUDI ARABIA
YEMEN
DJIBOUTI

GYPT

INDIA

MYANMAR
LAOS
THAILAND
CAM
VIETNAM

PACIFIC OCEAN

DAN

ETHIOPIA
SOMALIA
KENYA
TANZANIA
MALAWI
ZIMB
MOZAMBIQUE

MALDIVES

SRI LANKA

MALAYSIA

SINGAPORE

BRUNEI

PHILIPPINES

SEYCHELLES

CUMUROS

MADAGASCAR

MAURITIUS

INDONESIA

PAPUA NEW GUINEA

SOLOMON ISLANDS

WESTERN SAMOA

FIJI

AUSTRALIA

NEW ZEALAND

WHAT'S YOUR POISON?

INCREASE IN GLOBAL ALCOHOL CONSUMPTION *1965-80*
million hl of 100 percent alcohol

Source: WHO

Beer

1980
39

1965
22

Wine

1965
31

1980
37

Spirits

1965
20

1980
33

41

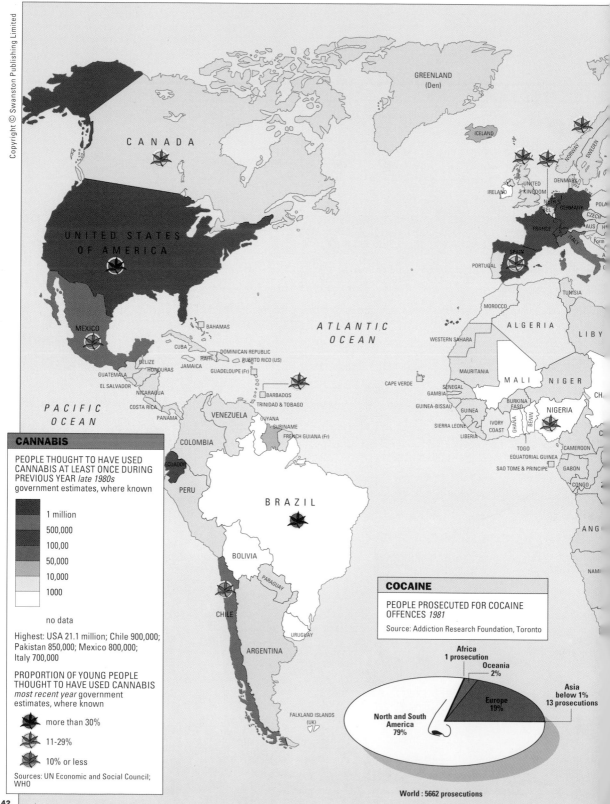

GREENLAND
(Den)

ICELAND

NORWAY
SWEDEN

DENMARK

IRELAND
UNITED
KINGDOM
POLA
NETH
BEL GERMANY
CZECH H
FRANCE AUS
S ITALY
PORTUGAL SPAIN Form

C A N A D A

U N I T E D   S T A T E S
O F   A M E R I C A

MEXICO

ATLANTIC
OCEAN

TUNISIA
MOROCCO
ALGERIA LIBY
WESTERN SAHARA
MAURITANIA
MALI NIGER
CAPE VERDE CH
SENEGAL
GAMBIA BURKINA
GUINEA-BISSAU FASO
GUINEA BENIN NIGERIA
IVORY GHANA
SIERRA LEONE COAST
LIBERIA
TOGO
CAMEROON
EQUATORIAL GUINEA
SAO TOME & PRINCIPE GABON
CONGO

BAHAMAS
CUBA
DOMINICAN REPUBLIC
BELIZE HAITI PUERTO RICO (US)
JAMAICA
GUATEMALA GUADELOUPE (Fr)
HONDURAS
EL SALVADOR BARBADOS
NICARAGUA TRINIDAD & TOBAGO
COSTA RICA
PANAMA VENEZUELA GUYANA
SURINAME
COLOMBIA FRENCH GUIANA (Fr)

P A C I F I C
O C E A N

ECUADOR

PERU

B R A Z I L

BOLIVIA

PARAGUAY

CHILE

URUGUAY

ARGENTINA

ANG

NAMI

FALKLAND ISLANDS
(UK)

CANNABIS

PEOPLE THOUGHT TO HAVE USED
CANNABIS AT LEAST ONCE DURING
PREVIOUS YEAR *late 1980s*
government estimates, where known

- 1 million
- 500,000
- 100,00
- 50,000
- 10,000
- 1000

no data

Highest: USA 21.1 million; Chile 900,000;
Pakistan 850,000; Mexico 800,000;
Italy 700,000

PROPORTION OF YOUNG PEOPLE
THOUGHT TO HAVE USED CANNABIS
most recent year government
estimates, where known

- more than 30%
- 11-29%
- 10% or less

Sources: UN Economic and Social Council;
WHO

COCAINE

PEOPLE PROSECUTED FOR COCAINE
OFFENCES *1981*

Source: Addiction Research Foundation, Toronto

Africa
1 prosecution
Oceania
2%

Asia
below 1%
13 prosecutions

Europe
19%

North and South
America
79%

World : 5662 prosecutions

Cannabis is by far the most commonly used illicit drug. There are about 15 million users of other illicit drugs worldwide. But since this includes only registered addicts and those picked up through the police and courts, it is a gross underestimate.

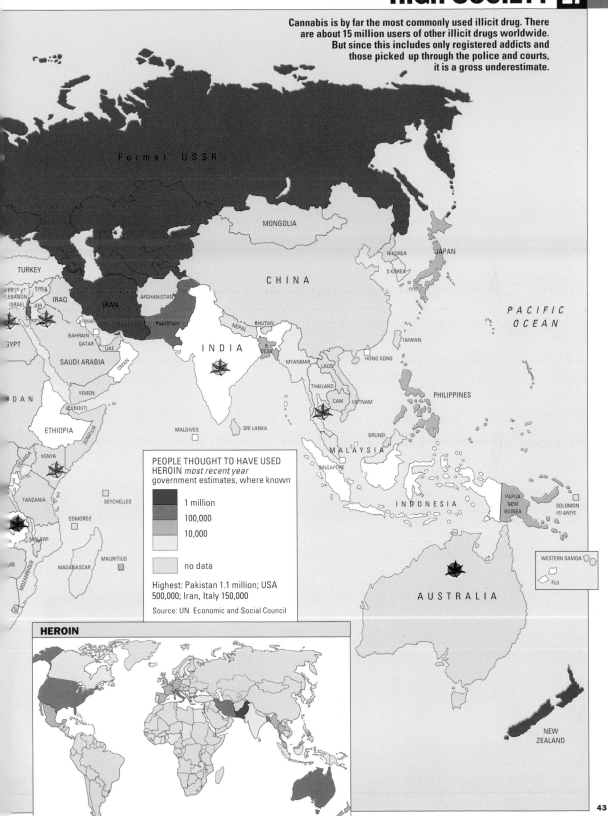

Former USSR

MONGOLIA

CHINA

N KOREA

JAPAN

S KOREA

TURKEY

CYPRUS
LEBANON SYRIA
ISRAEL JOR
IRAQ
IRAN
AFGHANISTAN

PACIFIC
OCEAN

EGYPT

KUWAIT
BAHRAIN
QATAR
UAE
OMAN
SAUDI ARABIA

PAKISTAN

NEPAL

BHUTAN

TAIWAN

INDIA

B DESH

HONG KONG

MYANMAR

LAOS

DAN

YEMEN

DJIBOUTI

ETHIOPIA

SOMALIA

MALDIVES

SRI LANKA

THAILAND

CAM

VIETNAM

PHILIPPINES

UGANDA
KENYA

BRUNEI

MALAYSIA

SINGAPORE

TANZANIA

SEYCHELLES

COMOROS

MALAWI

MAURITIUS

MADAGASCAR

INDONESIA

PAPUA
NEW
GUINEA

SOLOMON
ISLANDS

WESTERN SAMOA

FIJI

MB

MOZAMBIQUE

AUSTRALIA

PEOPLE THOUGHT TO HAVE USED HEROIN *most recent year*
government estimates, where known

- 1 million
- 100,000
- 10,000
- no data

Highest: Pakistan 1.1 million; USA 500,000; Iran, Italy 150,000

Source: UN Economic and Social Council

NEW
ZEALAND

HEROIN

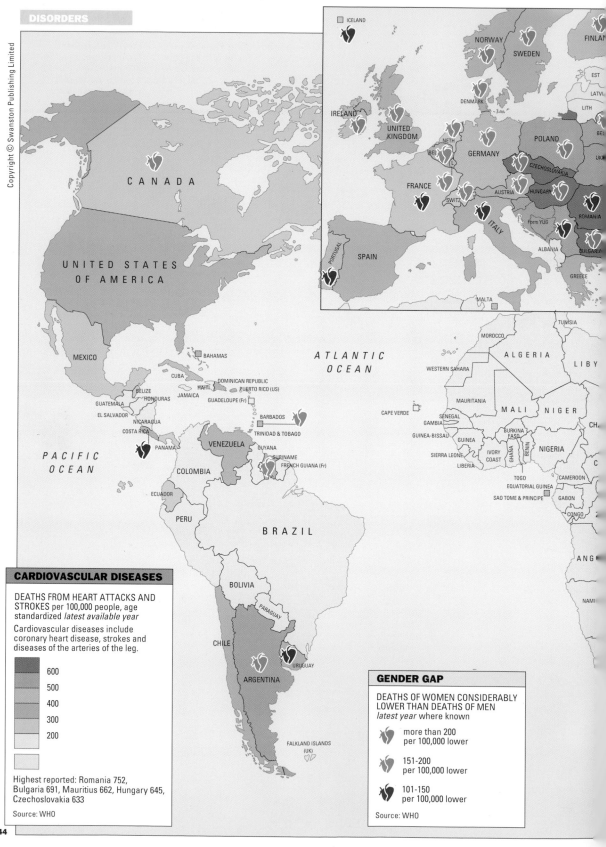

ICELAND

NORWAY SWEDEN FINLAN

EST

LATVI

DENMARK LITH

IRELAND BEL

UNITED POLAND

KINGDOM NETH

BEL GERMANY CZECHOSLOVAKIA UK

L

FRANCE AUSTRIA HUNGARY

SWITZ ROMANIA

form YUG

ITALY BULGARIA

PORTUGAL ALBANIA

SPAIN GREECE

MALTA

CANADA

UNITED STATES
OF AMERICA

ATLANTIC
OCEAN

TUNISIA

MOROCCO

MEXICO BAHAMAS ALGERIA LIBY

WESTERN SAHARA

CUBA DOMINICAN REPUBLIC

HAITI PUERTO RICO (US) MAURITANIA MALI NIGER

BELIZE JAMAICA

GUATEMALA HONDURAS GUADELOUPE (Fr) CAPE VERDE CH

EL SALVADOR BARBADOS SENEGAL

NICARAGUA TRINIDAD & TOBAGO GAMBIA BURKINA

COSTA RICA GUINEA-BISSAU FASO NIGERIA

PANAMA VENEZUELA GUINEA BENIN

PACIFIC GUYANA SIERRA LEONE IVORY GHANA

OCEAN COLOMBIA SURINAME LIBERIA COAST TOGO CAMEROON

FRENCH GUIANA (Fr) EQUATORIAL GUINEA

ECUADOR SAO TOME & PRINCIPE GABON

CONGO

PERU BRAZIL ANG

BOLIVIA

NAMI

PARAGUAY

CHILE

URUGUAY

ARGENTINA

FALKLAND ISLANDS
(UK)

CARDIOVASCULAR DISEASES

**DEATHS FROM HEART ATTACKS AND
STROKES** per 100,000 people, age
standardized *latest available year*

Cardiovascular diseases include
coronary heart disease, strokes and
diseases of the arteries of the leg.

	600
	500
	400
	300
	200

Highest reported: Romania 752,
Bulgaria 691, Mauritius 662, Hungary 645,
Czechoslovakia 633

Source: WHO

GENDER GAP

**DEATHS OF WOMEN CONSIDERABLY
LOWER THAN DEATHS OF MEN**
latest year where known

more than 200
per 100,000 lower

151-200
per 100,000 lower

101-150
per 100,000 lower

Source: WHO

Civilization is killing. One quarter of all deaths in the world are from cardiovascular diseases. More people die from them than from any other cause. Yet they are comparative newcomers on the world stage.

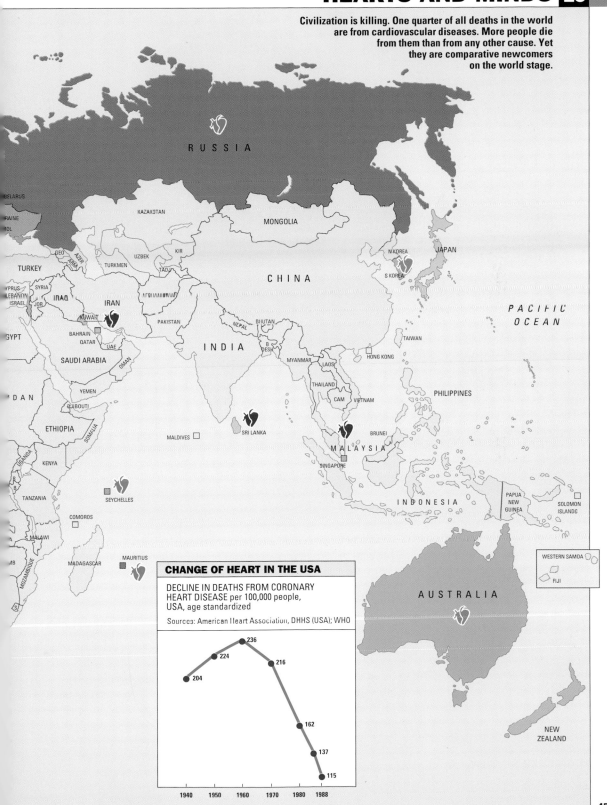

RUSSIA

BELARUS

RAINE

OL

KAZAKHSTAN

MONGOLIA

TURKEY

GEO
AZER
ARM

TURKMEN

UZBEK

KIR

TADJ

N.KOREA

JAPAN

S.KOREA

YPRUS
SYRIA
LEBANON
ISRAEL
JOR

INAQ

IRAN

KUWAIT

BAHRAIN
QATAR

UAE

OMAN

PAKISTAN

AFGHANISTAN

NEPAL

BHUTAN

B.
DESH

TAIWAN

CHINA

INDIA

GYPT

SAUDI ARABIA

YEMEN

DJIBOUTI

MYANMAR

LAOS

HONG KONG

PACIFIC
OCEAN

D A N

THAILAND

CAM

VIETNAM

PHILIPPINES

ETHIOPIA

SOMALIA

UGANDA

KENYA

R.

MALDIVES

SRI LANKA

MALAYSIA

SINGAPORE

BRUNEI

TANZANIA

SEYCHELLES

COMOROS

MALAWI

INDONESIA

PAPUA
NEW
GUINEA

SOLOMON
ISLANDS

MB

MOZAMBIQUE

MADAGASCAR

MAURITIUS

WESTERN SAMOA

FIJI

AUSTRALIA

CHANGE OF HEART IN THE USA

DECLINE IN DEATHS FROM CORONARY HEART DISEASE per 100,000 people, USA, age standardized

Sources: American Heart Association, DHHS (USA); WHO

204 — 224 — 236 — 216 — 162 — 137 — 115

1940   1950   1960   1970   1980   1988

NEW
ZEALAND

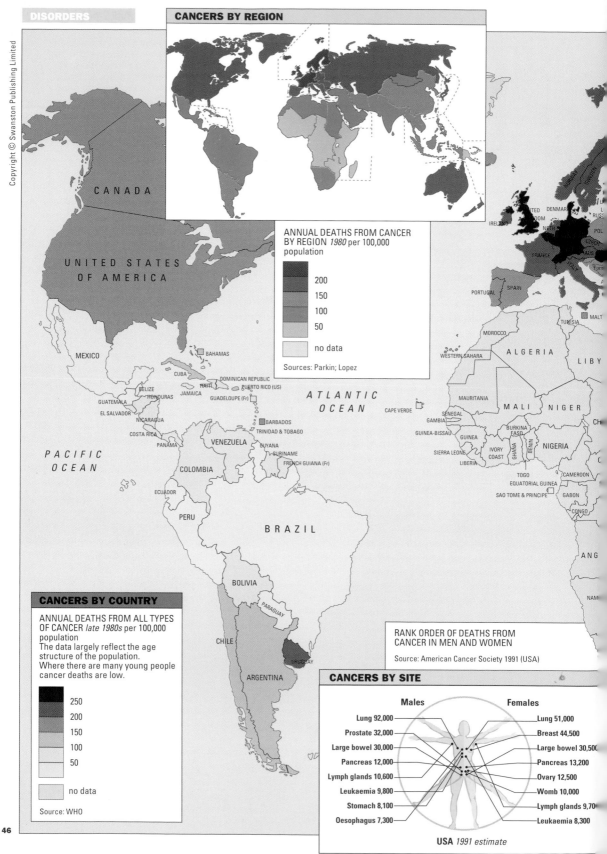

CANCERS BY REGION

ANNUAL DEATHS FROM CANCER BY REGION *1980* per 100,000 population

- 200
- 150
- 100
- 50
- no data

Sources: Parkin; Lopez

CANADA

UNITED STATES OF AMERICA

MEXICO

BAHAMAS

CUBA
DOMINICAN REPUBLIC
HAITI
PUERTO RICO (US)
JAMAICA
GUADELOUPE (Fr)

BELIZE
GUATEMALA
HONDURAS
EL SALVADOR
NICARAGUA
COSTA RICA
PANAMA

BARBADOS
TRINIDAD & TOBAGO

ATLANTIC OCEAN

CAPE VERDE

VENEZUELA
GUYANA
SURINAME
FRENCH GUIANA (Fr)

COLOMBIA

ECUADOR

PERU

PACIFIC OCEAN

BRAZIL

BOLIVIA

PARAGUAY

CHILE

URUGUAY

ARGENTINA

NORWAY
SWEDEN
IRELAND
UNITED KINGDOM
DENMARK
NETH
RUSS
POL
CZECH
FRANCE
AUS
ITALY

PORTUGAL
SPAIN

MALT

TUNISIA
MOROCCO
WESTERN SAHARA
ALGERIA
LIBY

MAURITANIA
MALI
NIGER
CH

SENEGAL
GAMBIA
GUINEA-BISSAU
GUINEA
SIERRA LEONE
LIBERIA
IVORY COAST
BURKINA FASO
GHANA
BENIN
TOGO
NIGERIA
CAMEROON

EQUATORIAL GUINEA
SAO TOME & PRINCIPE
GABON
CONGO

ANG

NAM

CANCERS BY COUNTRY

ANNUAL DEATHS FROM ALL TYPES OF CANCER *late 1980s* per 100,000 population
The data largely reflect the age structure of the population. Where there are many young people cancer deaths are low.

- 250
- 200
- 150
- 100
- 50
- no data

Source: WHO

RANK ORDER OF DEATHS FROM CANCER IN MEN AND WOMEN

Source: American Cancer Society 1991 (USA)

CANCERS BY SITE

Males

- Lung 92,000
- Prostate 32,000
- Large bowel 30,000
- Pancreas 12,000
- Lymph glands 10,600
- Leukaemia 9,800
- Stomach 8,100
- Oesophagus 7,300

Females

- Lung 51,000
- Breast 44,500
- Large bowel 30,500
- Pancreas 13,200
- Ovary 12,500
- Womb 10,000
- Lymph glands 9,700
- Leukaemia 8,300

USA *1991 estimate*

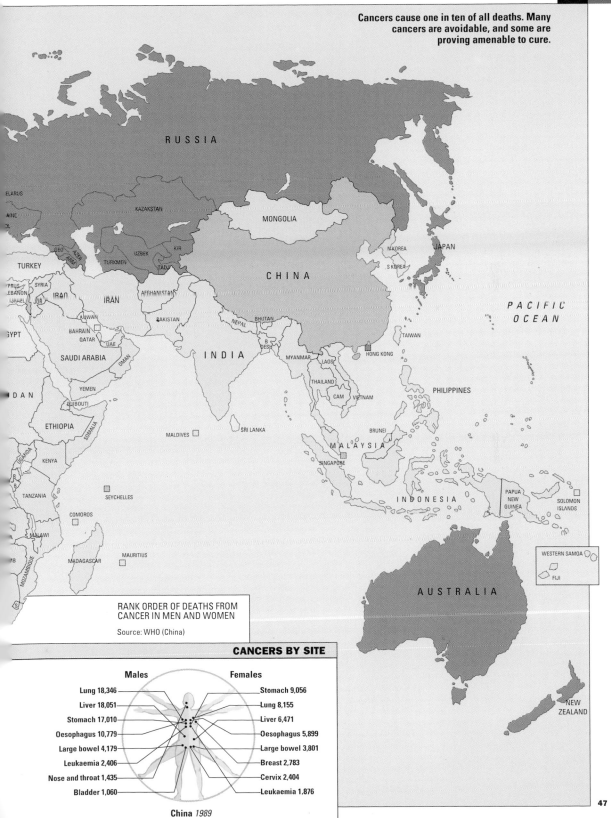

Cancers cause one in ten of all deaths. Many cancers are avoidable, and some are proving amenable to cure.

RUSSIA

BELARUS

KAZAKSTAN

MONGOLIA

GEO
AZER
ARM
TURKMEN
UZBEK
KIR
TADJ

TURKEY

N.KOREA
S.KOREA
JAPAN

CHINA

CYPRUS
LEBANON
SYRIA
ISRAEL
JOR
IRAN
IRAN

AFGHANISTAN

PACIFIC OCEAN

KUWAIT
BAHRAIN
QATAR
UAE
OMAN

PAKISTAN
NEPAL
BHUTAN
B.DESH
TAIWAN

EGYPT

SAUDI ARABIA

INDIA
MYANMAR
LAOS
HONG KONG

YEMEN

DAN

DJIBOUTI

THAILAND

CAM
VIETNAM

PHILIPPINES

ETHIOPIA

SOMALIA

MALDIVES

SRI LANKA

BRUNEI

UGANDA

KENYA

MALAYSIA

SINGAPORE

TANZANIA

SEYCHELLES

INDONESIA

PAPUA
NEW
GUINEA

SOLOMON
ISLANDS

COMOROS

MALAWI

MADAGASCAR

MAURITIUS

MOZAMBIQUE

WESTERN SAMOA

FIJI

AUSTRALIA

NEW
ZEALAND

RANK ORDER OF DEATHS FROM
CANCER IN MEN AND WOMEN

Source: WHO (China)

CANCERS BY SITE

Males	Females
Lung 18,346	Stomach 9,056
Liver 18,051	Lung 8,155
Stomach 17,010	Liver 6,471
Oesophagus 10,779	Oesophagus 5,899
Large bowel 4,179	Large bowel 3,801
Leukaemia 2,406	Breast 2,783
Nose and throat 1,435	Cervix 2,404
Bladder 1,060	Leukaemia 1,876

China *1989*

GREENLAND
(Den)

ICELAND

NORWAY   SWEDEN

IRELAND   UNITED
KINGDOM   DENMARK

NETH   POL
BEL   GERMANY
CZECH
FRANCE   S   AUS   F
Form
MONACO
PORTUGAL   SPAIN   ITALY

CANADA

UNITED STATES
OF AMERICA

MEXICO

BAHAMAS

CUBA
DOMINICAN REPUBLIC
BELIZE   HAITI   PUERTO RICO (US)
HONDURAS   JAMAICA
GUATEMALA   GUADELOUPE (Fr)
EL SALVADOR
NICARAGUA   GRENADA   BARBADOS
COSTA RICA   TRINIDAD & TOBAGO
PANAMA

VENEZUELA   GUYANA
SURINAME
COLOMBIA   FRENCH GUIANA (Fr)

ECUADOR

PERU

BRAZIL

BOLIVIA

PARAGUAY

CHILE

URUGUAY

ARGENTINA

FALKLAND ISLANDS
(UK)

ATLANTIC
OCEAN

PACIFIC
OCEAN

MOROCCO
ALGERIA   LIBY
WESTERN SAHARA
TUNISIA   MALT

MAURITANIA   MALI   NIGER
CAPE VERDE   CH
SENEGAL
GAMBIA   BURKINA
GUINEA-BISSAU   FASO
GUINEA   BENIN   NIGERIA
SIERRA LEONE   IVORY   GHANA
COAST   TOGO
LIBERIA   CAMEROON
EQUATORIAL GUINEA
SAO TOME & PRINCIPE   GABON
CONGO

ANG

NAM

TUBERCULOSIS

REPORTED NEW CASES
OF TUBERCULOSIS
Average per year per 100,000
people *1985-90* or latest available

	200
	150
	100
	50
	10
	no data

☸ HIV/AIDS already causing
major increase in tuberculosis

Highest: Djibouti 550; South Korea
241; Botswana 233; Namibia 204;
Philippines 203

Source: WHO

RISING CASES

RISE IN NUMBER OF NEW TB CASES:
NEW YORK CITY *1980-91*

Source: US Centers for Disease Control

Year	Cases
1980	1514
1981	1582
1982	1594
1983	1651
1984	1630
1985	1843
1986	2223
1987	2197
1988	2317
1989	2545
1990	3520
1991	3682

Tuberculosis is an infectious disease which is still increasing.
It thrives on overcrowding and poor nutrition. The twist
in the tail is the rise in cases caused
by the AIDS epidemic.

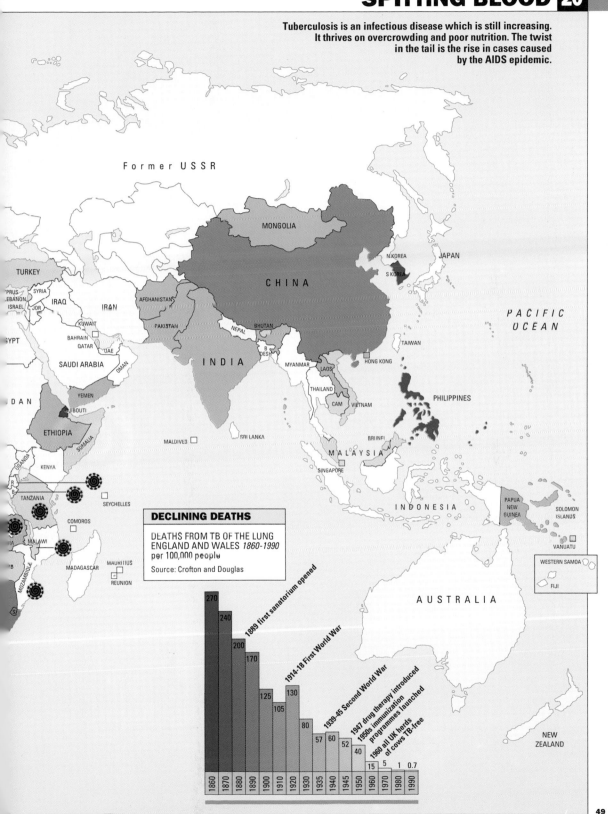

Former USSR

MONGOLIA

N. KOREA   JAPAN

S. KOREA

C H I N A

TURKEY

PRUS SYRIA IRAQ
LEBANON
ISRAEL JOR

IRAN

AFGHANISTAN

PACIFIC
OCEAN

KUWAIT

BAHRAIN
QATAR   UAE

PAKISTAN

NEPAL   BHUTAN

GYPT

SAUDI ARABIA

OMAN

B.
DESH

TAIWAN

I N D I A

MYANMAR

HONG KONG

D A N

YEMEN

LAOS

DJIBOUTI

ETHIOPIA

THAILAND

CAM   VIETNAM

PHILIPPINES

SOMALIA

MALDIVES

SRI LANKA

BRUNEI

UGANDA

KENYA

SEYCHELLES

M A L A Y S I A

SINGAPORE

TANZANIA

COMOROS

R
TANZANIA

MALAWI

MAURITIUS

REUNION

MADAGASCAR

I N D O N E S I A

PAPUA
NEW
GUINEA

SOLOMON
ISLANDS

VANUATU

WESTERN SAMOA

FIJI

MOZAMBIQUE

A U S T R A L I A

DECLINING DEATHS

DEATHS FROM TB OF THE LUNG
ENGLAND AND WALES *1860-1990*
per 100,000 people

Source: Crofton and Douglas

1889 first sanatorium opened

1914-18 First World War

1939-45 Second World War

1947 drug therapy introduced

1950s immunization
programmes launched

1960 all UK herds
of cows TB-free

NEW
ZEALAND

1860	1870	1880	1890	1900	1910	1920	1930	1935	1940	1945	1950	1960	1970	1980	1990
270	240	200	170	125	105	130	80	57	60	52	40	15	5	1	0.7

ICELAND

NORWAY SWEDEN FINL

EST

LATVI

C A N A D A

DENMARK

LITH

IRELAND

RUSSIA

UNITED
KINGDOM

BE.

POLAND

UK

NETH.

U N I T E D   S T A T E S
O F   A M E R I C A

GERMANY

CZECHOSLOVAKIA

BEL.

FRANCE

HUNGARY

AUSTRIA

ROMANIA

SWITZ.

SLO

ITALY

CRO

PORTUGAL

B-H   Form
YUG

BULGAR.

SPAIN

ALBANIA

GREECE

MEXICO

BAHAMAS

TUNISIA

MOROCCO

ATLANTIC
OCEAN

ALGERIA

LIBY

CUBA

WESTERN SAHARA

DOMINICAN REPUBLIC

BELIZE

HAITI   PUERTO RICO (US)

GUATEMALA   HONDURAS   JAMAICA

MAURITANIA

MALI

NIGER

CH.

EL SALVADOR

GUADELOUPE (Fr)

CAPE VERDE

NICARAGUA

SENEGAL

GAMBIA

BARBADOS

COSTA RICA

TRINIDAD & TOBAGO

GUINEA-BISSAU

GUINEA

BURKINA
FASO

NIGERIA

PANAMA

VENEZUELA

GUYANA

SIERRA LEONE

IVORY
COAST

GHANA

BENIN

PACIFIC
OCEAN

SURINAME

FRENCH GUIANA (Fr)

LIBERIA

COLOMBIA

TOGO

CAMEROON

EQUATORIAL GUINEA

GABON

ECUADOR

SAO TOME & PRINCIPE

CONGO

PERU

B R A Z I L

ANG

BOLIVIA

NAMI

PARAGUAY

AROUND THE WORLD IN 500 DAYS

APPEARANCES OF INFLUENZA VIRUS
A/BEIJING/353/89
November 1989 - March 1992
where known

Virus first isolated *November 1989*

November 1989 - March 1990
Recorded

CHILE

URUGUAY

April 1990 - September 1990
Recorded

ARGENTINA

October 1990 - March 1991
Recorded

April 1991 - March 1992
Recorded

FALKLAND ISLANDS
(UK)

General direction of flu virus

Sources: US Center for Disease Control, Atlanta, Georgia;
National Institute for Medical Research, London

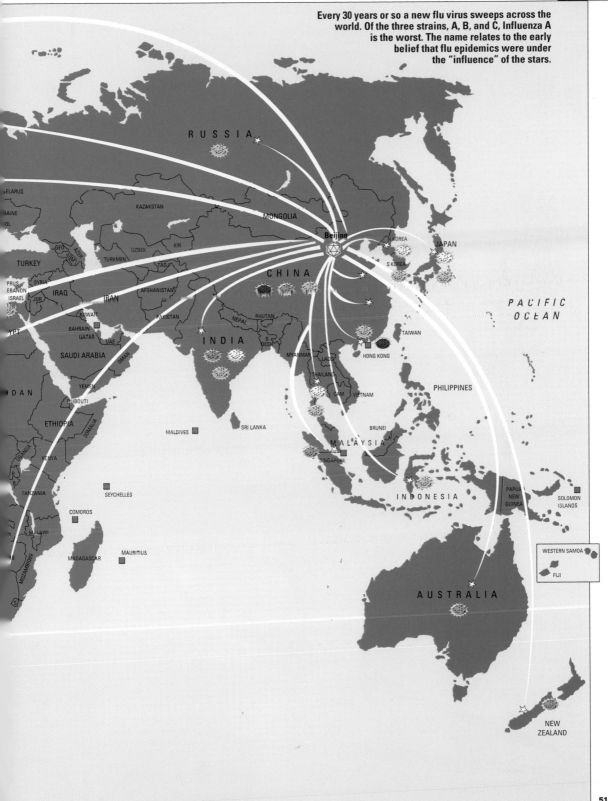

Every 30 years or so a new flu virus sweeps across the world. Of the three strains, A, B, and C, Influenza A is the worst. The name relates to the early belief that flu epidemics were under the "influence" of the stars.

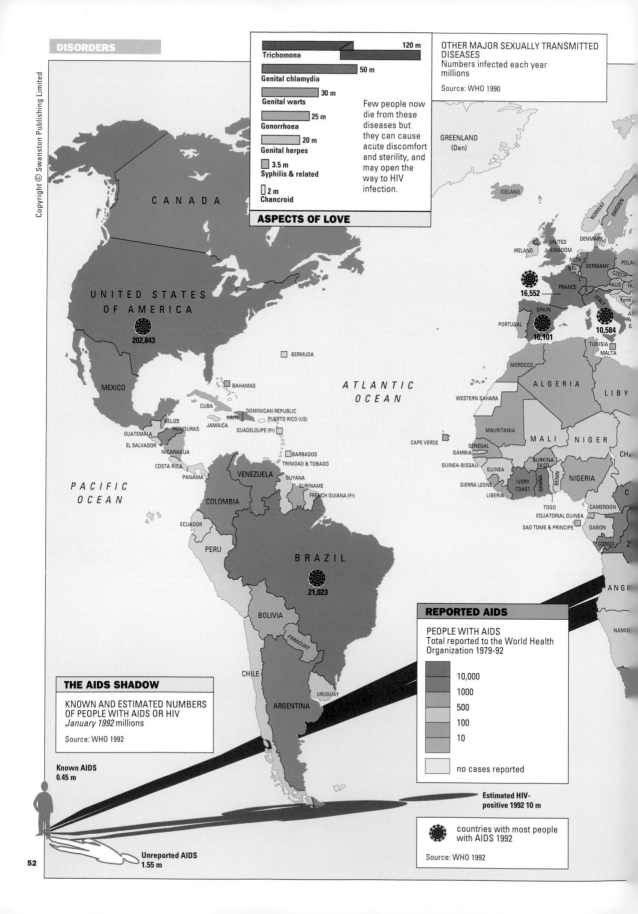

ASPECTS OF LOVE

OTHER MAJOR SEXUALLY TRANSMITTED DISEASES
Numbers infected each year millions

Source: WHO 1990

Trichomona	120 m
Genital chlamydia	50 m
Genital warts	30 m
Gonorrhoea	25 m
Genital herpes	20 m
Syphilis & related	3.5 m
Chancroid	2 m

Few people now die from these diseases but they can cause acute discomfort and sterility, and may open the way to HIV infection.

THE AIDS SHADOW

KNOWN AND ESTIMATED NUMBERS OF PEOPLE WITH AIDS OR HIV
January 1992 millions

Source: WHO 1992

Known AIDS
0.45 m

Estimated HIV-positive 1992 10 m

Unreported AIDS
1.55 m

REPORTED AIDS

PEOPLE WITH AIDS
Total reported to the World Health Organization 1979-92

	10,000
	1000
	500
	100
	10
	no cases reported

countries with most people with AIDS 1992

Source: WHO 1992

United States of America — 202,843
Brazil — 21,023
16,552
Spain — 10,101
10,584

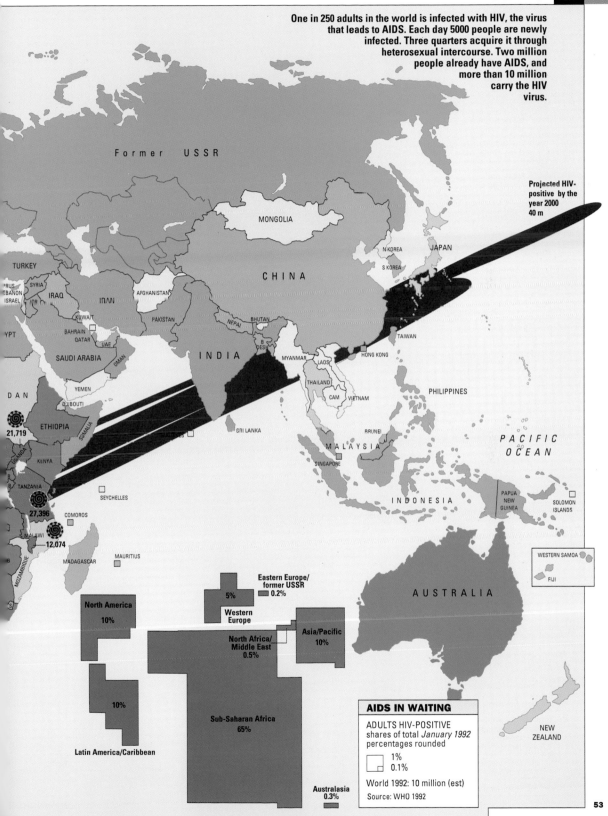

One in 250 adults in the world is infected with HIV, the virus that leads to AIDS. Each day 5000 people are newly infected. Three quarters acquire it through heterosexual intercourse. Two million people already have AIDS, and more than 10 million carry the HIV virus.

Projected HIV-positive by the year 2000 40 m

Former USSR

MONGOLIA

N KOREA
S KOREA
JAPAN

TURKEY
CYPRUS
LEBANON
SYRIA
ISRAEL
IRAQ
IRAN
AFGHANISTAN
CHINA
KUWAIT
BAHRAIN
QATAR
UAE
PAKISTAN
NEPAL
BHUTAN
TAIWAN
SAUDI ARABIA
OMAN
B DESH
YEMEN
MYANMAR
HONG KONG
DJIBOUTI
INDIA
LAOS
EGYPT
SUDAN
THAILAND
CAM
VIETNAM
PHILIPPINES

ETHIOPIA
21,719
SOMALIA
SRI LANKA
BRUNEI
PACIFIC OCEAN

UGANDA
KENYA
MALAYSIA
TANZANIA
27,396
SEYCHELLES
SINGAPORE
INDONESIA
PAPUA NEW GUINEA
SOLOMON ISLANDS

COMOROS
MALAWI
12,074
MADAGASCAR
MAURITIUS
MOZAMBIQUE

WESTERN SAMOA
FIJI

AUSTRALIA

NEW ZEALAND

Eastern Europe/
former USSR
5%   ▪ 0.2%

North America
10%

Western
Europe

Asia/Pacific
10%

North Africa/
Middle East
0.5%

Latin America/Caribbean
10%

Sub-Saharan Africa
65%

Australasia
0.3%

AIDS IN WAITING

ADULTS HIV-POSITIVE
shares of total *January 1992*
percentages rounded

☐ 1%
▪ 0.1%

World 1992: 10 million (est)

Source: WHO 1992

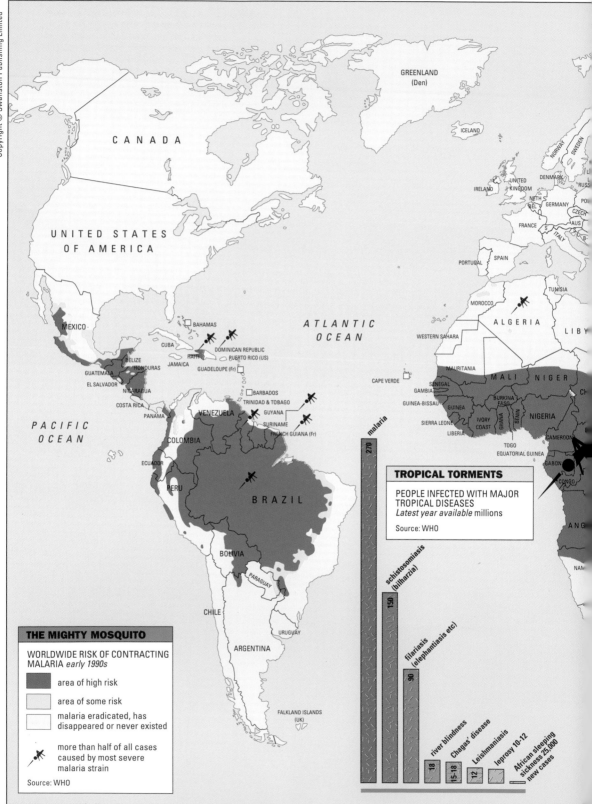

GREENLAND
(Den)

ICELAND

C A N A D A

NORWAY
SWEDEN

DENMARK
IRELAND UNITED
KINGDOM
NETH S
BEL GERMANY
FRANCE
ITALY

RUSS

POL
CZECH
AUS
S

U N I T E D S T A T E S
O F A M E R I C A

PORTUGAL SPAIN

TUNISIA

MOROCCO

ALGERIA

LIBY

MEXICO

BAHAMAS

CUBA
HAITI
JAMAICA

DOMINICAN REPUBLIC
PUERTO RICO (US)
GUADELOUPE (Fr)

WESTERN SAHARA

A T L A N T I C
O C E A N

CAPE VERDE

MAURITANIA

M A L I N I G E R

CH

BELIZE
HONDURAS
GUATEMALA
EL SALVADOR
NICARAGUA

COSTA RICA

BARBADOS
TRINIDAD & TOBAGO

PANAMA

VENEZUELA

GUYANA
SURINAME
FRENCH GUIANA (Fr)

SENEGAL
GAMBIA
GUINEA-BISSAU

GUINEA

SIERRA LEONE
LIBERIA

BURKINA
FASO
IVORY
COAST

GHANA
BENIN

TOGO

NIGERIA

CAMEROON

P A C I F I C
O C E A N

COLOMBIA

ECUADOR

EQUATORIAL GUINEA
GABON
CONGO

A N G

PERU

B R A Z I L

malaria

270

TROPICAL TORMENTS

PEOPLE INFECTED WITH MAJOR
TROPICAL DISEASES
Latest year available millions

Source: WHO

BOLIVIA

NAM

PARAGUAY

schistosomiasis
(bilharzia)

150

CHILE

URUGUAY

filariasis
(elephantiasis etc)

90

ARGENTINA

THE MIGHTY MOSQUITO

WORLDWIDE RISK OF CONTRACTING
MALARIA *early 1990s*

river blindness

Chagas' disease

Leishmaniasis

leprosy 10-12

African sleeping
sickness 23,000
new cases

area of high risk

area of some risk

malaria eradicated, has
disappeared or never existed

more than half of all cases
caused by most severe
malaria strain

18

15-18

12

FALKLAND ISLANDS
(UK)

Source: WHO

Half a billion people – 1 in 10 in the world – suffer from a 'tropical' disease. Most live in countries with less than US $400 per person annual income and where governments spend around US $4 per person on health care.

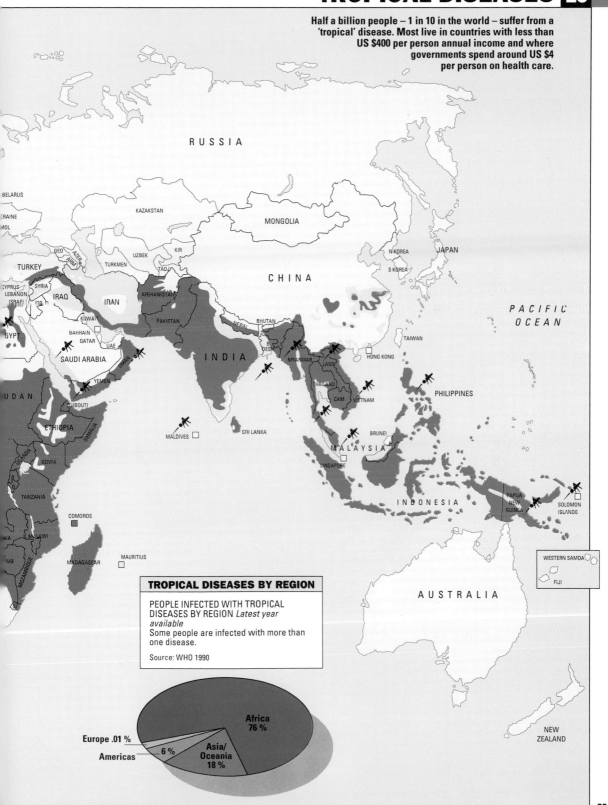

RUSSIA

BELARUS
KRAINE
MOL
KAZAKSTAN
MONGOLIA
N-KOREA JAPAN
S KOREA
GEO
AZER
TURKEY
ARM
TURKMEN
UZBEK
KIR
TADJ
CHINA
CYPRUS
LEBANON SYRIA
ISRAEL
IRAQ
IRAN
AFGHANISTAN
PAKISTAN
NEPAL BHUTAN
TAIWAN
KUWAIT
BAHRAIN
QATAR
UAE
SAUDI ARABIA
OMAN
YEMEN
INDIA
BL DESH
MYANMAR
LAOS
HONG KONG
GYPT
PACIFIC OCEAN
DIIBOUTI
ETHIOPIA
SOMALIA
THAILAND
CAM VIETNAM
PHILIPPINES
UDAN
UGANDA
KENYA
SRI LANKA
MALDIVES
BRUNEI
TANZANIA
MALAYSIA
SINGAPORE
COMOROS
I MALAWI
INDONESIA
PAPUA NEW GUINEA
SOLOMON ISLANDS
MB
MOZAMBIQUE
MADAGASCAR
MAURITIUS
WESTERN SAMOA
FIJI
AUSTRALIA
NEW ZEALAND

TROPICAL DISEASES BY REGION

PEOPLE INFECTED WITH TROPICAL DISEASES BY REGION *Latest year available*
Some people are infected with more than one disease.

Source: WHO 1990

Africa 76 %

Europe .01 %

Americas — **6 %**

Asia/ Oceania 18 %

GREENLAND
(Den)

ICELAND

C A N A D A

NORWAY
SWEDEN

IRELAND
UNITED
KINGDOM
DENMARK
NETH
BEL GERMANY POL
CZECH
AUS
FRANCE S C-B
ITALY

U N I T E D   S T A T E S
O F   A M E R I C A

PORTUGAL
SPAIN

TUNISIA MALT

MOROCCO

MEXICO

A T L A N T I C
O C E A N

ALGERIA
L I B Y

WESTERN SAHARA

BAHAMAS

CUBA
DOMINICAN REPUBLIC
HAITI PUERTO RICO (US)
BELIZE JAMAICA
GUATEMALA HONDURAS GUADELOUPE (Fr)
EL SALVADOR
NICARAGUA BARBADOS
COSTA RICA TRINIDAD & TOBAGO
PANAMA

CAPE VERDE

MAURITANIA

M A L I
N I G E R
CH

SENEGAL
GAMBIA
GUINEA-BISSAU
BURKINA
FASO
GUINEA
SIERRA LEONE IVORY
COAST GHANA BENIN NIGERIA

LIBERIA

VENEZUELA
GUYANA
SURINAME
FRENCH GUIANA (Fr)

TOGO
EQUATORIAL GUINEA
CAMEROON
SAO TOME & PRINCIPE GABON
CONGO

P A C I F I C
O C E A N

COLOMBIA

ECUADOR

PERU

B R A Z I L

A N G

NAM

'My teeth are
closer to me than
my relatives'
Spanish proverb

BOLIVIA

PARAGUAY

CHILE

URUGUAY

ARGENTINA

TEETH 1991

DECAYED, MISSING OR FILLED
TEETH PER 12-YEAR-OLD *1991*

0	very low
1.2	low
2.7	moderate
4.5	high
6.6	very high
	no data

Source: WHO

FALKLAND ISLANDS
(UK)

THE EMPTY MOUTH

PROPORTION OF 35-40 YEAR OLDS
WITH NO TEETH *1960s*

22%	32%	39%
UK	Netherlands	New Zealand

Dental health is improving in rich countries. Only one quarter of the world's dentists work in poor countries, so that while tooth decay is less common, few teeth are ever filled.

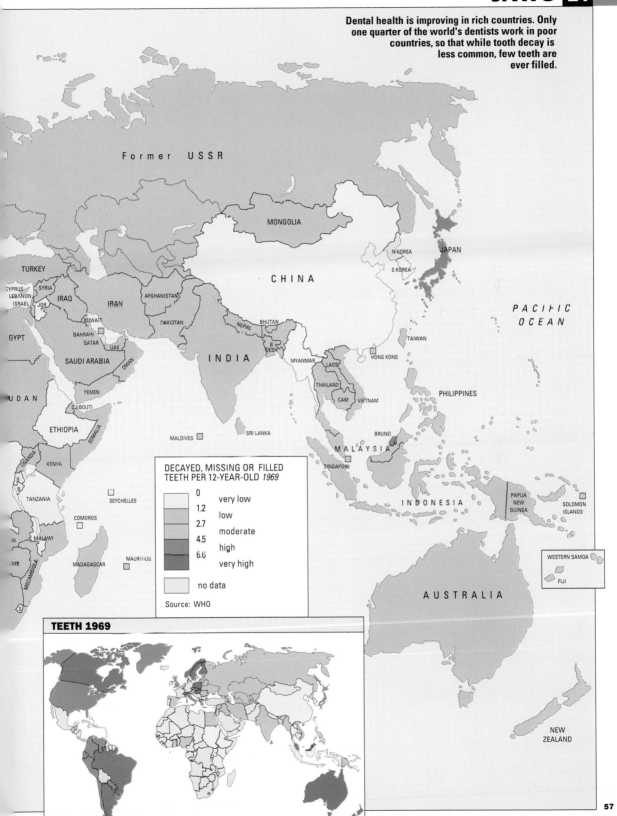

DECAYED, MISSING OR FILLED TEETH PER 12-YEAR-OLD *1969*

0	very low
1.2	low
2.7	moderate
4.5	high
6.6	very high
	no data

Source: WHO

TEETH 1969

CANADA

GREENLAND
(Den)

ICELAND

NORWAY SWEDEN

DENMARK

IRELAND UNITED
KINGDOM RUSS
NETH
BEL GERMANY POL
UNITED STATES CZECH
OF AMERICA FRANCE S AUS
ITALY

MEXICO PORTUGAL SPAIN

TUNISIA

BAHAMAS
MOROCCO
CUBA ALGERIA LIBY
DOMINICAN REPUBLIC WESTERN SAHARA
BELIZE HAITI PUERTO RICO (US)
JAMAICA GUADELOUPE (Fr)
GUATEMALA MAURITANIA MALI NIGER
HONDURAS CAPE VERDE
EL SALVADOR SENEGAL CH
NICARAGUA BARBADOS GAMBIA
COSTA RICA TRINIDAD & TOBAGO GUINEA-BISSAU BURKINA
PANAMA VENEZUELA GUINEA FASO NIGERIA
GUYANA SIERRA LEONE BENIN
SURINAME IVORY GHANA
FRENCH GUIANA (Fr) LIBERIA COAST
COLOMBIA TOGO CAMEROON

PACIFIC EQUATORIAL GUINEA
OCEAN ECUADOR SAO TOME & PRINCIPE GABON

PERU ATLANTIC CONGO
OCEAN
BRAZIL ANG

BOLIVIA
NAM
PARAGUAY

CHILE

URUGUAY

ARGENTINA

FALKLAND ISLANDS
(UK)

SEVERE MENTAL DISORDERS

PROPORTION OF POPULATION
SUFFERING FROM SCHIZOPHRENIA,
SEVERE DEPRESSION, OR DEMENTIAS
1990s percentages

☐ at least 1-2%

Source: WHO

WORLD MENTAL HEALTH

CENTRES COLLABORATING WITH THE
WORLD HEALTH ORGANIZATION ON
MENTAL HEALTH *1992*

● mental health

● biological psychiatry and
psychotropic drugs

● neurosciences

● health, psychosocial and
psychological factors

Source: WHO

No human community is free from severe mental disorder. Indeed, the proportion of people affected seems universal. One in seven people will suffer from a mental disorder during their lifetime.

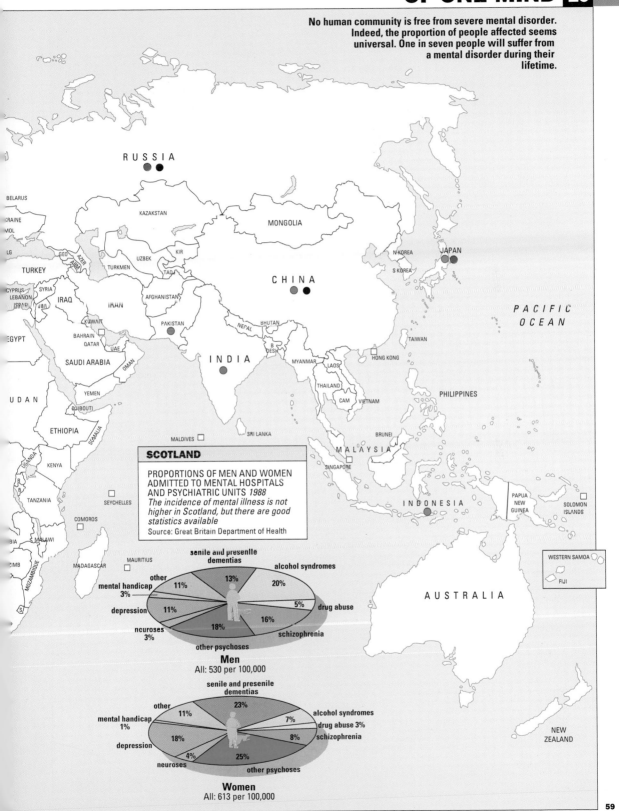

RUSSIA

BELARUS

KAZAKSTAN

MONGOLIA

UKRAINE

MOL

LG

TURKEY

KIR

UZBEK

TURKMEN

TAD

GEO
ARM
AZER

CYPRUS
LEBANON
ISRAEL
SYRIA
IRAQ
JOR

IRAN

AFGHANISTAN

KUWAIT
BAHRAIN
QATAR
UAE

EGYPT

SAUDI ARABIA

OMAN

YEMEN

DJIBOUTI

SUDAN

ETHIOPIA

SOMALIA

UGANDA

KENYA

PAKISTAN

NEPAL

BHUTAN

B
DESH

INDIA

MYANMAR

LAOS

THAILAND

CAM

VIETNAM

N KOREA

S KOREA

JAPAN

CHINA

TAIWAN

HONG KONG

PHILIPPINES

PACIFIC OCEAN

MALDIVES

SRI LANKA

BRUNEI

MALAYSIA

SINGAPORE

TANZANIA

SEYCHELLES

COMOROS

MALAWI

ZAMBIA

ZIMB

MOZAMBIQUE

MADAGASCAR

MAURITIUS

INDONESIA

PAPUA
NEW
GUINEA

SOLOMON
ISLANDS

AUSTRALIA

WESTERN SAMOA

FIJI

NEW
ZEALAND

SCOTLAND

PROPORTIONS OF MEN AND WOMEN ADMITTED TO MENTAL HOSPITALS AND PSYCHIATRIC UNITS *1988*
The incidence of mental illness is not higher in Scotland, but there are good statistics available
Source: Great Britain Department of Health

senile and presenile dementias
13%

alcohol syndromes
20%

other
11%

drug abuse
5%

mental handicap
3%

depression
11%

schizophrenia
16%

neuroses
3%

other psychoses
18%

Men
All: 530 per 100,000

senile and presenile dementias
23%

other
11%

alcohol syndromes
7%

mental handicap
1%

drug abuse 3%

schizophrenia
8%

depression
18%

neuroses
4%

other psychoses
25%

Women
All: 613 per 100,000

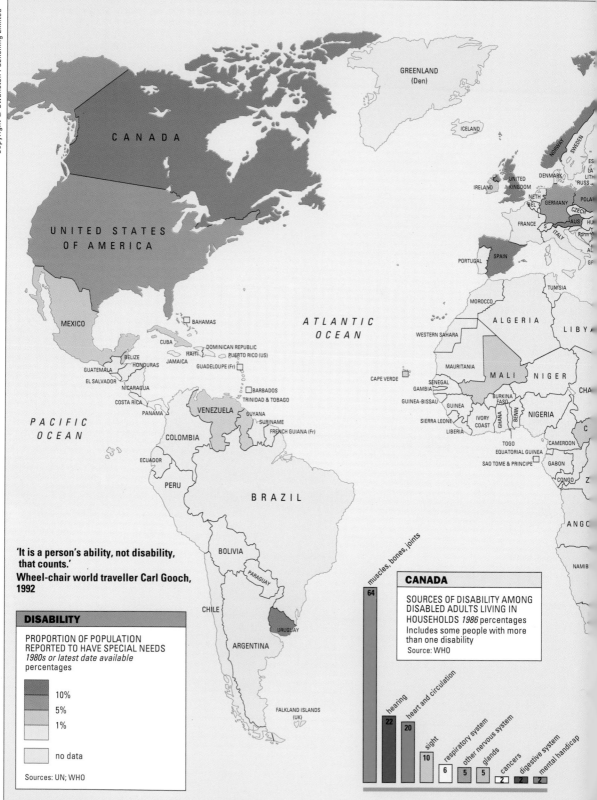

GREENLAND
(Den)

ICELAND

CANADA

UNITED STATES
OF AMERICA

MEXICO

BAHAMAS

CUBA
DOMINICAN REPUBLIC
HAITI   PUERTO RICO (US)
JAMAICA
GUADELOUPE (Fr)

BELIZE
HONDURAS
GUATEMALA
EL SALVADOR
NICARAGUA
COSTA RICA
PANAMA

ATLANTIC
OCEAN

BARBADOS
TRINIDAD & TOBAGO

VENEZUELA
GUYANA
SURINAME
FRENCH GUIANA (Fr)

PACIFIC
OCEAN

COLOMBIA

ECUADOR

PERU

BRAZIL

BOLIVIA

PARAGUAY

CHILE

URUGUAY

ARGENTINA

FALKLAND ISLANDS
(UK)

NORWAY
SWEDEN
ES
LA
LITH
DENMARK   RUSS
IRELAND   UNITED
KINGDOM
NETH   POLA
BEL   GERMANY
CZECH
FRANCE   S   AUS   HU
form
ITALY
AL
PORTUGAL   SPAIN   GF

TUNISIA

MOROCCO

WESTERN SAHARA

ALGERIA   LIBYA

MAURITANIA   MALI   NIGER   CHA

CAPE VERDE

SENEGAL   BURKINA
GAMBIA   FASO
GUINEA-BISSAU   GUINEA   NIGERIA
SIERRA LEONE   IVORY   GHANA   BENIN
LIBERIA   COAST   TOGO   CAMEROON   C
EQUATORIAL GUINEA
SAO TOME & PRINCIPE   GABON
CONGO   Z

ANGO

NAMIB

'It is a person's ability, not disability, that counts.'
Wheel-chair world traveller Carl Gooch, 1992

muscles, bones, joints

CANADA

SOURCES OF DISABILITY AMONG
DISABLED ADULTS LIVING IN
HOUSEHOLDS *1986* percentages
Includes some people with more
than one disability
Source: WHO

64

DISABILITY

PROPORTION OF POPULATION
REPORTED TO HAVE SPECIAL NEEDS
1980s or latest date available
percentages

- 10%
- 5%
- 1%

no data

Sources: UN; WHO

hearing

heart and circulation

22

20

sight

10

respiratory system

other nervous system

glands

6

5

5

cancers

digestive system

mental handicap

2   2   2

Some countries have gone much farther than others in recognizing and aiding people with disabilities.

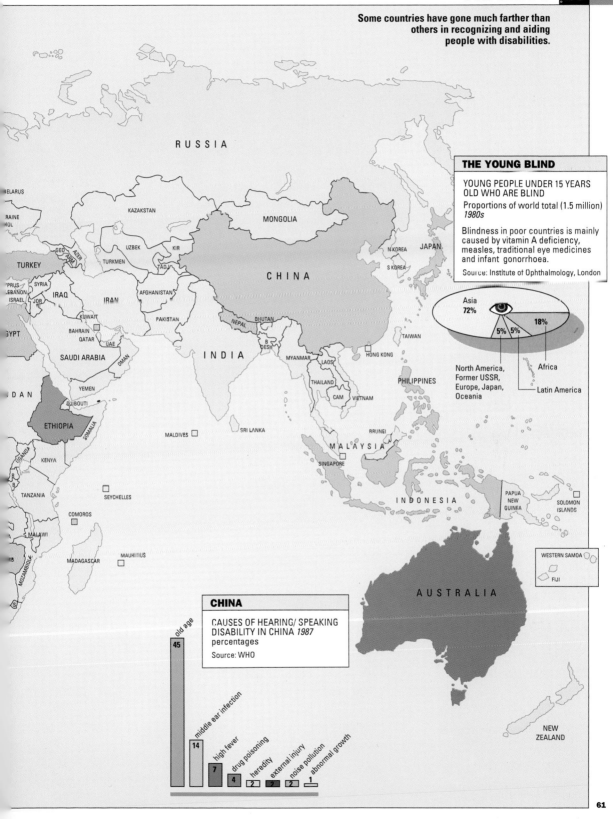

THE YOUNG BLIND

YOUNG PEOPLE UNDER 15 YEARS OLD WHO ARE BLIND

Proportions of world total (1.5 million) *1980s*

Blindness in poor countries is mainly caused by vitamin A deficiency, measles, traditional eye medicines and infant gonorrhoea.

Source: Institute of Ophthalmology, London

Asia 72%

18%

5% 5%

North America, Former USSR, Europe, Japan, Oceania

Africa

Latin America

CHINA

CAUSES OF HEARING/ SPEAKING DISABILITY IN CHINA *1987* percentages

Source: WHO

old age **45**

middle ear infection **14**

high fever **7**

drug poisoning **4**

heredity **2**

external injury **2**

noise pollution **2**

abnormal growth **1**

KILL OR CURE

Yugoslavia **53** <5
UAE **44** 7
Israel **26** 4
Jordan **26** 4
USA **25** 13

HEALTH SPENDING OF SOME HIGH
MILITARY SPENDERS *late 1980s*
percentages of government income

military spending
health spending

Source: World Bank; IMF

GREENLAND
(Den)

ICELAND

CANADA

UNITED STATES
OF AMERICA

ATLANTIC
OCEAN

MEXICO

BAHAMAS
CUBA
DOMINICAN REPUBLIC
HAITI
PUERTO RICO (US)
BELIZE
GUATEMALA   HONDURAS   JAMAICA   GUADELOUPE (Fr)
EL SALVADOR   NICARAGUA
COSTA RICA   PANAMA
BARBADOS
TRINIDAD & TOBAGO
VENEZUELA
GUYANA
SURINAME
COLOMBIA   FRENCH GUIANA (Fr)

PACIFIC
OCEAN

ECUADOR
PERU

BRAZIL

BOLIVIA

PARAGUAY

CHILE

URUGUAY

ARGENTINA

FALKLAND ISLANDS
(UK)

NORWAY   SWEDEN
DENMARK
IRELAND   UNITED KINGDOM
NETH   GERMANY   POLA
BEL   CZECH
FRANCE   AUS   H
S   ITALY   C   B
PORTUGAL   SPAIN

TUNISIA
MOROCCO
WESTERN SAHARA   ALGERIA   LIBY
MAURITANIA   MALI   NIGER   CH
CAPE VERDE   SENEGAL
GAMBIA   BURKINA
GUINEA-BISSAU   GUINEA   FASO
SIERRA LEONE   IVORY   GHANA   NIGERIA
LIBERIA   COAST   TOGO   CAMEROON   CA
EQUATORIAL GUINEA   GABON
SAO TOME & PRINCIPE   CONGO

ANG

NAMI

PAYING FOR HEALTH

SHARES OF GOVERNMENT INCOME
SPENT ON PUBLIC HEALTH
1987 percentages

6%
5%
4%
3%
2%
1%

no data

SPENDING ON PUBLIC HEALTH IN
1987 COMPARED WITH 1960
where known

doubled or more

declined

Source: UNDP

STATE SUPPORT

GOVERNMENT SHARES OF TOTAL
SPENDING ON HEALTH *late 1980s*
or latest year percentages

20%
40%
60%
80%

no data

Highest: Norway 100%; Sweden 95%;
UK 94%

Sources: World Bank; UNDP

To invest in health is to invest in people - not just their well-being but their prosperity. Most government health spending worldwide is on 'Western' medical services.

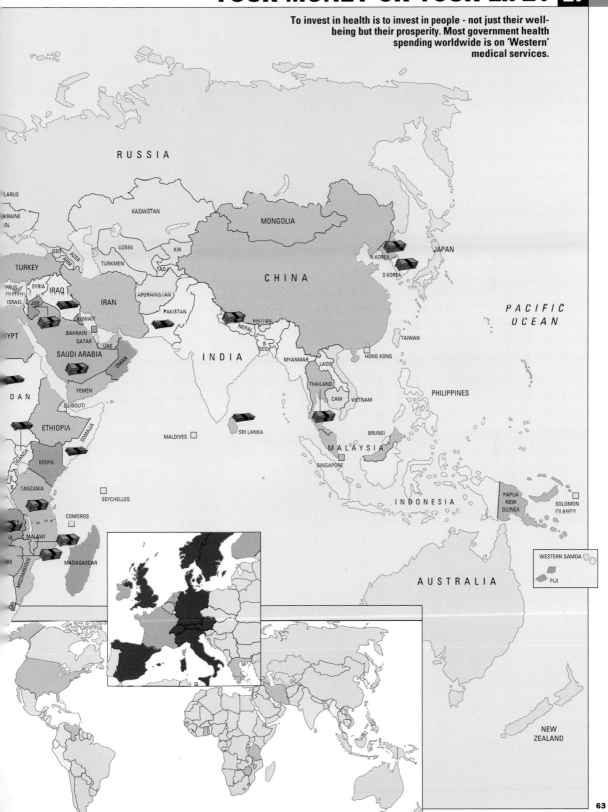

RUSSIA

LARUS

KRAINE
OL

KAZAKSTAN

MONGOLIA

JAPAN

N KOREA

S KOREA

GEO
AZER
ARM

UZBEK

KIR

TURKEY

TURKMEN

TAD

CHINA

PRUS
FD.RATION

SYRIA

IRAQ

AFGHANISTAN

ISRAEL

JOR

KUWAIT

IRAN

PAKISTAN

BHUTAN

NEPAL

TAIWAN

PACIFIC
OCEAN

YPT

BAHRAIN
QATAR

UAE

SAUDI ARABIA

OMAN

INDIA

B
DESH

MYANMAR

LAOS

HONG KONG

YEMEN

THAILAND

CAM

VIETNAM

PHILIPPINES

DAN

DJIBOUTI

ETHIOPIA

SOMALIA

MALDIVES

SRI LANKA

BRUNEI

MALAYSIA

UGANDA

KENYA

SINGAPORE

B

TANZANIA

SEYCHELLES

INDONESIA

PAPUA
NEW
GUINEA

SOLOMON
ISLANDS

COMOROS

IA

MALAWI

B

MOZAMBIQUE

MADAGASCAR

WESTERN SAMOA

FIJI

AUSTRALIA

NEW
ZEALAND

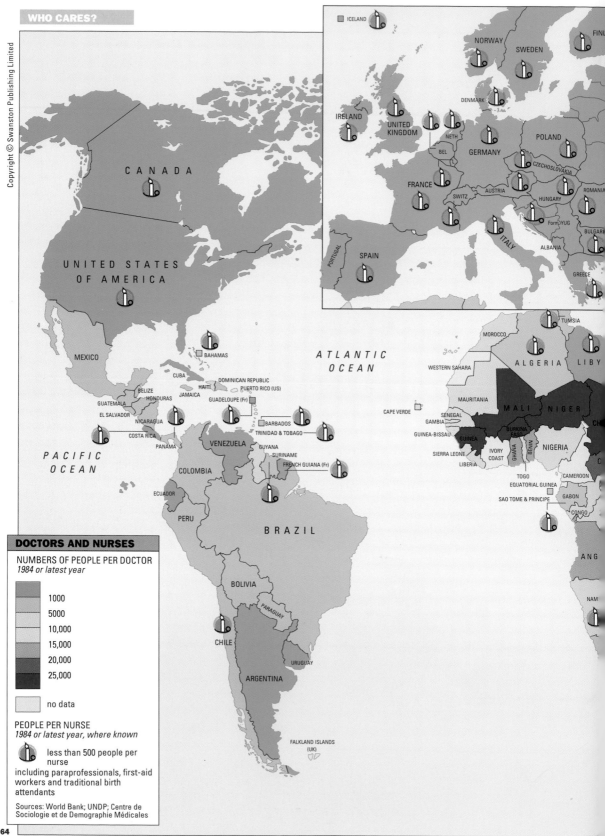

DOCTORS AND NURSES

NUMBERS OF PEOPLE PER DOCTOR
1984 or latest year

- 1000
- 5000
- 10,000
- 15,000
- 20,000
- 25,000

no data

PEOPLE PER NURSE
1984 or latest year, where known

less than 500 people per nurse

including paraprofessionals, first-aid workers and traditional birth attendants

Sources: World Bank; UNDP; Centre de Sociologie et de Demographie Médicales

There are five million doctors in the world and almost nine million nurses. But most health workers – including traditional and holistic healers, village elders, and caring relatives – cannot be shown on a map until their efforts are recorded.

Former USSR

MONGOLIA

CHINA

N.KOREA

S KOREA

JAPAN

PACIFIC OCEAN

TURKEY

PRUS.
LEBANON
ISRAEL
SYRIA
JDR
IRAQ
IRAN
AFGHANISTAN

KUWAIT
BAHRAIN
QATAR
UAE
OMAN

PAKISTAN

NEPAL
BHUTAN
B.
DESH

TAIWAN

HONG KONG

SAUDI ARABIA

YPT

INDIA

MYANMAR

LAOS

THAILAND

CAM
VIETNAM

PHILIPPINES

YEMEN

DJIBOUTI

DAN

ETHIOPIA

SOMALIA

KENYA

MALDIVES

SRI LANKA

BRUNEI

MALAYSIA

SINGAPORE

TANZANIA

SEYCHELLES

INDONESIA

PAPUA NEW GUINEA

SOLOMON ISLANDS

COMOROS

MALAWI

MADAGASCAR

MAURITIUS

WESTERN SAMOA

FIJI

AUSTRALIA

NEW ZEALAND

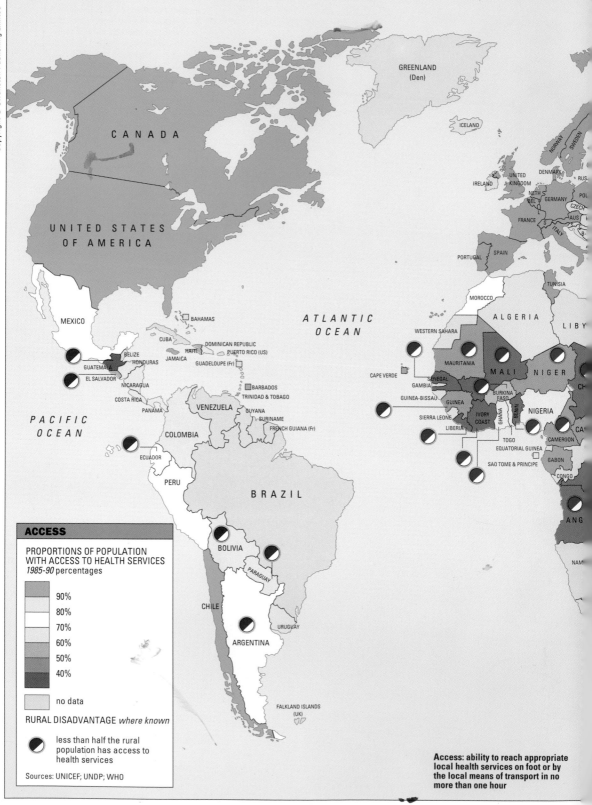

CANADA

UNITED STATES
OF AMERICA

GREENLAND
(Den)

ICELAND

NORWAY
SWEDEN

IRELAND
UNITED
KINGDOM
DENMARK
RUS.

NETH.
BEL. GERMANY
POL.
CZECH.
FRANCE
AUS.
ITALY B-

PORTUGAL
SPAIN

MEXICO

BAHAMAS

CUBA
DOMINICAN REPUBLIC
HAITI
PUERTO RICO (US)
BELIZE
HONDURAS
JAMAICA
GUATEMALA
GUADELOUPE (Fr)
EL SALVADOR
NICARAGUA
COSTA RICA
PANAMA

ATLANTIC
OCEAN

TUNISIA

MOROCCO

ALGERIA
LIBYA

WESTERN SAHARA

CAPE VERDE

MAURITANIA
MALI
NIGER
CH

SENEGAL
GAMBIA
BURKINA
FASO
NIGERIA
GUINEA-BISSAU
GUINEA
BENIN
CA
IVORY
COAST
GHANA
SIERRA LEONE
TOGO
CAMEROON
LIBERIA
EQUATORIAL GUINEA
GABON
SAO TOME & PRINCIPE
CONGO

BARBADOS
TRINIDAD & TOBAGO

VENEZUELA
GUYANA
SURINAME
FRENCH GUIANA (Fr)

PACIFIC
OCEAN

COLOMBIA

ECUADOR

PERU

BRAZIL

ANG

NAM

PARAGUAY

BOLIVIA

CHILE

URUGUAY

ARGENTINA

FALKLAND ISLANDS
(UK)

ACCESS

PROPORTIONS OF POPULATION
WITH ACCESS TO HEALTH SERVICES
1985-90 percentages

- 90%
- 80%
- 70%
- 60%
- 50%
- 40%

- no data

RURAL DISADVANTAGE *where known*

less than half the rural
population has access to
health services

Sources: UNICEF; UNDP; WHO

**Access: ability to reach appropriate
local health services on foot or by
the local means of transport in no
more than one hour**

It has been known for 30 percent of a nation's health budget to go on sending a privileged few abroad for treatment.

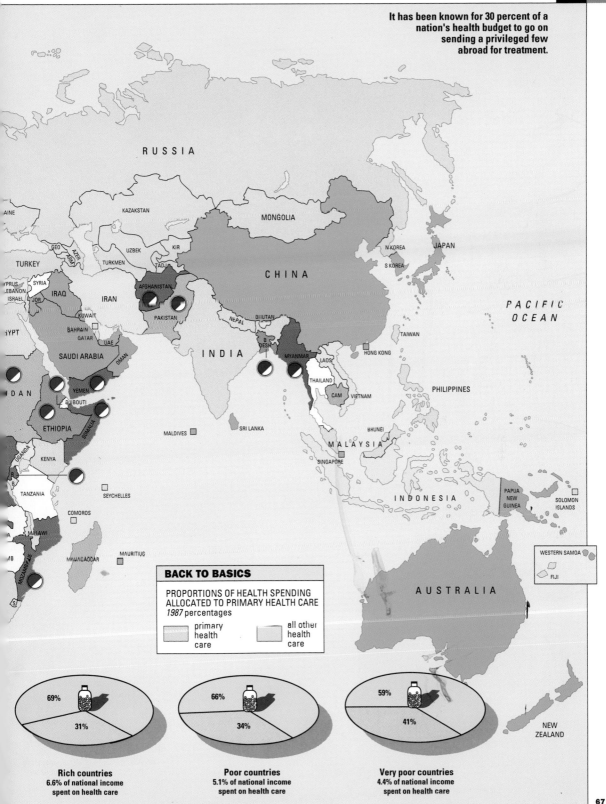

BACK TO BASICS

PROPORTIONS OF HEALTH SPENDING
ALLOCATED TO PRIMARY HEALTH CARE
1987 percentages

primary health care

all other health care

69%
31%

Rich countries
6.6% of national income
spent on health care

66%
34%

Poor countries
5.1% of national income
spent on health care

59%
41%

Very poor countries
4.4% of national income
spent on health care

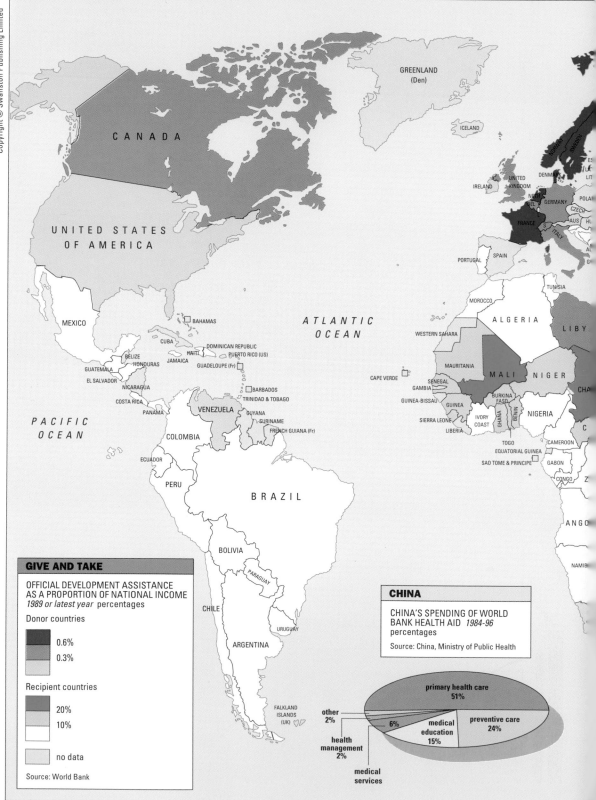

GREENLAND
(Den)

ICELAND

C A N A D A

NORWAY SWEDEN

ES
LA
LIT

DENMARK

IRELAND UNITED
KINGDOM

NETH
BEL GERMANY POLA
CZECH

UNITED STATES
OF AMERICA

FRANCE S AUS HU
ITALY

A
G

PORTUGAL SPAIN

TUNISIA

MOROCCO

MEXICO

ATLANTIC
OCEAN

WESTERN SAHARA

ALGERIA

LIBY

BAHAMAS

CUBA

DOMINICAN REPUBLIC
HAITI PUERTO RICO (US)

MAURITANIA

MALI

NIGER

CHA

BELIZE
HONDURAS JAMAICA

GUATEMALA

EL SALVADOR

GUADELOUPE (Fr)

CAPE VERDE

SENEGAL
GAMBIA

BURKINA
FASO

NICARAGUA

COSTA RICA

BARBADOS

GUINEA-BISSAU

GUINEA

BENIN

NIGERIA

PANAMA

TRINIDAD & TOBAGO

SIERRA LEONE

IVORY
COAST GHANA

PACIFIC
OCEAN

VENEZUELA

GUYANA

SURINAME

LIBERIA

TOGO

C

CAMEROON

FRENCH GUIANA (Fr)

EQUATORIAL GUINEA

COLOMBIA

SAO TOME & PRINCIPE

GABON

ECUADOR

CONGO

Z

PERU

BRAZIL

ANGO

BOLIVIA

NAMIB

PARAGUAY

CHILE

URUGUAY

ARGENTINA

FALKLAND
ISLANDS
(UK)

GIVE AND TAKE

OFFICIAL DEVELOPMENT ASSISTANCE
AS A PROPORTION OF NATIONAL INCOME
1989 or latest year percentages

Donor countries

0.6%

0.3%

Recipient countries

20%

10%

no data

Source: World Bank

CHINA

CHINA'S SPENDING OF WORLD
BANK HEALTH AID *1984-96*
percentages

Source: China, Ministry of Public Health

primary health care
51%

other
2%

6%

medical
education
15%

preventive care
24%

health
management
2%

medical
services

Loan repayments cost poor countries three times more than they receive in official development assistance from abroad. Less than 5 percent of this assistance goes on health care.

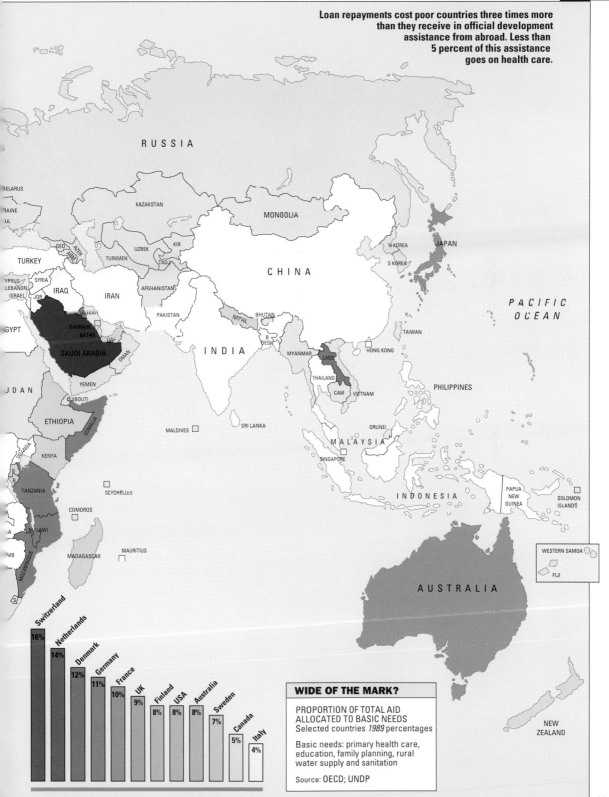

RUSSIA

BELARUS

RAINE

UL

KAZAKSTAN

MONGOLIA

TURKEY

GEO
AZER
ARM

UZBEK

TURKMEN

KIR

N-KOREA

JAPAN

YPRUS
LEBANON
ISRAEL

SYRIA

IRAQ

JOR

KUWAIT

BAHRAIN
QATAR

UAE

AFGHANISTAN

TAD

S-KOREA

CHINA

PACIFIC
OCEAN

IRAN

GYPT

PAKISTAN

NEPAL

BHUTAN

TAIWAN

JDAN

SAUDI ARABIA

OMAN

YEMEN

DJIBOUTI

INDIA

B
DESH

MYANMAR

LAOS

HONG KONG

THAILAND

VIETNAM

PHILIPPINES

ETHIOPIA

SOMALIA

MALDIVES

SRI LANKA

CAM

BRUNEI

UGANDA

KENYA

MALAYSIA

R

TANZANIA

SEYCHELLES

SINGAPORE

INDONESIA

PAPUA
NEW
GUINEA

SOLOMON
ISLANDS

COMOROS

A

MALAWI

MADAGASCAR

MAURITIUS

WESTERN SAMOA

FIJI

MB

MOZAMBIQUE

AUSTRALIA

NEW
ZEALAND

Bar chart

Country	Percentage
Switzerland	16%
Netherlands	14%
Denmark	12%
Germany	11%
France	10%
UK	9%
Finland	8%
USA	8%
Australia	8%
Sweden	7%
Canada	5%
Italy	4%

WIDE OF THE MARK?

PROPORTION OF TOTAL AID ALLOCATED TO BASIC NEEDS
Selected countries *1989* percentages

Basic needs: primary health care, education, family planning, rural water supply and sanitation

Source: OECD; UNDP

GREENLAND
(Den)

ICELAND

CANADA

UNITED STATES
OF AMERICA

ATLANTIC
OCEAN

PACIFIC
OCEAN

BERMUDA

MEXICO

BAHAMAS

CUBA
HAITI DOMINICAN REPUBLIC
        PUERTO RICO (US)
JAMAICA
BELIZE
HONDURAS GUADELOUPE (Fr)
GUATEMALA
EL SALVADOR
NICARAGUA   BARBADOS
                   TRINIDAD & TOBAGO
COSTA RICA
PANAMA   VENEZUELA GUYANA
                   SURINAME
COLOMBIA   FRENCH GUIANA (Fr)

ECUADOR

PERU

BRAZIL

BOLIVIA

PARAGUAY

CHILE

URUGUAY

ARGENTINA

FALKLAND ISLANDS
(UK)

NORWAY SWEDEN
UNITED
KINGDOM DENMARK
IRELAND
          NETH GERMANY
          BEL
          FRANCE
                  ITALY

PORTUGAL SPAIN

MOROCCO

WESTERN SAHARA

TUNISIA

ALGERIA   LIBYA

MAURITANIA MALI NIGER

CAPE VERDE
SENEGAL
GAMBIA
GUINEA-BISSAU
             GUINEA   BURKINA
SIERRA LEONE IVORY FASO NIGERIA
              COAST GHANA BENIN
LIBERIA
             TOGO
             EQUATORIAL GUINEA CAMEROON

SAO TOME & PRINCIPE GABON
                     CONGO

ANGO

NAMIB

CHIROPRACTIC

QUALIFIED CHIROPRACTORS *1991*

- 200
- 100
- 50
- 25
- 10
- 1
- no chiropractors

Highest: USA more than 50,000; Canada
2668; Australia 1267; UK 423; France 280;
Denmark 262

chiropractic colleges

Source: Dynamic Chiropractic

HOMEOPATHY IN INDIA

HOMEOPATHY COMPARED WITH
'WESTERN' MEDICINE IN INDIA
1980s

Source: Homeopathic Association of India

218,000
'Western' doctors

106 medical schools

143,000
registered homeopaths

96 colleges of homeopathy

UNITED STAT
OF AMERICA

MEXICO

The disaffected rich are turning to holistic health; the rural poor have no choice but to use traditional medicine. Both share modalities of treatment, such as acupuncture and herbal medicine, and emphasize the balance of mind, body and spirit.

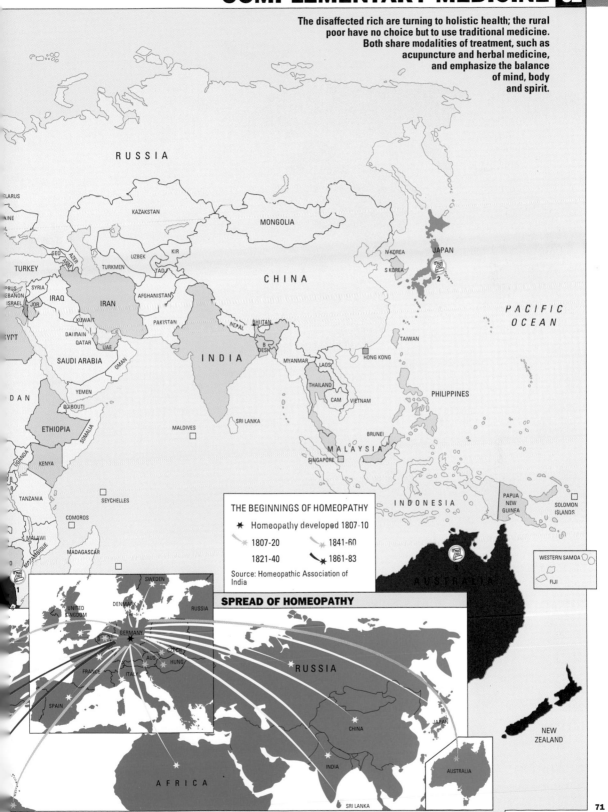

THE BEGINNINGS OF HOMEOPATHY

* ✱ Homeopathy developed 1807-10
* 1807-20
* 1821-40
* 1841-60
* 1861-83

Source: Homeopathic Association of India

SPREAD OF HOMEOPATHY

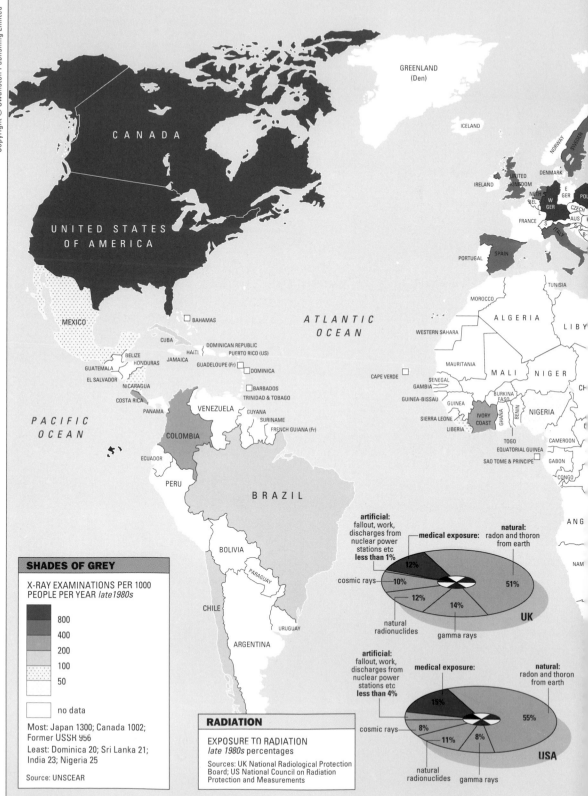

GREENLAND
(Den)

ICELAND

C A N A D A

UNITED STATES
OF AMERICA

NORWAY
SWEDEN

IRELAND
UNITED
KINGDOM
DENMARK

NETH
BEL
W
GER
E
GER
POL

CZECH

FRANCE
S
ITALY
AUS
B

PORTUGAL
SPAIN

MEXICO

BAHAMAS

CUBA
DOMINICAN REPUBLIC
HAITI   PUERTO RICO (US)
BELIZE   JAMAICA
GUATEMALA   HONDURAS   GUADELOUPE (Fr)
EL SALVADOR   DOMINICA
NICARAGUA
COSTA RICA   BARBADOS
PANAMA   TRINIDAD & TOBAGO

A T L A N T I C
O C E A N

TUNISIA

MOROCCO

WESTERN SAHARA

A L G E R I A
L I B Y

MAURITANIA
M A L I   N I G E R   CH

CAPE VERDE

SENEGAL
GAMBIA
GUINEA-BISSAU   GUINEA
BURKINA
FASO
NIGERIA

SIERRA LEONE   IVORY
COAST   GHANA   BENIN

TOGO
LIBERIA

VENEZUELA
GUYANA
SURINAME
FRENCH GUIANA (Fr)

COLOMBIA

ECUADOR

PERU

P A C I F I C
O C E A N

EQUATORIAL GUINEA
SAO TOME & PRINCIPE   CAMEROON
GABON
CONGO

B R A Z I L

A N G

NAM

BOLIVIA

PARAGUAY

CHILE

URUGUAY

ARGENTINA

artificial:
fallout, work,
discharges from
nuclear power
stations etc
less than 1%

medical exposure:

natural:
radon and thoron
from earth

12%

cosmic rays — 10%

12%

51%

14%

natural
radionuclides

gamma rays

UK

artificial:
fallout, work,
discharges from
nuclear power
stations etc
less than 4%

medical exposure:

natural:
radon and thoron
from earth

15%

55%

cosmic rays — 8%

11%

8%

natural
radionuclides

gamma rays

USA

SHADES OF GREY

X-RAY EXAMINATIONS PER 1000
PEOPLE PER YEAR *late1980s*

▓	800
▒	400
░	200
∴	100
	50
	no data

Most: Japan 1300; Canada 1002;
Former USSR 956

Least: Dominica 20; Sri Lanka 21;
India 23; Nigeria 25

Source: UNSCEAR

RADIATION

EXPOSURE TO RADIATION
late 1980s percentages

Sources: UK National Radiological Protection
Board; US National Council on Radiation
Protection and Measurements

Data compiled by Barrie Lambert, St Bartholomew's Hospital, London

70 percent of the world's population has little or no access to X-ray diagnosis and treatment.

Former USSR

MUNGOLIA

CHINA

JAPAN

N KOREA

S KOREA

TURKEY

CYPRUS
LEBANON
ISRAEL
SYRIA
IRAQ
JOR
IRAN
AFGHANISTAN
KUWAIT
BAHRAIN
QATAR
UAE
OMAN
SAUDI ARABIA
YEMEN
DJIBOUTI

PAKISTAN

NEPAL
BHUTAN
B
DESH
INDIA
MYANMAR
LAOS
THAILAND
CAM
VIETNAM

TAIWAN

HONG KONG

PHILIPPINES

EGYPT

UDAN

ETHIOPIA

SOMALIA

UGANDA

KENYA

TANZANIA

SEYCHELLES

COMOROS

MALAWI

ZIMB

MOZAMBIQUE

MADAGASCAR

MAURITIUS

MALDIVES

SRI LANKA

MALAYSIA

SINGAPORE

BRUNEI

INDONESIA

PAPUA
NEW
GUINEA

SOLOMON
ISLANDS

PACIFIC OCEAN

AUSTRALIA

WESTERN SAMOA

FIJI

NEW ZEALAND

ON SCREEN

X-RAY INVESTIGATIONS PER 1000 PEOPLE *late 1980s*

Sources: UK National Radiation Protection Board; US National Council on Radiological Protection and Measurements

	UK	Netherlands	France	Italy	USA	Japan
Mammograms	4	8	5	7	6	1
CT Scans	4		5	13	14	123
Mass chest screening	12	12	166	81		242

MEDICINES

ANNUAL EXPENDITURE ON
PHARMACEUTICAL PRODUCTS PER
PERSON latest available year US $

100
50
10

no data

Source: WHO

NEW DRUGS

NUMBER OF DRUGS NEEDED
COMPARED WITH NEW DRUGS
LAUNCHED *late 1980s*

Source: WHO

new drugs launched every year

teaching hospital

district hospital

dispensary or health centre

village health post

1500

200

100

30-40

10-15

We spend US $100 billion a year on pharmaceutical products – well over $100 a person in some rich countries, down to less than $1 per person in sub-Saharan Africa.

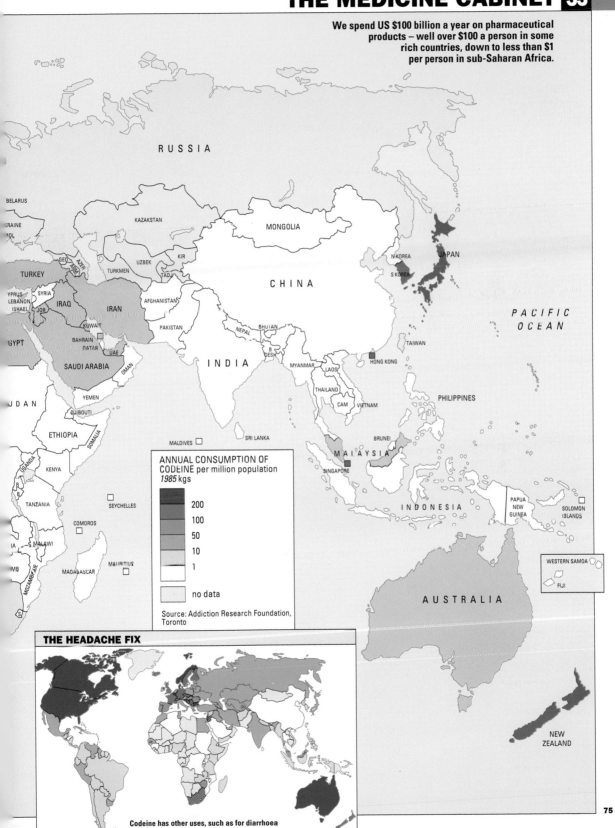

RUSSIA

BELARUS

KRAINE

IOL

KAZAKSTAN

MONGOLIA

N.KOREA

JAPAN

S.KOREA

TURKEY

GEO AZER ARM

UZBEK

KIR

TURKMEN

TADJ

CHINA

PACIFIC OCEAN

YPRUS LEBANON ISHAEL SYRIA JOR

IRAQ

IRAN

AFGHANISTAN

KUWAIT

BAHRAIN QATAR UAE

OMAN

SAUDI ARABIA

GYPT

PAKISTAN

NEPAL

BHUTAN

B DESH

INDIA

MYANMAR

TAIWAN

HONG KONG

YEMEN

DJIBOUTI

LAOS

THAILAND

CAM VIETNAM

PHILIPPINES

JDAN

ETHIOPIA

SOMALIA

MALDIVES

SRI LANKA

BRUNEI

MALAYSIA

UGANDA

R B

KENYA

SEYCHELLES

SINGAPORE

INDONESIA

PAPUA NEW GUINEA

SOLOMON ISLANDS

TANZANIA

COMOROS

MALAWI

MOZAMBIQUE

MADAGASCAR

MAURITIUS

WESTERN SAMOA

FIJI

AUSTRALIA

NEW ZEALAND

ANNUAL CONSUMPTION OF CODEINE per million population
1985 kgs

- 200
- 100
- 50
- 10
- 1

no data

Source: Addiction Research Foundation, Toronto

THE HEADACHE FIX

Codeine has other uses, such as for diarrhoea

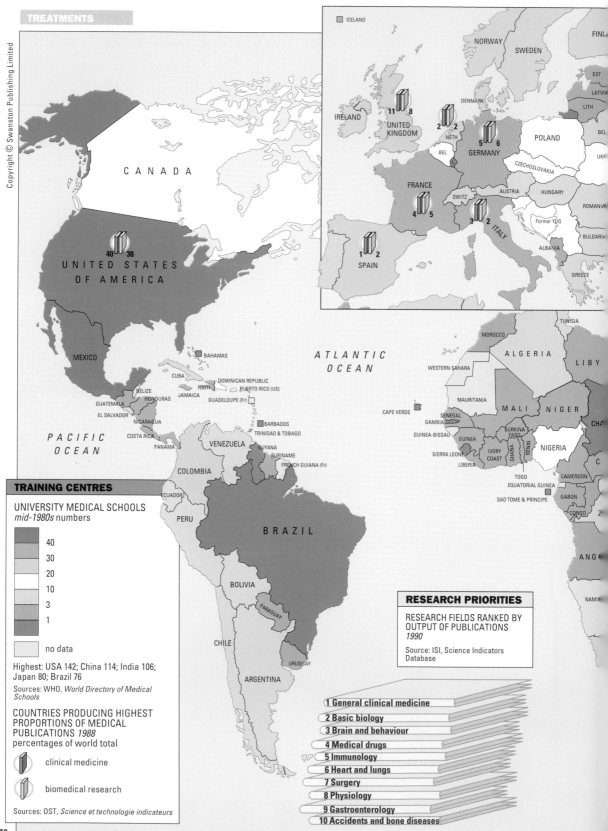

ICELAND

NORWAY

SWEDEN

FINL

IRELAND

UNITED
KINGDOM

11 8

DENMARK

EST

LATVIA

LITH

BEL

UKF

NETH

BEL

2 2

GERMANY

5 6

POLAND

CZECHOSLOVAKIA

FRANCE

4 5

SWITZ

AUSTRIA

HUNGARY

ROMANIA

Former YUG

3 2

ITALY

BULGARIA

ALBANIA

GREECE

SPAIN

1 2

C A N A D A

UNITED STATES

OF AMERICA

40 38

MEXICO

BAHAMAS

CUBA

DOMINICAN REPUBLIC

HAITI

PUERTO RICO (US)

JAMAICA

GUADELOUPE (Fr)

BELIZE

HONDURAS

GUATEMALA

EL SALVADOR

NICARAGUA

COSTA RICA

PANAMA

BARBADOS

TRINIDAD & TOBAGO

ATLANTIC
OCEAN

CAPE VERDE

MOROCCO

WESTERN SAHARA

ALGERIA

LIBY

TUNISIA

MAURITANIA

MALI

NIGER

CHA

SENEGAL

GAMBIA

GUINEA-BISSAU

GUINEA

SIERRA LEONE

LIBERIA

IVORY
COAST

GHANA

BURKINA
FASO

BENIN

TOGO

NIGERIA

CAMEROON

EQUATORIAL GUINEA

SAO TOME & PRINCIPE

GABON

CONGO

C

PACIFIC
OCEAN

VENEZUELA

GUYANA

SURINAME

FRENCH GUIANA (Fr)

COLOMBIA

ECUADOR

PERU

B R A Z I L

BOLIVIA

PARAGUAY

CHILE

URUGUAY

ARGENTINA

ANG

NAMI

Z

TRAINING CENTRES

UNIVERSITY MEDICAL SCHOOLS
mid-1980s numbers

- 40
- 30
- 20
- 10
- 3
- 1

no data

Highest: USA 142; China 114; India 106;
Japan 80; Brazil 76

Sources: WHO, *World Directory of Medical
Schools*

COUNTRIES PRODUCING HIGHEST
PROPORTIONS OF MEDICAL
PUBLICATIONS *1988*
percentages of world total

clinical medicine

biomedical research

Sources: OST, *Science et technologie indicateurs*

RESEARCH PRIORITIES

RESEARCH FIELDS RANKED BY
OUTPUT OF PUBLICATIONS
1990

Source: ISI, Science Indicators
Database

1 General clinical medicine
2 Basic biology
3 Brain and behaviour
4 Medical drugs
5 Immunology
6 Heart and lungs
7 Surgery
8 Physiology
9 Gastroenterology
10 Accidents and bone diseases

Data compiled by Harriet Muir Moxham and Lesley A. Rogers, Wellcome Trust, London

While rich countries spend US $30 per person on health-related research and development, poor countries spend barely 30 cents. In the USA, cancer and AIDS are the diseases which receive most funding.

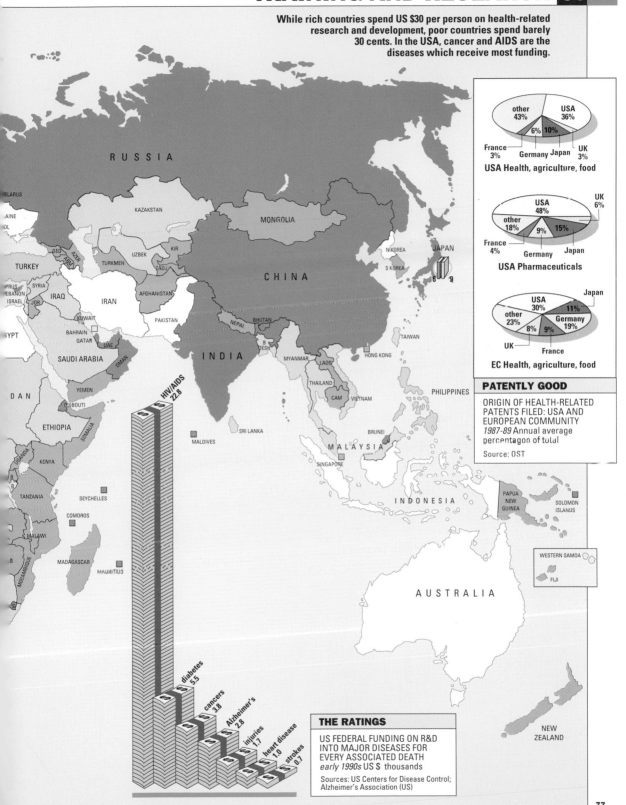

USA Health, agriculture, food

other 43%
USA 36%
France 3%
Germany 6%
Japan 10%
UK 3%

USA Pharmaceuticals

USA 48%
UK 6%
other 18%
France 4%
Germany 9%
Japan 15%

EC Health, agriculture, food

USA 30%
Japan 11%
other 23%
Germany 19%
UK 8%
France 9%

PATENTLY GOOD

ORIGIN OF HEALTH-RELATED PATENTS FILED: USA AND EUROPEAN COMMUNITY
1987-89 Annual average percentage of total

Source: OST

HIV/AIDS 22.8

diabetes 5.5
cancers 3.8
Alzheimer's 2.8
injuries 1.7
heart disease 1.0
strokes 0.7

THE RATINGS

US FEDERAL FUNDING ON R&D INTO MAJOR DISEASES FOR EVERY ASSOCIATED DEATH
early 1990s US $ thousands

Sources: US Centers for Disease Control; Alzheimer's Association (US)

THE UNDER-ONES

PROPORTION OF INFANTS IMMUNIZED
BY THE AGE OF ONE YEAR AGAINST
DIPHTHERIA, WHOOPING COUGH AND
TETANUS *1990* percentages

- 90
- 80
- 70
- 60
- 50
- 40

no data

Sources: WHO, UNICEF

Each year immunization saves the lives of three million children. Two million more are now walking and running who would otherwise have been crippled by polio.

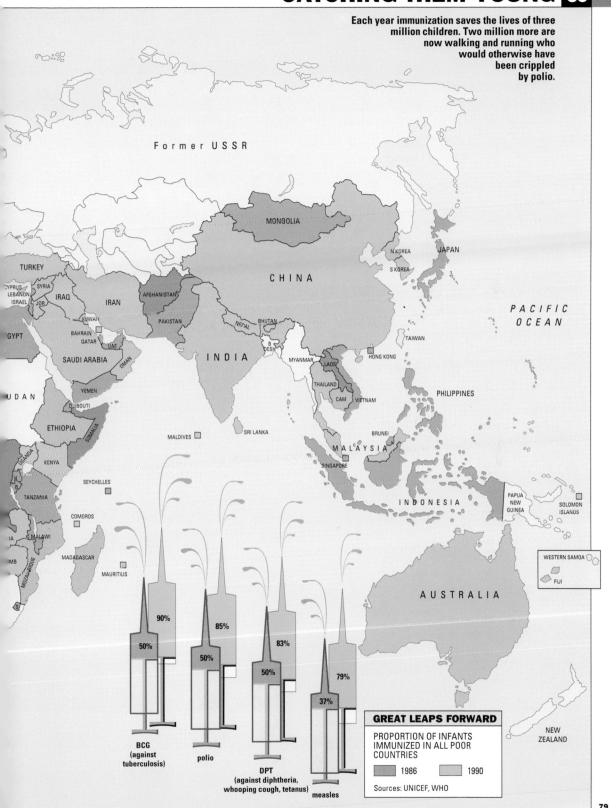

Former USSR

MONGOLIA

N.KOREA

JAPAN

S.KOREA

CHINA

PACIFIC OCEAN

TURKEY

CYPRUS
LEBANON
ISRAEL
SYRIA
IRAQ
JOR
KUWAIT
IRAN
AFGHANISTAN
PAKISTAN
NEPAL
BHUTAN

EGYPT

BAHRAIN
QATAR
UAE
SAUDI ARABIA
OMAN

YEMEN

DJIBOUTI

SUDAN

ETHIOPIA

SOMALIA

UGANDA
KENYA

B
TANZANIA

COMOROS

MALAWI

MB

MOZAMBIQUE

MADAGASCAR

MAURITIUS

SEYCHELLES

MALDIVES

INDIA

SRI LANKA

B
DESH

MYANMAR

THAILAND

LAOS

CAM
VIETNAM

HONG KONG

TAIWAN

PHILIPPINES

BRUNEI

MALAYSIA

SINGAPORE

INDONESIA

PAPUA
NEW
GUINEA

SOLOMON
ISLANDS

WESTERN SAMOA

FIJI

AUSTRALIA

NEW
ZEALAND

90%

50%

BCG
(against
tuberculosis)

85%

50%

polio

83%

50%

DPT
(against diphtheria,
whooping cough, tetanus)

79%

37%

measles

GREAT LEAPS FORWARD

PROPORTION OF INFANTS
IMMUNIZED IN ALL POOR
COUNTRIES

| 1986 | 1990 |

Sources: UNICEF, WHO

State	Projected population 1995 thousands	Population per sq km 1995 numbers	Life expectancy those born years 1990-95	Average births in woman's lifetime numbers 1990
Afghanistan	23,122	35	43.5	6.9
Albania	3,521	121	72.8	2.9
Algeria	28,704	12	66.2	5.1
Angola	11,531	9	46.5	6.4
Argentina	34,264	12	71.4	2.9
Australia	17,901	2	76.9	1.8
Austria	7,601	90	75.3	1.5
Bahamas	249	18	—	—
Bahrain	602	602	71.6	—
Bangladesh	132,219	918	52.9	5.3
Barbados	259	647	75.6	—
Belarus	10,200	—	—	2.1
Belgium	9,845	317	75.6	1.6
Belize	184	8	—	—
Benin	5,421	48	48.0	7.1
Bhutan	1,698	36	50.0	5.5
Bolivia	8,422	8	55.9	5.9
Botswana	1,549	3	61.1	6.7
Brazil	165,083	19	66.3	3.3
Brunei	249	41	—	—
Bulgaria	9,036	81	73.1	1.9
Burkina Faso	10,396	38	49.2	6.5
Burundi	6,362	227	49.5	6.8
Cambodia	9,205	51	51.0	4.6
Cameroon	14,037	30	55.0	6.9
Canada	27,557	3	77.3	1.7
Cape Verde	438	109	67.8	—
Central African Republic	3,511	6	50.5	6.2
Chad	6,447	5	47.5	5.8
Chile	14,237	19	72.1	2.7
China	1,222,562	128	70.9	2.4
Colombia	36,182	32	69.3	3.0
Comoros	658	329	56.0	—
Congo	2,678	8	54.7	6.3
Costa Rica	3,374	66	75.2	3.1
Cuba	11,091	100	75.7	1.9
Cyprus	733	81	76.6	—
Czechoslovakia	15,874	124	72.4	2.0
Denmark	5,158	120	76.2	1.5
Djibouti	474	21	49.0	—

Note: *Some independent states with small populations, such as St. Kitts-Nevis-Anguilla (pop. 20,000) and some dependencies or otherwise non-independent states*
Sources: Cols. 1 & 2: *as for map 1;* **Col. 3:** *as for map 6;* **Col. 4:** *as for map 2;* **Col. 5:** *as for map 11;* **Col. 6:** *as for map 16;* **Col. 7:** *as for map 27;* **Col. 8:** *as for map 28;* **C**

:ality of children er five per 1000 e births 1990	Alcohol consumption litres per adult p.a. latest data 1992	Government income spent on health percentages 1987	People per doctor numbers 1984	Medical schools numbers mid-1980s	Immunized by 1 year against DPT percentages 1990
292	—	—	10,000 (est.)	2	25
37	0.57	—	727	1	94
98	0.37	1.3	2,340	9	89
292	0.80	1.0	17,790	1	23
35	12.59	1.5	370	9	85
10	10.05	—	440	10	93
9	9.72	7.1	390	3	90
—	12.09	—	1,100	0	86
17	—	2.6	1,000	—	95
180	—	0.6	6,730	8	62
12	6.76	4.0	1,133	0	91
—	—	—	—	3	—
9	11.33	4.2	??0	11	80
29	4.01	—	2,200	—	84
147	1.35	0.8	15,940	1	67
189	2.38	—	9,730	0	95
160	2.94	0.4	1,540	3	41
85	2.66	3.8	6,900	—	86
83	2.55	1.7	1,080	76	81
—	4.29	0.8	2,025	0	89
18	11.77	—	280	5	100
228	—	1.0	265,250	1	37
192	8.07	0.8	21,030	—	86
193	0.58	—	—	1	40
148	8.60	0.8	—	1	56
9	8.61	—	510	16	85
56	1.25	—	5,800	0	88
169	2.33	1.2	23,530	1	82
216	0.36	0.6	38,360	0	20
27	6.72	2.1	1,230	6	99
42	1.20	1.4	1,010	114	97
50	2.68	0.7	1,240	21	87
151	0.03	—	17,742	0	94
110	2.66	2.1	8,320	1	79
22	3.03	5.0	960	2	95
14	2.26	3.0	530	4	92
13	4.46	2.0	1,100	0	90
13	10.29	—	280	10	99
9	9.73	3.7	400	3	99
164	—	—	1,000	0	85

o Rico, do not feature here. Information on the new republics of Yugoslavia and on the former USSR, not listed here, may appear on the appropriate map.
ap 34; **Col. 10:** as for map 35.

State	Projected population 1995 thousands	Population per sq km 1995 numbers	Life expectancy those born years 1990-95	Average births in woman's lifetime numbers 1990
Dominican Republic	7,915	162	67.5	3.5
Ecuador	11,934	42	66.6	4.1
Egypt	58,388	58	61.6	4.3
El Salvador	5,943	283	66.5	4.7
Equatorial Guinea	400	14	48.0	—
Estonia	1,573	—	—	2.2
Ethiopia	57,140	47	47.0	6.8
Fiji	824	46	65.9	—
Finland	5,031	15	75.9	1.7
France	57,138	104	76.8	1.8
Gabon	1,382	5	53.5	5.2
Gambia	984	89	45.0	—
Germany	77,330	217	75.0	1.5
Ghana	17,608	74	56.0	6.3
Greece	10,124	77	76.5	1.7
Grenada	94	313	—	—
Guatemala	10,621	97	64.8	5.6
Guinea	6,700	27	44.5	7.0
Guinea-Bissau	1,073	30	43.5	5.8
Guyana	829	4	65.2	—
Haiti	7,215	258	56.7	4.9
Honduras	5,968	53	65.8	5.2
Hong Kong	6,080	6,080	77.6	1.4
Hungary	10,509	113	71.6	1.8
Iceland	264	3	78.1	—
India	946,716	288	60.4	4.2
Indonesia	201,797	106	62.7	3.3
Iran	60,390	37	67.1	5.0
Iraq	22,411	51	66.2	6.1
Ireland	3,900	56	75.1	2.4
Israel	4,958	236	76.3	2.9
Italy	57,114	190	76.4	1.4
Ivory Coast	14,535	45	54.4	7.4
Jamaica	2,603	237	73.6	2.5
Japan	125,904	333	78.8	1.7
Jordan	4,738	53	67.9	5.8
Kenya	28,978	50	61.0	6.9
Korea, North	23,966	198	71.1	2.5
Korea, South	44,655	451	70.8	1.7
Kuwait	2,347	130	73.9	3.7

Note: *Some independent states with small populations, such as St. Kitts-Nevis-Anguilla (pop. 20,000) and some dependencies or otherwise non-independent states*
Sources: Cols. 1 & 2: *as for map 1;* **Col. 3:** *as for map 6;* **Col. 4:** *as for map 2;* **Col. 5:** *as for map 11;* **Col. 6:** *as for map 16;* **Col. 7:** *as for map 27;* **Col. 8:** *as for map 28;*

rtality of children ler five per 1000 ve births 1990	Alcohol consumption litres per adult p.a. latest data 1992	Government income spent on health percentages 1987	People per doctor numbers 1984	Medical schools numbers mid-1980s	Immunized by 1 year against DPT percentages 1990
78	2.49	1.7	1,760	12	69
83	1.89	1.9	820	6	68
85	0.05	1.1	770	11	87
87	1.31	0.9	2,830	5	76
206	—	—	—	—	78
—	—	—	—	1	—
220	0.76	1.3	78,770	3	44
31	1.90	2.4	2,200	1	97
7	6.64	5.9	440	5	90
9	16.23	6.6	320	37	95
164	9.37	1.6	2,290	1	78
238	1.14	1.6	11,600	0	90
9	11.55	7.5	380	30	95
140	1.03	1.2	20,460	2	57
11	7.31	—	350	6	83
38	4.82	—	1,954	1	80
94	2.52	1.2	2,180	2	66
237	0.06	1.0	46,420	1	17
246	2.52	—	7,500	—	38
71	2.32	4.4	6,200	0	83
130	4.64	1.3	7,130	1	41
84	1.60	3.3	1,510	1	84
7	2.24	—	1,070	2	88
16	12.90	—	310	4	99
—	3.28	—	354	1	99
142	0.01	0.9	2,520	106	92
97	0.37	0.5	9,460	14	87
59	0.33	1.5	2,840	19	93
86	0.39	0.8	1,740	6	75
9	5.97	5.3	680	5	77
11	2.89	—	350	4	87
10	12.55	5.7	230	31	85
136	2.30	1.7	—	1	48
20	1.88	2.8	2,040	1	86
6	6.75	—	660	80	87
52	0.32	2.7	1,120	2	92
108	1.61	2.0	10,050	2	74
35	3.72	1.0	420	10	98
30	8.10	0.4	1,160	31	74
19	—	2.8	640	1	94

State	Projected population 1995 thousands	Population per sq km 1995 numbers	Life expectancy those born years 1990-95	Average births in woman's lifetime numbers 1990
Laos	4,788	20	51.0	6.7
Latvia	2,681	—	—	2.2
Lebanon	3,014	301	67.1	3.6
Lesotho	2,053	68	58.5	5.8
Liberia	3,032	27	55.4	6.8
Libya	5,446	3	63.1	6.8
Lithuania	3,690	—	—	2.2
Luxembourg	376	145	75.3	—
Madagascar	14,113	24	55.5	6.6
Malawi	10,494	89	49.1	7.6
Malaysia	20,037	61	70.8	3.8
Maldives	210	700	—	—
Mali	10,799	9	46.0	7.1
Mauritania	2,335	2	48.0	6.5
Mexico	97,967	50	70.4	3.3
Mongolia	2,503	16	63.7	4.9
Morocco	28,301	63	63.3	4.5
Mozambique	17,922	22	48.5	6.3
Myanmar (Burma)	46,275	68	62.5	3.9
Namibia	2,079	3	58.8	5.9
Nepal	21,521	153	53.5	5.7
Netherlands	15,409	416	77.6	1.6
New Zealand	3,534	13	75.6	2.0
Nicaragua	4,539	35	66.3	5.3
Niger	9,104	7	46.5	7.1
Nigeria	127.694	138	52.5	6.8
Norway	4,271	13	77.4	1.7
Oman	1,811	9	67.9	7.1
Pakistan	141,522	178	59.0	6.2
Panama	2,659	35	72.7	3.0
Papua New Guinea	4,341	9	55.9	5.0
Paraguay	4,893	12	67.3	4.5
Peru	23,854	19	64.6	3.8
Philippines	69,935	233	65.0	4.1
Poland	39,365	126	72.0	2.2
Portugal	10,429	113	74.5	1.7
Qatar	436	40	70.0	—
Romania	23,816	100	71.5	2.1
Russia	147,386	—	—	2.2
Rwanda	8,602	331	50.5	8.1

Note: *Some independent states with small populations, such as St. Kitts-Nevis-Anguilla (pop. 20,000) and some dependencies or otherwise non-independent states*
Sources: Cols. 1 & 2: *as for map 1;* **Col. 3:** *as for map 6;* **Col. 4:** *as for map 2;* **Col. 5:** *as for map 11;* **Col. 6:** *as for map 16;* **Col. 7:** *as for map 27;* **Col. 8:** *as for map 28;* C

tality of children er five per 1000 ve births 1990	Alcohol consumption litres per adult p.a. latest data 1992	Government income spent on health percentages 1987	People per doctor numbers 1984	Medical schools numbers mid-1980s	Immunized by 1 year against DPT percentages 1990
152	1.20	—	1,360	1	18
—	—	—	—	1	—
56	2.05	—	683	3	82
129	2.26	1.8	18,610	0	76
205	2.62	1.8	9,350	1	28
112	0.02	3.2	690	2	84
—	—	—	—	2	—
—	18.27	—	526	0	90
176	0.98	2.0	9,780	2	46
253	3.12	1.9	11,340	1	81
29	6.26	1.5	1,930	3	91
85	—	—	20,300	0	94
284	0.46	0.7	25,390	1	42
214	0.07	2.0	11,900	—	28
49	2.59	2.3	1,242	57	66
84	1.54	1.4	400	1	84
112	0.33	1.0	4,760	2	81
297	0.35	1.8	37,960	1	46
88	0.05	0.7	3,740	3	69
167	—	0.6	6,453	—	53
189	0.15	0.8	30,220	1	79
9	8.94	6.7	450	8	94
12	9.13	—	580	2	69
78	2.30	5.0	1,500	2	65
221	0.13	0.7	39,670	1	13
167	3.57	0.2	6,440	14	57
10	4.15	7.5	450	4	87
49	—	2.2	1,700	0	96
158	—	0.2	2,910	17	83
31	3.12	5.7	1,000	1	82
80	0.96	3.0	6,070	1	69
60	3.66	0.3	1,460	1	78
116	2.38	0.8	1,040	9	72
69	2.76	0.7	6,570	27	88
18	7.38	—	490	10	96
16	11.60	—	410	5	92
36	—	—	1,300	0	82
34	7.79	—	570	6	96
—	—	—	—	49	—
198	14.73	0.6	35,090	1	84

o Rico, do not feature here. Information on the new republics of Yugoslavia and on the former USSR, not listed here, may appear on the appropriate map.
ap 34; Col. 10: as for map 35.

State	Projected population 1995 thousands	Population per sq km 1995 numbers	Life expectancy those born years 1990-95	Average births in woman's lifetime numbers 1990
St Lucia	139	232	—	—
Sao Tome & Principe	120	120	—	—
Saudi Arabia	17,124	8	65.8	7.1
Senegal	8,423	43	49.3	6.3
Seychelles	67	134	—	—
Sierra Leone	4,740	66	43.0	6.5
Singapore	2,874	4,790	74.5	1.8
Somalia	8,441	13	47.1	6.6
South Africa	39,348	22	62.9	4.3
Spain	39,915	79	77.4	1.6
Sri Lanka	18,338	278	71.6	2.6
Sudan	29,128	12	51.8	6.4
Suriname	460	3	70.3	—
Swaziland	943	55	58.0	—
Sweden	8,509	19	77.8	1.9
Switzerland	6,682	163	77.8	1.5
Syria	15,001	81	67.2	6.5
Taiwan	21,155	588	—	—
Tanzania	32,971	35	55.0	7.1
Thailand	59,605	116	67.1	2.4
Togo	4,138	73	55.0	6.6
Trinidad & Tobago	1,376	275	72.2	2.8
Tunisia	9,076	55	67.8	3.7
Turkey	61,577	79	66.2	3.5
Uganda	22,666	96	53.0	7.3
Ukraine	51,704	—	—	2.1
United Arab Emirates	1,777	21	71.0	4.6
United Kingdom	57,864	236	76.1	1.8
USA	258,162	28	76.4	1.8
Uruguay	3,186	18	72.5	2.4
Vanuatu	152	13	—	—
Venezuela	22,212	24	70.3	3.6
Vietnam	74,475	226	63.9	3.9
Western Sahara	95	0.4	—	—
Western Samoa	163	54	—	—
Yemen	13,993	26	52.6	7.7
former Yugoslavia	24,389	95	73.2	1.9
Zaire	41,813	18	54.0	6.1
Zambia	10,222	14	55.4	7.2
Zimbabwe	11,340	29	60.8	5.6

Note: *Some independent states with small populations, such as St. Kitts-Nevis-Anguilla (pop. 20,000) and some dependencies or otherwise non-independent states*
Sources: Cols. 1 & 2: *as for map 1;* **Col. 3:** *as for map 6;* **Col. 4:** *as for map 2;* **Col. 5:** *as for map 11;* **Col. 6:** *as for map 16;* **Col. 7:** *as for map 27;* **Col. 8:** *as for map 28;* **C**

rtality of children ler five per 1000 ve births 1990	Alcohol consumption litres per adult p.a. latest data 1992	Government income spent on health percentages 1987	People per doctor numbers 1984	Medical schools numbers mid-1980s	Immunized by 1 year against DPT percentages 1990
23	6.36	—	3,971	1	89
55	2.93	—	2,500	0	66
91	0.04	3.6	740	4	94
185	0.40	1.1	13,060	1	60
21	—	—	2,200	0	82
257	5.05	0.6	13,620	0	83
9	1.64	1.3	1,310	1	85
215	0.01	0.2	16,080	1	18
88	5.93	0.6	1,604	7	67
10	11.92	5.0	320	23	73
35	0.41	1.7	5,520	5	90
172	1.48	0.2	10,190	3	62
38	4.48	—	1,379	1	83
167	3.35	2.3	23,879	0	89
7	5.63	8.5	390	6	99
9	11.03	7.2	700	5	90
59	0.18	0.4	1,260	3	90
8	—	—	1,080	9	—
170	3.59	1.1	24,980	1	85
34	0.91	1.1	6,290	7	92
147	2.27	1.7	8,700	1	61
17	5.07	3.2	950	0	82
62	0.74	2.2	2,150	4	90
80	0.89	1.5	1,390	22	74
164	10.24	0.3	21,900	1	77
—	—	—	—	15	—
30	—	1.0	1,020	0	85
9	6.90	5.7	700	29	75
11	8.36	5.0	470	142	97
25	4.15	1.0	510	1	88
—	0.79	—	5,500	0	76
43	4.37	2.0	700	7	63
65	0.43	—	950	8	87
—	—	—	—	—	—
—	0.26	—	2,500	0	66
187	0.31	1.5	5,639	1	89
23	6.79	—	550	11	91
130	2.39	0.9	12,940	3	32
122	3.28	2.0	7,150	1	79
87	3.94	3.7	6,700	1	73

o Rico, do not feature here. Information on the new republics of Yugoslavia and on the former USSR, not listed here, may appear on the appropriate map.
ap 34; **Col. 10:** as for map 35.

DATA SOURCES

World Health Organization (WHO)
WHO was the biggest single source of data and particular thanks must go to:

Dr Jane Ferguson, Technical Officer, Adolescent Health Programme; Mrs Carole Torel, Technical Officer, Expanded Programme on Immunization; Dr F. Luelmo, Medical Officer, Tuberculosis Unit; Dr F. S. Antezana, Director, Drug Action Programme, and Dr German Velasquez; Dr Claire Chollat Traquet, Tobacco or Health; Dr Tipani Piha, Regional Adviser, Tobacco or Health, WHO Regional Office for Europe; Dr Jennifer Sardo Infirri, Scientist, Oral Health Programme; Dr Jose Antonio Najera-Morrondo, Director, Division of Control of Tropical Diseases, Dr Ken Mott, Chief, Shistosomiasis and Trematode Infections, and Dr A.E.C. Rietveld, Malaria Unit; Dr Olayiwola Akerele, Programme Manager, Traditional Medicine Programme; Dr Hilary King, Diabetes and Other Noncommunicable Diseases Unit; Dr Paul Sato, Surveillance, Forecasting and Impact Assessment Unit (SFI), Global Programme on AIDS; Dr W. Gulbinat, Senior Scientist, Division of Mental Health; Dr Erica Royston, Maternal Health and Safe Motherhood; Ms Karin Esteves, Division of Communicable Diseases

United Nations Children's Fund (UNICEF), New York: Dr Beverley Carlson, Senior Adviser, Monitoring and Statistics
United Nations Development Programme (UNDP), New York: Dr Bernard Hausner, Senior Information Officer
The World Bank: Dr Stayce Brown, Consultant, Population, Health and Nutrition Division, Population and Human Resources Department
Population Division, UN, New York: Dr Larry Heligman, Chief, Estimates and Projections Section
Statistical Office, UN, New York: Dr Marie Chamie, Statistician, Demographic and Social Statistics Branch
UN International Drug Control Programme, Vienna: Dr Gale U. Day, Head Technical Services Division
International Agency for Research on Cancer (IARC), Lyon: Dr Max Parkin, Chief of the Descriptive Epidemiology Unit
Organisation for Economic Co-operation and Development (OECD), Paris: Dr Jean-Pierre Poullier, Chief, Statistics Section; Mr Bevan B. Stein, Head, Reporting Systems Division; Yasmin Ahmad, Creditor Reporting System.
Centre de Sociologie et de Demographie Medicales, Paris: Dr Bui Dang Ha Doan, Director
Addiction Research Foundation, Toronto: Dr M. Adrian, Dr P. Juli, Dr R. Williams
World federation of Chiropractic, Toronto: Dr David Chapman-Smith
Dynamic Chiropractic, Dr Donald Petersen

Professor Richard Feachem, Dean, London School of Hygiene and Tropical Medicine, kindly sent me *The Health of Adults in the Developing World*, published for The World Bank.

Data for Taiwan and Hong Kong were kindly provided by their respective Departments of Health.

NOTES TO THE MAPS

1 THE WEIGHT OF NUMBERS

Each day the world's population increases by just over a quarter of a million (the population of the Bahamas, Barbados, Brunei or Iceland). This is equivalent to 2 million more people a week (the population of Kuwait or Namibia) or 8 million more people each month (the population of Sweden or Paris). Each year the world's population expands by 96 million, the population of Mexico. Ninety million of these are born in poor countries and a mere 6 million in rich countries.

This rise will continue even if birth rates fall, because in the early 1990s one third of the world's population is under 15 years old, and will soon enter the child-bearing age. In contrast, only six percent of the world's inhabitants are over 65 years old. The inset map 'The three ages' highlights countries with the lowest median age, where the population is likely to grow at the fastest rate. Africa is experiencing the largest growth rate ever seen. Even given the worst-case scenario for AIDS in Africa, the cartogram 'Shifting shares' shows that the population will still have increased dramatically by 2025.

This large global increase in population is caused principally by falling death rates, due to improved living conditions, better nutrition and access to health care systems. It has little to do with increasing birth rates. A health official once said of the increase of the world's population 'It is not that people started breeding like rabbits; it is just that they stopped dying like flies.'

About half of the world's population live in just four countries: China, India, USA and Indonesia. If the next six largest countries (Brazil, Russia, Pakistan, Bangladesh, Nigeria and Japan) are included, then the proportion rises to nearly two thirds.

The population in Europe and North America is now fairly stable, and in Germany and Hungary has even begun to decline. The share of the world's population living in rich countries will have fallen from one third in 1950 to less than 20 percent in 2025, while in poor countries it will have risen from two thirds to more than 80 percent. At least 95 percent of the increase in growth of the world's population will take place in poor countries.

Sources:
United Nations (UN), *World Population Prospects 1990*, UN, 1991; UN, *The Sex and Age Distributions of Populations: The 1990 Revision*, UN, 1991; The World Bank, *World Development Report 1991*, New York and London: Oxford University Press, 1991; World Health Organization (WHO), *Global Estimates for Health Situation Assessment and Projections*, Geneva: WHO, 1990, Walker, Alison, 'Population: more than a numbers game', *British Medical Journal*, 303, November 1991.

Acknowledgements:
Dr Larry Heligman, Chief, Estimates and Projections Section, Population Division, United Nations; Dr Stayce Brown, Consultant, Population, Health and Nutrition Division, Population and Human Resources Department, The World Bank.

2 BIRTH COUNTS

Sixty-nine children, the greatest officially-recorded number of children born to one woman, were produced by a Russian peasant in the 18th century. Necessarily, amongst these numbers are twins, triplets and quadruplets. Currently, the world's most prolific mother lives in Birmingham, England, having had 22 single pregnancies.

Currently, there are 147 million births in the world each year, 130 million in poor countries and only 17 million in rich countries. On average, women nowadays each give birth to three children – women in rich countries give birth to two and women in poor countries to four children. However, this average for poor countries can be misleading. Because of comprehensive family programmes in China women give birth to one or two children, while in Africa women tend to have at least six children. Women in poor countries with no schooling have twice as many children as those with schooling of seven years or more.

The world average has fallen from five children in 1950 and is expected to fall to two by 2025. This fall is principally influenced by rising incomes, the education of women, reduced child deaths and the availability of family planning. When women come to feel confident that their children are likely to survive, they then have fewer children.

The inset map 'In practice' shows the percentage of women aged 15-49 years, currently married or in a union, who use any form of contraception. However, this measure says nothing about contraception among individuals who are not in a long-term relationship but who may be at risk of an unwanted pregnancy. Contraception includes both 'modern' methods (the Pill, condoms, intra-uterine devices [IUDs], injectables, implants and sterilization); and also periodic abstinence, withdrawal (coitus interruptus) and other varied traditional techniques. Modern methods have, if used properly, higher effectiveness in enabling couples to control fertility, but the proportion of couples using any method gives a better indication of the numbers who are actively trying to influence their family size. Because some 7-8 per cent of couples are always infertile, and at any given time some women will be trying to achieve pregnancy, or are pregnant or breast-feeding, a rate of around 70 percent indicates that most of those couples who wish to do so are using contraception. Where very few couples appear to be practising contraception it is usually because modern forms of contraception are not readily available or have only recently become so. Once percentages reach the mid-20s, its popularity begins to spread quickly.

The rates of couples using contraception, shown on the map, give an indication rather than an exact measure, of the situation in different countries. Even where contraception is said to be available, the range of methods may be restricted, and access to the services (in rural areas, for example, or by unmarried people) may be limited.

Family planning reduces rapid childbearing and child mortality; for example, if four children are born within a period of six years the risk of dying in infancy or early childhood for the next child is more than doubled.

The benefit of contraception is not confined to children; maternal deaths could be reduced by half within a decade if family planning services and improved maternal health care were made available, according to the Safer Motherhood Initiative. This campaign is undertaken jointly by the World Health Organization (WHO), the World Bank, the United Nations Development Programme (UNDP), United Nations Population Fund (UNPF) with the International Planned Parenthood Federation (IPPF) and the Population Council (PC).

Some couples have problems in having a family. Infertility affects up to 15 percent of people, caused mainly by blocked Fallopian tubes in women and disorders of the testes in men. In a large proportion of both men and women (20-25 percent of women) no cause can be found, yet the problem often causes untold anguish affecting not only mental but also physical health. In some cultures, women can face family and social discrimination.

Sources:
Population Reference Bureau, Inc., *1991 World Population Data Sheet*, Washington DC, 1991; IPPF (International Planned Parenthood Federation) People, *Reproductive Right Wallchart*, London: IPPF, 1990; *Better Health Through Family Planning: recommendations of the International Conference on Better Health for Women and Children Through Family Planning*, London: IPPF, 1987;*World Population Prospects 1990*. United Nations (UN); United Nations Children's Fund (UNICEF), *The State of the World's Children 1992*, New York and Oxford: Oxford University Press for UNICEF, 1992; World Health Organization (WHO),*World Health Statistics Annual*, Geneva: WHO, 1985; WHO, *Global Estimates for Health Situation Assessment and Projections*, Geneva: WHO, 1990.

Acknowledgements:
For data for the map and other information: Dr Penny Kane, President, Family Planning Federation of Australia; Sunetra Puri, International Planned Parenthood Federation (IPPF) London; Dr Beverley Carlson, Senior Adviser, Monitoring and Statistics, UNICEF. Paragraph 1 above: From "*The Guinness Book of Records 1993*", Copyright © Guinness Publishing Ltd 1992.

3 THE PERILS OF PREGNANCY

90   'Every four hours a jumbo jet crashes and all on board are killed. The 250 passengers are all women in the prime of life, many still in their teens. They are pregnant or have just delivered a child. Most have small children at home and families that depend on them.' Dr Malcolm Potts, 1985.

There has been a remarkable absence of concern about the magnitude of maternal deaths, and the hazards to women's health associated with their reproductive role.

Maternal mortality data is not collected in many countries and the figures given here may therefore be estimates. The worst category, above 800, includes countries where rates are extremely high: Mali 2000; Bhutan 1310; Somalia 1100; Ghana 1000. But any rate above 500 indicates quite appalling health hazards for women, and for every woman who dies, many more suffer serious illness or permanent disability.

In rich countries deaths in pregnancy and childbirth are now rare, but in most of the poor world maternal mortality is among the leading, if not the leading, cause of death among women of reproductive age.

More than half a million women die each year in pregnancy and childbirth. All but 4000 of these deaths (99%) occur in poor countries: more than half (61%) occur in Asia, 33% in Africa and 5% in Latin America. Even so, these figures probably understate the problem, as most deaths occur in poor countries where they are least likely to be registered.

Although the risks in pregnancy are decreasing, the total number of births in the world is increasing, this means that the actual numbers of women dying remains about the same. For instance, the risks per birth in Asia are falling but the number of births is rising, so the number of women who die is also increasing. The risks per birth in some countries in Africa are increasing, and as the number of births is also increasing, maternal mortality in Africa is now higher than anywhere else.

The maternal mortality rate in poor countries is on average more than 14 times higher than in rich countries and can be as much as a hundred times higher. This difference is greater than for any other measure of public health. Despite this, maternal mortality has been ignored by the health care professions until very recently.

Very high levels of maternal mortality are nothing new. During the 18th and 19th centuries the rate of maternal mortality in Europe was comparable to what is now reported from Africa and parts of Asia. Reviewing trends in maternal mortality in Europe and North America over the last 100 years has made it clear that most maternal deaths are preventable by simple medical care.

In poor countries, very few women are attended in childbirth by trained personnel, on average, 52 percent (see inset map 'You're on your own'). Even when the attendant is trained she will often be a local woman, who has been on a short training course, but who is likely to be illiterate.

Among other factors contributing to maternal mortality are: the lack of roads or transport to get women to medical care; having the first pregnancy shortly after puberty; short intervals between pregnancies; poor access to family planning services; and unsafe traditional birthing practices, such as the insertion of herbs, leaves, cow dung, mud or various oils into the vagina during labour.

This helps to explain why maternal mortality is high, but why has so little been done about it? The fundamental causes lie rooted in traditional customs and practices that give preferential treatment to boys in nutrition, education and access to health care. As they enter pregnancy, many girls and women are malnourished and anaemic and many young girls are married and bear children when they are hardly more than children themselves.

Maternal mortality will never improve until women are better valued, better educated, better nourished. Compulsory schooling, a minimum age of marriage, and equal rights for women are important for reducing maternal mortality.

Sources:

Potts, Malcolm, 'Maternal mortality: helping women off the road to death', *WHO Chronicle*, 40 (5), 1986; World Health Organization (WHO) *World Health Statistics Annual 1989*; WHO, *Global Estimates for Health Situation Assessment and Projections*, Geneva: WHO, 1990; 'Safe motherhood South Asia: challenge for the nineties', *Medical Bulletin*, International Planned Parenthood Federation; *Maternal Mortality Ratios and Rates, Maternal Health and Safe Motherhood Programme*, 3rd ed, Geneva: WHO, 1991; United Nations Children's Fund (UNICEF), *The State of the World's Children 1992*, New York and Oxford: Oxford University Press for UNICEF, 1992; AbouZahr, C. & E. Royston, *Maternal Mortality A Global Factbook*, Geneva: WHO, 1991; Loudon I, 'Maternal Mortality: 1880-1950, some regional and international comparisons', Social History of Medicine vol 1; Rosenfield, A. & D. Maine, 'Maternal mortality: a neglected tragedy. Where is the M in MCH?' *Lancet* ii, 1985; Royston, E. & S. Armstrong, eds., *Preventing Maternal Deaths*, Geneva: WHO ,1989; WHO, 'New estimates of maternal mortality', *Weekly Epidemiological Record*, 47, 1991.

Acknowledgements:
For data for the map and other information: Lelia Duley, National Perinatal Epidemiology Unit, Radcliffe Infirmary, Oxford.

4 THE FIRST YEAR MILESTONE

The infant mortality rate is the number of deaths in the first year after live birth per 1000 live births. The difference between rates for rich and poor countries is not as great as in the rates for maternal mortality, but the gaps are still very wide. In 1990, the rates ranged from five to six deaths per thousand live births in Japan, Sweden and Finland to over 150 in Afghanistan and some African countries. This makes the much repeated comparisons between the infant mortality rate in the USA or the UK and those of other Western countries seem relatively minor.

The 1990 rates for the USA, about nine per 1000 births, or eight in England and Wales, were higher than the rates of five to seven for Japan and the Nordic countries. Nevertheless, the infant mortality rates for East European countries were two to three times higher, those for Latin American countries were eight to nine times higher and those for African countries were 15 to 20 times higher than the rates for the UK.

The infants of the poor within rich countries are at much higher risk than average. In the USA, black infants are twice as likely to die in their first year of life as white infants. Thus, despite the encouraging decline in infant mortality, there is no room for complacency.

In total, about 10 million infants under one-year-old die annually. In general, in rich countries, over half of infant deaths occur within a month of birth, and are related to congenital malformations and problems centred around the time of birth. In poor countries, by far the majority of infant deaths occur after the first month of life and are related to communicable and diarrhoeal diseases and respiratory illnesses.

As comparison with the inset map shows, there were dramatic falls in infant mortality rates in all countries between 1960 and 1990. In many countries they have fallen by more than half. Improved nutrition accounts for as much as 40 percent of the decline. The biggest improvements in rates were in Oman (214 to 37), Turkey (190 to 69), Egypt (179 to 61), Iran (169 to 46), China (150 to 30) and the United Arab Emirates (145 to 24). The countries whose rates have fallen less markedly are some in Asia and sub-Saharan Africa, which have the highest rates.

The relationship between infant mortality and low birthweight is complex. In rich countries, the birthweight of a baby is the single most important determinant as to whether it will live or die. Low birthweight babies – the official WHO definition of low birthweight is under 2500g (5lbs 5oz) – have an increased risk of being ill or dying. Women who are disadvantaged or in poor health are more likely to have a baby which is born too soon or whose growth is retarded.

In most poor countries birthweights are also low where there is a high infant mortality. However in others, such as the Congo, Kenya and Sri Lanka, the link is less strong.

Sources :
United Nations Children's Fund (UNICEF), *The State of the World's Children 1992*, New York and Oxford: Oxford University Press for UNICEF, 1992; 'White infant mortality down', *The Nation's Health*, American Public Health Association, March 1992; The World Bank,*World Development Report 1991*, Oxford: Oxford University Press, 1991.

Acknowledgements:
For data for the map and other information: Alison Macfarlane, National Perinatal Epidemiology Unit, Radcliffe Infirmary, Oxford.

5 A PICTURE OF HEALTH?

Only you can gauge how well or ill you feel, and even then not reliably. You might not know what is possible for your age; you might be trapped in prevailing expectations; without experience of a different pattern of behaviour and diet; habituated to chronic disease or debility; or simply unable to express what you feel in words.

There is no easy way round these problems. But they pale into insignificance beside the problem of judging how others feel, which is what doctors, welfare workers, law enforcers and all the other spokespersons for social norms aspire to.

The maps represent both approaches – the external and the subjective. The main map – 'The quality of life' – rests on a composite index of wellbeing constructed by the United Nations Development Programme (UNDP). The index combines longevity as measured by life expectancy at birth, knowledge as measured by adult literacy and average years of schooling, and real income per head adjusted to account for the fact that the effect of income in satisfying needs declines as income rises.

The index does not capture the less easily quantifiable aspects of life: the emotional, spiritual, aesthetic or social sides; nor does it break with the twin abstractions favoured by economists – average and state. It reflects the prejudices of its compilers about what constitutes essential prerequisites for a good life, prejudices held by a narrow circle of Western-educated, liberal intellectuals steeped in world affairs. There is little reason to suppose that those on whom we wish these fortunate circumstances think similarly. But that is a risk that accompanies all 'objective' assessments.

By contrast the telephone symbols – 'Sorry, I can't make it' – attempt the subjective route. They assume that, by and large, people know whether they are well or ill. They assume, more precariously, that if you do not turn up at work when expected for reasons other than holidays, strikes, lockouts, maternity leave, bad weather, disrupted transport, or family and personal reasons, and you declare that you are ill, that is what you are. The data does not account for fake or phantom illnesses – logged in order to take up unused entitlements to sick leave, to join a public rally, to pursue romance or revenge, to care for children or others ... There are many, many reasons to avoid work, even in a work-orientated society that ultimately punishes absenteeism. Even more precariously, the data assumes that the people who do turn up for work feel well. Well...

The allocation of symbols rests on Labour Force Survey studies of absence from work in a single reference week in 1988 (mainly) or in the following two years in certain rich countries. It covers declared absences of one hour or more for reasons of illness or injury. These ranged from 60% of all time lost in the USA to 6% in Greece. Of the larger countries Germany registered 35%, France 28%, Canada 25% and the UK 20%. The rate of absence due to illness and injury ranged from 0.9% of the total work-time expected in Belgium to 3.9% in the Netherlands (and 6.1% in Sweden where, exceptionally, part-time workers were included in the survey). It was 2.5% in the UK, 2.1% in France, 1.7% in the USA, 1.6% in Germany, and 1.1% in Italy. In every case declared illness or injury constitute either the prime factor or the second most important one (behind holidays and vacations) in total absences from work.

The graphic – 'Future (im)perfect' rests on an external, 'objective' evaluation of health. It shows that in North America and Western Europe with a generally long life expectancy, men and women can anticipate very different fates: on average men live for a shorter time, but enjoy a higher proportion of healthy years. Although the number of years both men and women can expect to live in these countries is still rising, the number of years of healthy living is not rising as fast. Although the graphic does not show this, the most affluent in rich countries enjoy the most years of both life and healthy life.

Sources:
OECD Employment Outlook, Paris: OECD, 1991; Robine, Jean Marie & Karen Ritchie, 'Healthy life expectancy: evaluation of global indicator of change in population health', *British Medical Journal*, 1991, vol 302; United Nations Development Programme (UNDP), *Human Development Report 1992*, New York and Oxford: Oxford University Press, 1992.

Acknowledgements:
For data for the map and for the above text: Michael Kidron, who thanks: Irvine Hoffmann, Chief, Statistics of Employment and Unemployment Section, Bureau of Statistics, International Labour Office (ILO), Geneva; Roland Sigg, International Social Security Association, ILO; Joe Thurman, Working Conditions and Environment Department, ILO; Dr Alan Lopez, WHO; Meghnad Desai, London School of Economics; Abrar Hasan, Head, Central Analysis Unit, Department of Education, Manpower and Social Affairs, OECD, Paris.

6 THREE SCORE YEARS AND TEN

Life expectancy at birth reflects first and foremost the risks of dying below the age of five years; and second the risks of dying between 5-35 years. In fact, if you live to 35 years of age in rich countries, you will, on average, live another 40-45 years. Life expectancy is therefore primarily an indicator as to whether communicable diseases, especially those that affect children such as diarrhoea and respiratory infections, are either rampant or are under control. Thus, the main reason people are living longer is that communicable diseases are being prevented: by a combination of improved nutrition, better housing, clean water supply, immunization, low-level primary health care and improved education, particularly of women.

People in rich countries can now expect to live to the age of 75; 30 years longer than their great-grandparents. Although people in poor countries generally live to only 63 years (52 years in Africa), their life expectancy is also rising, contributing to substantial population increases.

The graphic 'Japan in the fast lane' illustrates one of the most dramatic improvements in life expectancy this century, and shows Japan surpassing all other long-living populations. In 1900 Japan's average life expectancy was below 45 years. By the year 2000 it could well be over 80 years.

There have been some extraordinary claims of longevity – one Chinese man claimed in 1933 to have been born in 1680 (therefore 253 years old) – but there has never been a proven 121st birthday party. Four out of every five centenarians are women; yet while married men live longer than bachelors, spinsters live longer than married women. Does marriage suit men but not women?

Sources:
United Nations (UN), *World Population Prospects 1990*, UN, 1991; World Health Organization (WHO), *Global Estimates for Health Situation Assessment and Projections*, Geneva: WHO, 1990; The World Bank, *World Development Report 1991*, Oxford University Press, 1991; Dr Alan Lopez, WHO, personal communication, February 1992.

Acknowledgements:
Dr Larry Heligman, Chief of the Estimates and Projections Section, Population Division, UN; Dr Stayce Brown, Population, Health and Nutrition Division, The World Bank. Information in last paragraph above: From *"The Guinness Book of Records 1993"*, Copyright © Guinness Publishing Ltd 1992.

7 THE GRIM REAPERS

50 million people in the world die each year, many prematurely. Infant and child deaths constitute one third of these deaths and in poor countries 40 percent of all deaths occur among children under 15 years old. In contrast, over two thirds of deaths in rich countries occur in people over 65 years old, and only four per cent in children under 15 years.

Because country-specific data from poor countries is scanty, the map does not show the deaths of children. Diarrhoeal diseases and acute respiratory infections cause one half of these deaths, and neonatal tetanus, measles and whooping cough a further quarter. Diseases may be present concurrently, and many have multiple underlying factors, particularly malnutrition. There has been a decrease in death rates among children everywhere in the world. This is nowhere more striking than in China, where the rates, albeit still double those of rich countries, are now one fifth of those in 1960, and are currently only a quarter of the death rates in sub-Saharan Africa. One of the most impressive achievements in reducing children's deaths has been immunization (see **35. Catching Them Young**).

Detailed annual statistics on causes of death are available from less than half the countries in the world, principally rich countries, a number of Latin American countries, and a handful of Asian ones. In poor countries, deaths are often not attended by a health professional, the death is not certified, and the cause of death is not established with any degree of accuracy.

In rich countries diseases of life-style are the cause of three quarters of deaths. An infant born in a rich country has a greater than 30% chance of dying eventually from heart disease, 20% from cancer, 15% from stroke, 7% from respiratory diseases and 5% from injury and poisoning. Trends of causes of death in rich countries since 1950 show a substantial increase in lung cancer in men and more recently among women (90 percent due to smoking) and a decrease in coronary heart disease and stroke, which partially reflects reduction in smoking, but which has not yet been fully explained.

The symbol of the burning motor car highlights some (mainly rich) countries where there are high death rates from road accidents. But there are no worldwide data available. Among young adults, traffic accidents are still the main cause of death, although in the 1970s and 1980s the number of deaths declined, in spite of a sharp increase in road traffic. This decline can be attributed to a combination of factors, including stricter traffic regulations, campaigns and legislation against drinking alcohol when driving, and the use of safety belts. Road accidents typically disable at least 15 times more often than they kill. For example, in the USA, motor vehicle accidents cause 50,000 deaths each year but almost 40 times more (two million) disabling injuries.

In both rich and poor countries, up to one third of hospital admissions and one in 15 of all deaths are the result of accidents: either motor vehicle accidents, falls, drownings, burns or poisoning. Accidents in the home account for one third of all accidental deaths, particularly affecting the very young and the very old. In many rich countries, suicide has risen among men since 1950, and more recently among women (with the striking exception of Australia). In the USA, falls cause 12,000 deaths but 11 million injuries; and burns kill 5000 but 60,000 are admitted to hospitals with burns injuries.

Sources.
World Health Organization (WHO), *Global Estimates for Health Situation Assessment and Projections*, Geneva: WHO, 1990; *World Health Statistics Annual 1990*, Geneva: WHO, 1990; '200 million may die prematurely in the 1990s', *Bulletin of International Union Against Tuberculosis and Lung Disease*, vol 65, no 2-3. June-September 1990.

Acknowledgements:
Dr Stayce Brown, Consultant, Population, Health and Nutrition Division, Population and Human Resources Department, The World Bank; Dr Bernard Hausner, Senior Information Officer, UNDP; Ms Susan van Niekerk, Department of National Health and Population Division, South Africa.

8 THE ELEMENTS

Nature is far from even-handed when it comes to distributing disasters. Certain areas of the world have more than their fair share of earthquakes, volcanoes, floods, droughts, storms, monsoons, cyclones (which are called hurricanes in the Caribbean, the Atlantic and the eastern Pacific, and typhoons in the western Pacific), landslides, heat waves or cold waves. Nevertheless human activity may contribute to or even cause 'natural' disasters, such as when flooding is the result of earlier deforestation.

Some countries are more likely than others to suffer from several different sources of 'natural' disaster. Bangladesh, for example, is frequently flooded when its great rivers overflow with monsoon rains descending from the Himalayas, but its delta-coastline is also highly vulnerable to cyclones sweeping up the Bay of Bengal. Yet Bangladesh is also liable to drought, cold waves and earthquakes.

Nor is the impact of a disaster, of a given physical extent and intensity, the same in every country. Extreme natural events are much more destructive where social and economic conditions make people vulnerable. In 1989 an earthquake in California killed 63 people. The following year, an earthquake of less intensity (6.8 as opposed to 7.1 on Richter scale) killed 25,000 in Armenia. Poorly-constructed buildings were blamed for the high death toll in the 1992 Cairo earthquake. California has been preparing for such events for decades, with earthquake proofing of buildings, and extensive planning by relief services.

In almost every disaster, the poorest countries, and the poorest within each country, suffer disproportionately more. In Bangladesh, for instance, the poorest farmers live on the most vulnerable marginal land such as shifting islands in the delta. A cyclone in 1991 led to such widespread floods, famine and epidemic disease that more than 100,000 people were killed.

During the 1980s, in an average year, around 50,000 people were internationally recorded as having died as a direct result of 'natural disasters'. Earthquakes killed about 5000 people a year, volcanoes about 2000, and floods about 2000.

The annual average number of people injured and in other ways seriously affected by disaster is very much larger than the numbers of deaths. Worldwide, around 30 million people are recorded as being affected by floods and at least 10 million by drought. Earthquakes have a profound impact on more than two million people every year, and volcanoes on 40,000.

But global long-term averages conceal individual events that are almost apocalyptic in their local intensity. In 1985, a volcano in Chile annihilated a whole town, killing practically everyone – 21,800 people. No other parts of the country were affected. In 1976, an earthquake in Tangshan, China, killed more than 240,000 people.

Published figures may be a poor guide to the numbers of people killed, injured or otherwise seriously affected by 'natural' violence. For one thing, deaths and injuries resulting from disasters are notoriously difficult to quantify, and published data may even be seriously misleading. The very nature of the events, and in some cases their geographic isolation, means that precision is impossible. As a result, the United Nations Disaster Relief Organisation (UNDRO) and the US Office of Foreign Disaster Relief (OFDA) often vary considerably in their estimates. Sometimes the situation is so confused that OFDA, for instance, will not even hazard a guess at numbers involved (and hence records numbers killed or injured as '0'). Moreover, long-term health damage is generally excluded from all published data.

It should further be noted that such figures are restricted to officially-reported and declared 'disasters' only; overall numbers affected by the violence of natural events are probably far higher. The published data exclude deaths from generally less severe – but more frequent – weather or earth-moving events that did not kill, injure, or affect sufficient numbers of people, or damage enough property, to qualify as 'disasters'.

Indeed, what counts as a 'disaster', and hence is reported in detail, can seem arbitrary. One of the most important sources, the US Office of Disaster Assistance, publishes detailed breakdowns of all disasters to which the office responded with relief assistance, together with data on some 'non-declared' disasters that are deemed significant. For example, earthquakes and volcanoes are not included unless at least six people were killed, or the total number of dead and injured was 25 or more, or at least 1000 people were homeless or 'affected', or damage amounted to US$1 million or more. Weather disasters are not included unless they are known to have killed or injured at least 50 people.

The inset 'Major disasters' provides some historical background and shows that China and Bangladesh have suffered particularly badly. Some of the deaths in the Irish famine were caused by the famine itself; others were caused by typhus, which spread rapidly in the weakened population. The floods in 1970 in Bangladesh were caused by a cyclone.

'Natural' disasters are certain to take an ever-increasing toll in the future. Whatever advances are made in disaster-prediction, or in technical advances in terms of building design or flood barriers to ward off their worst effects, the numbers of people – particularly poor people – living near major earthquake zones, or volcanoes, or in areas prone to drought, are increasing rapidly. It is also likely that rising sea levels, already up 30 cm this century, will magnify the impact of cyclones. Long-term global warming would put billions at risk.

Sources:
Disaster History: Significant Data on Major Disasters World-wide, 1900-Present, Washington, DC: Office of Foreign Disaster Assistance/Agency for International Development, 1990; United Nations Environment Programme (UNEP) *Environmental Data Report 1991-92*, Oxford: UNEP/Basil Blackwell, 1991.

Acknowledgements:
For data for the map and for the above text: Philip Boys.

9 THE COSTS OF WAR

96 For this map, war is defined as an open armed conflict in which the regular uniformed

forces of a state are engaged on at least one side; there is a degree of central organization on both sides; there is some continuity between clashes; and there are no minimum numbers killed. It includes deaths from both conventional and chemical weapons.

Most of today's wars are civil wars. They do not always or even usually begin with a formal declaration. They often have no clear starting date or endpoint. They tend to last a long time but they are not fought at the same level of intensity for their whole duration. The pattern is for war to splutter into action, subside, kick viciously again, tick over at a relatively low level of mayhem, seem to stop, return to find more victims.

Most of those killed in modern wars, and even more of those harmed by them, are civilians. Data on casualties are extremely unreliable because no agency takes responsibility for counting non-combatants who are killed in war. Almost all casualty figures are estimates whose range is not infrequently greater than an order of magnitude. This is the chief reason for choosing wide bands for presenting information on mortality in war. The figures for several countries – Cambodia, Ethiopia, Mozambique, Sudan and Uganda – include deaths attributable to large scale famines which were caused or exacerbated by warfare. Countries such as the UK and India, who have casualties from civil wars, have also fought – and even experienced deaths – on other territory.

War has health effects beyond immediate casualties and famine: health care resources are disrupted and diverted; water and sanitation systems break down; birth rates fall. Always, the heaviest burden is borne by children, who miss their chance forever to grow up normal in mind and body. Not only are there an estimated 200,000 soldiers aged under 15 engaged in today's predominantly civil wars, but in the last decade, more than one and a half million children have been killed in wars and more than four million have been physically disabled – limbs amputated, brains damaged, eyesight and hearing lost. Five million children live in refugee camps because of war; a further 12 million have lost their homes. Ten million children in the world are estimated to have suffered psychological trauma in international and civil wars.

A new Convention on the Rights of the Child, which especially demands 'all feasible measures to ensure protection and care of children who are affected by armed conflict' has now been ratified by over 100 nations. Some nations have made unusual interpretations of this convention. In El Salvador, civil war which ended in 1992 was suspended on three separate days in each of its last seven years so that children could be immunized. In Lebanon, 'days of tranquillity' allowed children to be immunized, even at the height of the troubles. In the Sudan, both sides eventually agreed to 'corridors of peace', through which essential supplies could reach millions of civilians, mostly women and children, trapped in the war zone. Similar agreements have since been negotiated in Angola and Ethiopia. In Iraq, essential medical supplies were delivered even at the height of the Gulf War. In 1992 in Bosnia-Herzegovina, however, both the UN and Western rescue operations were often frustrated in their attempts to provide food and medical relief for Sarajevo and other cities.

War rarely brings improvements in health, but it can bring improvements in health services. Modern nursing was inaugurated in the Crimean war by Florence Nightingale. Accident and emergency surgery rapidly improved in both World Wars. World War I initiated the concept of rehabilitating physically mutilated victims. After World War II governments developed programmes to rehabilitate amputees, paralysed, blind, deaf and 'shell-shocked' war victims into the community. Nowadays virtually every medical school and medium-to-large hospital has a department of rehabilitation.

In the cartogram 'Refugees' the size of countries relates to the number of refugees created by each country as a proportion of the total number of refugees in the world. A few countries were too small to include: Togo at 0.03%; Albania, Panama, Suriname, 0.02%; Indonesia, 0.016%; Cuba, 0.003%; Lesotho, 0.002%. The colour-coding shows the percentage range of refugees who are internal, living within their own country. The cartogram shows people who have left home involuntarily because of war, repression, discrimination, famine, environmental degradation and other disasters. More than half of the world's refugees are internal. There are 18 million refugees displaced beyond their national border, and in addition more than 30 million internally displaced persons globally. Most are in Asia and Africa, only two million live in Europe and North America. Although a privileged few refugees enjoy better conditions than whence they came, most are malnourished, and live in squalid, unhealthy conditions, with inadequate health care provision.

Sources:
Kohn, *Dictionary of Wars*, New York: Doubleday, 1987; Sivard, R.L., *World Military and Social Expenditures*, Washington DC: World Priorities Inc. annual; *Strategic Survey*, London: International Institute for Strategic Studies, annual; Stockholm International Peace Research Institute, *SIPRI Yearbook: World Armaments and Disarmament*, Oxford: Oxford University Press, annual; Wallensteen, P., ed., *States in Armed Conflict 1988* and *1989*, Uppsala University, 1989 and 1991; *Amnesty International Report*, London: Amnesty International, annual; Minority Rights Group, *World Directory of Minorities*, Harlow: Longman, (1989/90); *World Refugee Survey 1992*, Washington DC: US Committee for Refugees, 1992; Kidron, Michael and Dan Smith, *The New State of War and Peace*, London: Grafton Books and New York: Simon & Schuster, 1991; further data from Uppsala University, Department of Peace and Conflict Research; press reports.

The World Bank, *World Development Report 1991*, Oxford: Oxford University Press, 1991; United Nations Children's Fund (UNICEF), *The State of the World's Children 1992*, New York and Oxford: Oxford University Press for UNICEF, 1992; World Health Organization (WHO), *Global Estimates for Health Situation Assessment and Projections, 1990*, Geneva: WHO; Kuntz, Diane, 'Comment: The world's refugees and displaced persons: The untold story', *The Nation's Health*, American Public Health Association, July 1991.

Acknowledgements:
For data for the map and cartogram and other information: Dan Smith, Transnational Institute, Amsterdam and International Peace Research Institute, Oslo.

10 PERSONAL VIOLENCE

Homicide statistics have serious limitations, since they reside in the intersection between the medical and legal systems and are therefore subject to a wide variety of bureaucratic and procedural influences. They provide a preliminary indication of the levels of violence in a particular society. But as the map shows, many countries and large areas of the world do not provide statistics for comparison.

Worldwide the reported incidence of murders of men varies from a high of 207 per 100,000 population in Guatemala to less than 1 in the Scandinavian countries. Of rich countries, the USA is by far the most violent. There were 23,000 killings (three every hour) in the USA in 1990, more than twice the rate of Northern Ireland, which is torn by civil war, four times that of Italy, nine times that of Britain and 11 times more than that of Japan. More than 1.8 million Americans were murdered, raped, robbed or assaulted during that single year. The crime rate in the USA is now the highest ever, and Americans are more likely than ever to become victims of violent crime.

Men are more likely to die violently than women in almost all societies, although Israel and Denmark provide interesting exceptions. Men are also more likely to kill. In the UK, about 25 percent of all homicides are domestic, almost all of them men killing women. In the USA some 50 percent of all female murder victims are killed by men with whom they have intimate relationships, but only 10 percent of male victims are killed by their wives.

The number of murders of women gives only a very small indication of the huge burden of domestic violence borne by women around the world. These attacks are almost invisible with women being reluctant to report them out of embarrassment, guilt, loyalty or fear of reprisal. One British study indicated that the police were informed in only 2 percent of cases and often failed to record the violence, seeing it as 'just domestic'. Similar problems exist in the reporting of rape.

The inset 'Dowry deaths' shows the reported numbers of young married women in parts of India who suffer sudden death, often by burning, thus freeing their husbands to marry again and receive a second dowry. It is estimated that around 9000 such deaths occurred in India in 1987 and at least two women are said to be burned to death in New Delhi each day. These homicides, combined with an increase in reported rapes, suggests a high level of violence against women. Dowry deaths have been reported from India, Bangladesh and Pakistan among both Hindu and Muslim families. Indian women have been organizing in recent years to publicize and prevent the growing number of dowry murders. The dowry deaths in the graphic do not include female infanticide prompted by fear of the eventual cost of providing a dowry

The inset 'Sex offences' represents only the numbers reported to Interpol. Interpol cautions about the validity of comparisons between countries. It may be that Canada appears as the worst case on the map simply because it keeps better statistics and is more likely to bring a case to prosecution. The countries with the highest number of sex offences may well submit no statistics at all.

In recent years campaigns have been launched to bring the violence committed against women to public attention, and to develop strategies for prevention. They have shown that personal violence is part of the dynamic of many families around the world, with women being murdered, assaulted, raped, sexually abused and humiliated in their own homes. A recent US crime survey suggested that some 2.1 million American women are the victims of domestic violence each year.

Most research on rape and domestic violence has been conducted in the rich countries but there is now increasing enquiry being undertaken in the poor countries. A national survey has been undertaken in Papua New Guinea and case studies have been carried out in several other countries including Nigeria, Colombia, Bangladesh and Chile.

Policy initiatives are growing around the world, both to change the laws and judicial processes relating to rape and domestic violence, and to provide support for women survivors. The number of refuges and rape crisis centres is increasing with shelters recently opened in Egypt, Hong Kong, Malaysia, Thailand and Trinidad and Tobago. However, many remain dependent on charity for their funding and demand for their services continues to exceed supply.

Sources:
Asian and Pacific Women's Resources Centre, *Collection Network, Asian and Pacific Women's Resources Centre*, Health, 1989; Connors, J., *Violence Against Women in the Family*, United Nations (UN), 1989; Manushi. *In Search of Answers: Indian Women's Voices from Manushi.*, Zed Press, 1984; Smith L.J., *Domestic Violence: An overview of the literature*, Great Britain, Home Office Research and Training Report 1989; *United Nations Demographic Yearbook, 1989*, UN; *The World's Women: Trends and Statistics 1970-1990.*, UN, 1991; *Worldwide Action on Violence Against Women*, Welsh Women's Aid, 1988; World Health Organization (WHO), *World Health Statistics Annual 1990*, WHO, 1991; Dobash, R. & R. Dobash. *Women, Violence and Social Change.*, Routledge and Kegan Paul, 1992; 'Report on [US] Senate Judiciary Committee Report for 1990'. *South China Morning Post*, 14 March 1992.

Acknowledgements:
For data for the map and other information: Lesley Doyal, Professor of Nursing, Health and Social Studies, University of the West Country, Bath, UK.

11 WEALTH AND HEALTH

This cartogram titrates deaths of children under five against a country's national income (GNP) expressed as a share of world income. It dramatically confirms that the greater a country's wealth, the more likely will its children survive beyond the age of five.

Gross national product (GNP) is known to be flawed as a measure of a country's wealth but it is still the most widely used and accepted. It has two major weaknesses: it excludes the movement of goods and services outside the market economy; and for comparative purposes it has to be expressed through a possibly capricious exchange rate for the US dollar. The GNP data used here were originally calculated for the 4th edition of *The New State of the World Atlas*, 1991.

Health can be measured in a number of ways, for example, by comparing data on life expectancy, the birthweight of babies, or nutrition. However, the mortality rate of children under five years old has been selected by UNICEF as the single most important indicator of the state of a nation's children and is a sensitive indicator of a country's general health.

The average income per person in rich countries is 50 times greater than that of the poorest and this gap is widening. The International Labour Organization (ILO) estimates that in 1995 there will be 913 million people living in 'extreme poverty' in poor countries, 90 percent of them living in rural areas. The proportion of children living in poverty has risen from 14 percent in the 1960s to 22 percent today.

Worsening poverty is particularly serious in Africa, and not surprisingly this is where the highest mortality rates of children under five are found. Extreme poverty is increasing to a lesser extent in South America while in Asia, the numbers are actually declining, despite an absolute increase in population.

Health is best in countries where there is a more equal distribution of wealth. In China, far from being a wealthy country in terms of gross national product, the richest fifth earn only three times more than the poorest fifth. In the Philippines the rich earn 10 times more, and in Brazil 28 times more. China has a far better under-five mortality rate (42) than the **99**

Philippines (69) and Brazil (83). And Japan, with relatively egalitarian income distribution, has the lowest under-five mortality rate in the world.

The map cannot show, for example, that in the USA one fifth of children live in poverty – poverty being defined as the income level below which a minimum nutritionally adequate diet plus essential non-food requirements is not affordable. While there is a substantial and widening economic (and therefore health) gap between black and white Americans, and ethnic minorities are over-represented, most of America's 12 million poor children are white, living in small families, outside big cities, and with one or more parent working. The Children's Defence Fund attributes 40% of the increase in poverty in the USA to a reduction in government benefits, 30% to a fall in real wages among the poor and 30% to the rise in mother-only families. Today, less than 10 percent of all cash benefits go to poor families with children.

The map also cannot show the inequalities in health, even in relatively wealthy countries, between rich and poor of all ages. The poor live less long and their life spans are less healthy than the richer members of any society (see notes to **5. A Picture of Health?**).

Sources:
World Health Organization (WHO), *Global Estimates for Health Situation Assessment and Projections, 1990*, Geneva: WHO; United Nations Children's Fund (UNICEF), *The State of the World's Children 1992*, New York and Oxford: Oxford University Press for UNICEF, 1992; United Nations (UN), World Population Prospects 1990: UN,1991; Wilkinson, R. G., 'Income distribution and life expectancy', *British Medical Journal*, vol 304, 1992; Robine, Jean Marie and Karen Ritchie, 'Healthy life expectancy: evaluation of global indicator of change in population health', *British Medical Journal*, vol 302, 1991; Kidron, Michael and Ronald Segal, *The New State of the World Atlas*, 4th ed., New York and London: Simon and Schuster 1991.

Acknowledgements:
Dr Beverley Carlson, Senior Adviser, Monitoring and Statistics, UNICEF.

12 FAT AND THIN

With the exception of Africa, there is enough food produced within each region of the world to meet local demand. Yet about one fifth of the world's people – especially in Africa and South Asia – do not get enough food to lead productive lives.

In many countries the daily calorie supply is far in excess of needs. Countries with a supply of more than 140 percent of their needs are the United Arab Emirates 151%; Greece 148%; Ireland 147%; Belgium 146%; Bulgaria 145%; Czechoslovakia 144%; Spain 144%; Libya 143%; and Italy 142%. At the other end of the spectrum, countries with a daily calorie supply below 80 percent of their needs are all in Africa: Ethiopia 69%; Mozambique 70%; Angola 74%; Somalia 74%; Chad 76%; Rwanda 78%; and Sierra Leone 79%.

There is much more food available in the world than in 1960 and average calorie intake has increased in spite of rising populations. Only nine countries, with a total population of 196 million, now have a daily calorie supply per person below 1900 calories – compared to 23 countries with a total population of 985 million in 1961.

The map cannot show the adequacy of food distribution within countries. In all countries, some people have more to eat than others. The symbols, which show where children are stunted or obese, indirectly show unequal food distribution in that both stunted and obese children can co-exist in the same country: Bolivia, Honduras, Peru and Zambia for example. Besides, some people need more than others: for example growing children, the more physically active, the less healthy, and pregnant women.

In fact, those most at risk of sub-nutrition are children. The symbol identifying countries where young children are stunted in height fails to show the strong disparity between regions: 48% of children in Asia are stunted; 38% in Africa; 26% in the Eastern Mediterranean, 19% in the Western Pacific region, 19% in the Americas and 4% in Europe. Most sub-nourished children come from poor families where parents lack knowledge about the use of foods and may live in societies where there are many taboos about food. But child sub-nutrition is caused as much by infection as by lack of food. Diarrhoeal, respiratory and parasitic diseases are critical determinants of malnutrition in infants and children.

Reducing sub-nutrition is not wholly dependent on increasing production and a more
equitable distribution. Increasing food supply is only of use if the people can afford to buy

it; if not, governments export the food and plant cash crops for export to relieve foreign debt. The problems are best addressed by a combination of approaches: meeting nutritional needs; immunization; the promotion of breast feeding; oral rehydration when diarrhoea occurs; improving sanitation and water supplies; personal hygiene; and education (see **13. The Hand that Rocks the Cradle, 14. Air and Water, 35. Catching Them Young**).

The world could be losing millions of tonnes of grain output each year because of environmental damage to land and crops. Control of 'natural' disasters, that cause acute variation in the food supply, are sometimes beyond human control. In particular, droughts are causing serious food shortages in many countries, especially in Africa and Asia (see **8. The Elements**). Currently, over 100 nations depend on food imports from the USA. China is currently facing a major challenge: how to feed 22 percent of the world's population on seven percent of the world's arable land. China currently predicts that the demand for food will outstrip supply by the year 2000, when China's population will reach 1.28 billion.

Meanwhile, the rich world has too much to eat. The 'fat child' symbol and the inset 'Overample proportions' are not to be taken as the only countries where children and adults are fat; they show only those few countries where studies have been reported.

The 'fat child' symbol shows the pattern of obesity is set early. Overweight infants and children do not necessarily become obese adults, but fatness at the age of 13 years is a good predictor of adult fatness. 'Overweight' is not a description or a comment on fashion. People who are seriously overweight are predisposed to many health problems, including heart disease, high blood pressure, higher cholesterol and other fats like triglycerides, adult-onset diabetes, lowered lung function, gallstones, menstrual problems in women and osteoarthritis of weight-bearing joints (especially the hip, knees and back).

Obesity and associated health problems are not only confined to rich countries. Half the world's deaths from coronary heart disease occur in poor countries (see note to **7. The Grim Reapers**); about half the world's 50 million diabetics now live in poor countries, and the rest live principally in the disadvantaged communities of the rich countries.

Nutritional problems are not only created by poverty. As national income (GNP) rises, so does the proportion of animal fat in the diet. If the GNP is under US$1200 per head per year, the percentage of animal fat is six percent; if the GNP is more than US$11,500, the percentage is 29 percent. Compared to the 1940s, Europeans – especially in the north – now eat more animal and less vegetable food. Nearly half the deaths in people under the age of 65 in Europe result from cardiovascular diseases and cancer, to which diet makes an important contribution.

Sources:
China Daily, 26 February 1992; Walker, Alison, 'Population: more than a numbers game', *British Medical Journal*, vol 303, 1991; Walsh, Julia A. and Kenneth S. Warren, eds., *Strategies for Primary Health Care: Technologies Appropriate for the Control of Disease in the Developing World*, Chicago and London: The University of Chicago Press, 1986; Warren, Kenneth S. and Adel A.F. Mahmoud, *Tropical and Geographical Medicine*, 2nd ed, McGraw-Hill Inc.,1990; World Health Organization (WHO), *World Health*, May-June1991; O'Connor, Michael, 'Europe and nutrition: prospects for public health', *British Medical Journal*, vol 304, 1992; Garrow, J.S., *Obesity and overweight*, London: Health Education Authority, 1991; United Nations Children's Fund (UNICEF), *The State of the World's Children 1992*, New York and Oxford: Oxford University Press for UNICEF, 1992; WHO, *Diet, Nutrition, and the Prevention of Chronic Diseases*, (report) WHO Technical Report Series 797, Geneva: WHO, 1990.

Acknowledgements:
Dr Beverley Carlson, Senior Adviser, Monitoring and Statistics, UNICEF; Dr Stayce Brown, Consultant, Population, Health and Nutrition Division, Population and Human Resources Department, The World Bank; Dr Kenneth S. Warren, Director for Science, Maxwell Macmillan Group, New York; Dr Hilary King, Diabetes and Other Noncommunicable Diseases Unit, WHO; Dr Donald Reid, Director, Programmes Division, and Ms Catherine Lowe, Nutrition and Dental Health Programme Officer, Health Education Authority, London.

13   THE HAND THAT ROCKS THE CRADLE

Education is the passport to health. The educated are healthier, have fewer children, eat better and have access to better jobs.

Out of 3.2 billion adults in the world, 2.3 billion are literate and 0.9 billion are illiterate – more than a quarter of the world's adult population. Although the proportion of illiterate people has fallen, absolute increases in populations mean that numbers are now higher. **101**

One in two women in Asia is illiterate compared with two in three women in Africa. Poor countries have a much higher proportion of illiterate women, a fact which the colour- coding of the main map clearly shows. The symbols, representing countries where more than one child in ten dies before the age of five, confirm the link between the literacy of women and the survival of children.

The inset 'School benefits' illustrates how improved schooling for women over almost over 30 years has produced a direct annual improvement in child survival. A single extra year of schooling for girls is associated with a two percent drop in the rate of infant mortality.

Countries with near universal primary education for boys, but low enrollment for girls, have much higher infant mortality (and fertility) rates. Up to 100 girls could be given primary education for the cost of educating one university graduate. Closing the gender gap would be a far more cost-effective way of improving health and wealth in a society than providing higher education for boys.

The inset 'Goose and gander' compares the literacy rates of men and women in rich and poor countries. Because women are generally valued less, girls receive less schooling than boys. One in every three women is illiterate compared to only one in five men. To deprive women of education not only locks them into their own cycle of poverty and poor health, but is extremely short-sighted for the health and well-being of society as a whole.

Sources:
United Nations Children's Fund (UNICEF), *The State of the World's Children 1992*, New York and Oxford: Oxford University Press for UNICEF, 1992; World Health Organization (WHO), *Global Estimates for Health Situation Assessment and Projections*, Geneva: WHO, 1990; The World Bank, *World Development Report 1991*, Oxford University Press, 1991.

Acknowledgements:
Dr Beverley Carlson, Senior Adviser, Monitoring and Statistics at UNICEF; Dr Stayce Brown, Consultant, Population, Health and Nutrition Division, Population and Human Resources Department, The World Bank; and Dr Bernard Hausner, Senior Information Officer, UNDP.

14 AIR AND WATER

'We never know the worth of water until the well run dry.' Thomas Fuller MD, *Gnomologia*, 1732

'Access' to a safe water supply is defined as being within the home or within 15 minutes' walk. The international organizations use this as a target for all dwellings in the world. It is hard to see more than a very few people in the rich world being prepared to tolerate such a walk to safe water. More than one billion people have little or no access to safe drinking water. Almost two billion lack basic sanitation. Most live in poor countries, where sanitation reaches 66 percent of those in urban areas but only 17 percent of those in rural areas.

Keeping improvements in water supply and sanitation ahead of population expansion is a major problem. During the WHO International Drinking Water Supply and Sanitation Decade of the 1980s, an estimated 225 million urban residents in poor countries were newly supplied with a safe water supply. But as the estimated urban population increased in poor countries by 37 percent during the same period, there was only a small increase in coverage, from 76 to 78%. The greatest improvement was to rural water supplies, with 310 million additional people served, although this only brought coverage to 46 percent. Even this is not necessarily being maintained.

But 80 percent of the US$12 billion spent annually by governments on water supply systems goes to putting private taps in the homes of the relatively well off, about $600 per person served. Only 20 percent goes to the public wells and stand-pipes which can bring clean water to the majority of the poor at a cost of US$30-50 per person. Re-allocation of even a moderate proportion of total expenditures could provide a safe water supply for almost every community by the year 2000.

Most people in rich countries have access to a safe water supply, thanks to the visions of the ancient Roman Empire and, much more recently, a London doctor. By the end of the
first century A.D., nine aqueducts were channelling water to Rome, with purification

achieved en route by settling basins and intermediate reservoirs, by keeping drinking water separate from the rest and by a complex series of sewers to dispose of sewage. In a classic breakthrough in public health, John Snow, in mid-19th century London, aborted a cholera epidemic long before anyone had seen a cholera germ under a microscope. He removed the handle of the Broad Street water pump, thus cutting off the source of the water-borne cholera bacteria to the whole district.

In the 1990s domestic drinking water in the rich world may be reprocessed or go through water treatment plants. Drinking water is stored, treated, sedimented and filtered, organic matter is removed, and the water is finally disinfected with chlorine, ozone or exposure to ultra-violet light; pH is adjusted, and fluoride may be added. But there is a growing level of distrust in water supplies. Sales of bottled mineral and distilled water have rocketed in the last decade in rich countries, and a survey in London and the Midlands in the UK showed that over one quarter of people never drink water directly from the tap.

Domestic water comes from groundwater, rivers, reservoirs or, less commonly, desalinated sea water. Whatever the origin, all sources need some form of cleansing, a particularly difficult problem when the source of water is a river that runs through several countries. Pollution from pesticides and fertilizers can and do filter into water supplies. Chemical contaminants which cause human illness include aluminium, nitrates, lead and pesticides.

The problems in poor countries are much greater, where children often suffer five or more diarrhoeal episodes each year, much of this because of unclean water (see symbols on the map). There are dozens of water-borne diseases, including cholera, shistosomiasis, Hepatitis A, typhoid and campylobacter. These bacteria may be present because of contamination, broken or blocked sewage pipes or inadequate chlorination. Diarrhoeal diseases could be substantially reduced by children washing their hands after defaecating, but if scarce water is fetched from a well several kilometres away, it may be thought far too precious to be used for such a purpose.

Research clearly shows the link between atmospheric pollution and health. The 'Air pollution' symbol gives the most recent results on 20 cities from the Global Environment Monitoring System, which has been monitoring air pollution in urban areas since 1974. The results are not reassuring. Some 1.2 billion city dwellers worldwide are exposed to excessive levels of sulphur dioxide and even more are exposed to excessive levels of dust and dirt. Nearly one third of the cities have levels of nitrogen dioxide that exceed official WHO guidelines. Overall, only 20 percent of the world's 2.26 billion urban dwellers live in cities where air quality is acceptable, and levels of urban air pollution are increasing rapidly in poor countries.

Air pollution, especially sulphur dioxide and smoke, affects the lung and induces chronic bronchitis. The two great London smogs of 1952 and 1962 both caused an increase in deaths from bronchitis, correlating with high concentrations of sulphur dioxide and smoke. Studies in Canada, the USA and Japan have confirmed this relationship. Sulphur dioxide, also the major cause of acid rain, is produced by burning fossil fuels, metal-smelting and from volcanic emissions. Dust and dirt comes mainly from industrial sources, volcanoes, plant pollen and incomplete fuel combustion. Nitrogen oxides, from fuel combustion, fertilizers, volcanic activity and forest fires, also affect the lung. Ozone, causing photochemical smogs, is found in high quantities in Los Angeles and several other cities.

Other pollutants affect the blood, such as lead, mostly generated by motor vehicles and smelters. Carbon monoxide, one of the most widely distributed of all pollutants, also affects the blood, and again comes mainly from motor vehicles.

Cigarette smoking remains a far more important cause of bronchitis than atmospheric pollution. Studies carried out by the US Environmental Protection Agency on eleven chemicals in the air (such as cigarette smoke, cleaning agents, building materials and gasoline) concluded that outdoor exposure was relatively insignificant compared to indoor pollution and other 'life-style exposures'. In some cases the indoor levels of exposure were 70 times higher than outdoors.

Sources:
United Nations Environmental Programme (UNEP), *Global Environment Monitoring System, Urban Air Pollution*, UNEP/GEMS Environmental Library No 4, UNEP, 1991; World Health Organization (WHO), *Global Estimates for Health Situation Assessment and Projections*, Geneva: WHO 1990; United Nations Children's Fund (UNICEF), *The State of the* **103**

World's Children 1992, New York and Oxford: Oxford University Press for UNICEF, 1992; *World Health Statistics Annual 1988*, Geneva: WHO; Walker, Alison, 'Drinking water - doubts about quality', *British Medical Journal*, vol 304, 1992; '11 chemicals pose greater hazards in home'. Business News, *South China Morning Post*, 12 June 1985; Seager, Joni,*The State of the Earth*, A Pluto Project, London & New York: HarperCollins & Simon and Schuster, 1990.

Acknowledgements:
For data for the map: John Jackson and Anthony Webster, Monitoring and Assessment Research Centre, King's College London; Dr Beverley Carlson, Senior Adviser, Monitoring and Statistics, UNICEF; Dr Bernard Hausner, Senior Information Officer, UNDP.

15 THE SUPERFIX

One third of all regular cigarette smokers are killed by tobacco. Half of these will die in middle age. They will lose on average more than 20 years of life compared with non-smokers.

Smoking among men in rich countries is declining, and the map shows that they now smoke less than men in poor countries. On average about 30% of men (and 30% of women) smoke in rich countries, compared to about 50% of men (and only 5% of women) in poor countries.

The main map focusses on men, since for much of the 20th century smoking has been a predominantly male habit. Smoking rates of manufactured cigarettes were chosen as these are both the most reliable data and this is the most harmful way of using tobacco. But tobacco can also be sucked, chewed, sniffed, rubbed on the gums, smoked in pipes, water pipes, cigars, 'roll-your-own' cigarettes and bidis, and used in other ways.

There is no known way of using tobacco safely. Cigarettes are radioactive and contain over 4000 chemicals, including formaldehyde, benzene, cyanide, phenol and arsenic. In rich countries where cigarette smoking has been an established habit for decades, it accounts for the large majority of all deaths from chronic lung disease and from cancers of the lung, mouth and throat, as well as a substantial share of all heart and stroke deaths (see **18. Hearts and Minds**, **19. Cancers**). It contributes to many other cancers (such as cancers of the pancreas, bladder and cervix) and causes problems as diverse as duodenal ulcers and reduced fertility. Smoking harms others, even causing cancer in non-smokers who live or work with smokers. Smoking in pregnancy is hazardous to the foetus and also to the mother. The smoking of parents or other adults is a form of child abuse, causing documented illness in children.

The addictive habit starts in childhood. On average, out of every 1000 young men in the UK who smoke cigarettes regularly, about one will be murdered, about six will die on the roads and at least 350 will be killed before their time by tobacco.

In the USA, about 434,000 smokers die each year from smoking, a greater number than deaths of Americans between 1941-46 in World War II (407,316), World War I (116,708), the Vietnam War (58,151) or the Korean War (54,246). Cigarettes cause almost half a million deaths in Europe each year. Overall, at least one third, and probably close to one half, of all regular cigarette smokers are killed by tobacco. Half of these deaths will be in middle-age, not old age. Those killed in middle-age lose an average of more than 20 years of life compared with non-smokers. In rich countries, smoking kills more than alcohol, AIDS, car accidents, accidents at work, all other drugs (legal and illegal), homicide, suicide and drowning, combined.

Smoking also has an economic cost, including costs of medical care, of land used to grow tobacco instead of food, of lost productivity, higher cleaning and ventilation costs, property damage and fires – between a quarter to a third of fires are due to careless smoking. There is also an environmental cost: one in 25 trees in the world is cut down to dry tobacco; a modern cigarette manufacturing machine uses four miles of paper an hour; and discarded matches, cigarette ends and empty packets litter urban and rural areas.

The 'lips' symbol shows areas where rates of smoking are high among women. In countries where women have been smoking for a long time, for example, the UK, the USA, Australia and Denmark, deaths from lung cancer are as high or have already overtaken those from breast cancer. This will increase further as smoking among women increases.

The bar chart 'Future shock' shows that the current three million annual deaths worldwide from tobacco will more than treble by 2025. Seven million of these deaths will be in poor countries. In China alone, about 50 million of all the children alive today will eventually be killed prematurely by smoking. This reflects the changing global patterns of smoking, which is slowly decreasing in rich countries at a rate of one percent annually, and rising in poor countries at over two percent annually, partly due to population expansion and particularly due to an increase in smoking, especially in China. Poor countries can least afford the health, social and economic consequences of smoking; already two-thirds spend more money importing tobacco than they earn exporting it. Their governments are often preoccupied by other general or health problems, do not yet have adequate policies, laws or health education programmes against tobacco, and lack experience in dealing with transnational tobacco cartel tactics.

Sources:
Chollat-Traquet, Dr Claire, ed.,*Women and Tobacco*, Geneva: World Health Organization (WHO), 1992; Chapman, S. & W. W. Leng, *Tobacco Control in the Third World: A Resource Atlas*, 1990; Lopez, A.D., 'Lung cancer overtakes breast cancer in some parts of the world', *WHO Tobacco Alert*, January 1990; *1991 World Almanac*, Centers for Disease Control, National Safety Council, National Center for Health Statistics; *Health or Smoking*, London: Royal College of Physicians, 1983; WHO, The Health of Youth, Facts for Action: Youth and Tobacco, A42/*Technical Discussions* 3, Geneva: WHO, 1989; Masironi, R. & Rothwell, K., 'Tendences et effets du tabagisme dans le monde', *WHO World Statistics Quarterly*, 41, Geneva: WHO, 1988; US Department of Health and Human Services, *Smoking and Health in the Americas*, Atlanta, Georgia: US Department of Health and Human Services, Public Health Service, Centers for Disease Control, National Center for Chronic Disease Prevention and Health Promotion, Office on Smoking and Health, 1992; United Nations Development Programme (UNDP), *Human Development Report 1992*, New York and Oxford: Oxford University Press, 1992.

Acknowledgements:
Tobacco or Health Unit, WHO; Dr Jane Ferguson, Adolescent Health Unit, WHO; Dr Tipani Piha, WHO Regional Office for Europe; Dr Luk Joossens, Director, European Bureau for Action on Smoking Prevention (BASP); Professor Richard Peto, University of Oxford.

Contributors of national data for updating prevalence statistics: Mervi Hara, Director, Finland's ASH; Dr Kyoichi Miyazaki, ASH, Japan; Ms Janie Weir, ASH, New Zealand; Dr David Yen and Mr Ma, The John Tung Foundation, Taiwan; Dr Prakash C. Gupta, Tata Institute of Fundamental Research, Bombay, India; Mr David Pollock, Director, ASH, UK; Dr Seth Emont, Office on Smoking and Health, Centers for Disease Control, USA; Drs Jan van Reek and Hans Adriaanse in the Netherlands; Mr Ken Kyle and Dr Cheryl Moyer, Canadian Cancer Society; Dr Rose Vaithinathan, Ministry of Health, Singapore; Dr Myint Myint Sann, Singapore Cancer Society; Ms Bang On, Thai Anti-Smoking Campaign Project; Ms Marina Emmanuel, International Organization of Consumers Unions, Malaysia; Dr Margaretha Haglund, National Board of Health & Welfare, Sweden; Mrs L.A. Hanafiah, Indonesian Heart Foundation and Mrs Lisa Harun, International HealthCare, Indonesia; Professsor Il Suh, Korean ASH; Dr Natasha Herrera, Department of Smoking and Health, Ministry of Health and Social Assistance, Venezuela; Dr Witold Zatonski; Deputy Chair, Tobacco Control Eastern Europe, UICC; Dr Kjell Bjartveit, Director, National Health Screening Service, Norway; Dr Derek Yach, Dr Yusuf Saloojee, Dr Di McIntyre, Medical Research Council, South Africa.

16 BACCHUS BECKONS

People in rich countries drink on average double the amount of alcohol drunk by people in poor countries. The French drink more than any people in the world, and although per capita alcohol consumption among adults in France has fallen by half over the last twenty years, it is still higher than Luxembourg and Spain, currently second and third in the European drinking league. The national statistics on the map cannot show drinking patterns or attitudes. In Scotland, for example, three percent of the population consume 30 percent of the alcohol. In the USA, alcohol is increasingly regarded as antisocial and alcoholic beverages are required to carry a health warning.

While modest drinking of one half to two drinks daily might have some beneficial effect upon the heart, anyone who regularly drinks more than five pints of beer a day (or the equivalent) runs a high risk of liver cirrhosis, stomach damage, depression of the protective immune system, and an increased risk of several cancers. Women are more at risk than men, because of lower body weight, a smaller liver and possibly other as yet unknown factors. Pregnant women are advised not to drink at all.

After a single pint of beer (or equivalent) the chance of a driver having a road accident increases; after two and a half pints of beer the likelihood is increased 25 times. 40 percent of all people in the USA will be involved in alcohol-related road crashes some time in their lives. In places as diverse as the USA and Africa, 50 percent of all road deaths are attributable to alcohol. In Europe, excessive drinkers account for 40-60 percent of hospital days and sick leave from work (see **5. A Picture of Health?**).

Eighteen million Americans have a serious drinking problem. The annual costs of alcohol in the USA, including medical bills and the costs of lost workdays, are US$117 billion. In the UK, between 8-14 million working days are lost each year, and absenteeism through alcohol misuse is estimated to cost about UK£700 million a year.

Drinking three-quarters of a bottle of spirits usually leads to oblivion and coma, and immediate death is possible after one bottle of spirits. Alcoholism is defined as when alcohol affects physical and mental health, and interferes with social and personal functioning. Alcoholism has profound effects upon family, work and social life, and can lead to debt, violence in marriage, child neglect, separation and divorce.

Treatment for alcoholism has ranged from individual psychotherapy, social skills training, group therapy, family therapy and drug treatment. The most successful is Alcoholics Anonymous (AA). The AA symbol on the map shows countries with an established group registered with the international wing of AA in New York. Established in 1935 to help people to recover from alcoholism, AA now has about 94,000 groups worldwide with over two million active members. Its membership is increasing at a rate of 15 percent each year.

Since 1965 both the total volume and consumption of alcohol per person has increased. The global volume consumed has risen from 74 to 110 million hectolitres of 100 percent alcohol. The inset 'Nectar of the gods' shows that this is true for all kinds of alcohol – beer (22 to 39), wine (31 to 37) and spirits (20 to 33). Although part of this increase is explained by population growth, alcohol consumption per person is rising in all regions except for Africa (where it is falling) and Latin America (where it is static). Young people, particularly boys, are drinking more heavily, and are starting to drink at a younger age. The distinctions in drinking habits that used to separate cultures, social classes and sexes are fast disappearing.

Sources:
Adrian, M., P. Jull and R. Williams, *Statistics on Alcohol and Other Drug Use in Canada and Other Countries, 1988*, Toronto: Addiction Research Foundation, 1989; 'French drink the most in Europe', *British Medical Journal*, vol 303, 1991; *Journal of the Hong Kong Medical Association*, vol 41, no 1, March 1989; Dight, S.E., *Scottish Drinking Habits*, London: Population and Censuses and Surveys Office, HMSO, 1976; Rimm, E. B. et al., 'Prospective study of alcohol consumption and the risk of coronary disease in men', *Lancet*, vol 338, 1991; Jackson, R. et al., 'Alcohol consumption and risk of coronary heart disease', *British Medical Journal*, vol 303, 1991; 'Anti-drunk driving efforts thought to be successful', *The Nation's Health*, American Public Health Association, January 1992; World Health Organization (WHO), *Global Estimates for Health Situation Assessment and Projections*, Geneva: WHO, 1990; 'Alcohol and work', *British Medical Journal*, vol 298, 1989; *The Health of Youth, Facts for Action: Youth and Alcohol*, WHO, 1989. A42/Technical Discussions/4; The Health of Youth. Background Document, Technical Discussions, WHO, May 1989.

Acknowledgements:
Dr M. Adrian, Dr P. Jull and Dr R. Williams, Addiction Research Foundation, Toronto; Ms Lois Fischer, Overseas Desk, General Service Board, Alcoholics Anonymous, New York; Dr Jane Ferguson and Dr H.L. Friedman, Adolescent Health Programme, WHO.

17 HIGH SOCIETY

This map examines only illegal drugs (for legal drugs see **15. The Superfix**; **16. Bacchus Beckons**; **33. The Medicine Cabinet**). By its nature, no one knows the extent of illegal drug use. Therefore the data on the map are incomplete, representing information available from less than half the countries in the world. Some countries provide data from health records, others from police records, some conduct population surveys, while others simply guess. Some countries keep statistics on the weight of drugs seized or the number of arrests or prosecutions. Some countries report any person thought to have used a drug even once during the previous year, some list those who are daily users, while others record only registered abusers. Some countries multiply the numbers of known abusers by a factor (for example, ten) to estimate total numbers of abusers, but the multiplication factor itself varies from country to country.

In an attempt to standardize the information as much as possible, this map shows the numbers of people reported as having used a drug during the previous year. Where such data do not exist, the numbers of registered or daily users have been multiplied by a factor of ten. Thus, the map given can only offer an overall impression.

Drug use has spread far beyond its areas of origin. Substantially more young people than before are using drugs, and using them at a younger and younger age. More powerful forms of drugs are being developed: cannabis today is up to 50 times stronger than that grown in the 1960s. Drug users expose themselves to the dangers of HIV and AIDS through contaminated needles. AIDS has therefore added a new sense of urgency to efforts to control injectable drugs.

Cannabis is the most commonly used illegal drug. There are 21 million users in the USA alone. Men and women use it in fairly equal numbers in North America and some European countries, but in Asia and Africa it is predominantly a male habit. The leaf symbol shows, in the few countries researched, the popularity of cannabis among young people.

In addition to users of cannabis, the United Nations estimates that there are about 15 million other illicit drug users worldwide. This is an underestimate, as their figure only includes registered addicts and those picked up through the police and courts.

The total number of heroin users (see the inset map 'Heroin') is small (1.6 million reported cases) compared to users of other drugs. However, in all regions of the world there are reports of increasing use. The typical heroin user is young, male, single, little educated, socially deprived and unemployed. Another million people reportedly use other opiates. Opium consumption has remained stable and has even declined in Asia and the Middle East, while in South America heroin and opiate use is almost unknown.

In contrast, use of cocaine is escalating dramatically in most regions of the world, especially in the Americas and in Europe. The total number of reported cases is 13 million. The pie inset shows that by far the largest number of prosecutions for cocaine offences are in the Americas (78%), followed by Europe (19%), compared with only 3% in Africa, Asia and Oceania combined where, except for Nigeria, the Ivory Coast, Ghana, Australia and Japan, cocaine problems are very rare.

It is estimated that in some parts of the world as many as 10-30 percent of adolescents are users of some form of illicit drug, though the majority are only occasional users. In general, the first drug tried by youth in South America is coca paste; in Asia, an opiate; in rich countries, cannabis; and in Africa, barbiturates; but a wide range of additional substances are used. In general, and for all drugs, long-term users tend to be the least privileged in societies, and to come from families where parents are heavy drinkers or take tranquillizers.

Illicit drugs cannot be divorced from legal drugs. Tobacco and alcohol, addictive in themselves, also act as 'gateway' drugs for illegal drug use. Also, users of illicit drugs tend to be heavy cigarette smokers and drinkers. In the USA, 70 percent of 20 cigarette-a-day smokers had also used illicit drugs during the previous month. In Norway, regular cigarette smokers are ten times more likely than non-smokers, and heavy drinkers 30 times more likely than non-drinkers, also to use cannabis.

Sources:
World Health Organization (WHO), *Global Estimates for Health Situation Assessment and Projections*, Geneva: WHO, 1990; *The Health of Youth, Facts for Action: Youth and Drugs*, A42/Technical Discussion 7, Geneva: WHO, 1989; *The Health of Youth, Facts for Action: Youth and Drugs*, A42/Technical Discussion 2, Geneva: WHO, 1989; United Nations Economic and Social Council, E/CN.7/1992/8, *Commission on Narcotic Drugs*, 35th Session, Vienna, 6-15 April 1992; Adrian, M. & P. Jull and R. Williams, *Statistics on Alcohol and Other Drug Use in Canada and Other Countries*, Toronto: Addiction Research Foundation, 1989.

Acknowledgements:
Dr Gale U. Day, Head, Technical Services Division, UN International Drug Control Programme, Vienna; Dr Jane Ferguson Adolescent Health Programme, WHO; Dr M. Adrian, Dr P. Jull and Dr R. Williams, Addiction Research Foundation, Toronto.

18 HEARTS AND MINDS

'Cardiovascular disease' refers to diseases caused by hardening, narrowing and clogging of the arteries, reducing the vital blood supply to the heart muscle, brain or legs. In the heart, the disease (coronary heart disease) affects the coronary arteries that run over the surface of the heart and supply the heart muscle with blood, leading to angina or, if the process is more severe, to heart attacks. If the arteries to the brain are affected, the same process causes strokes; if the legs, it leads to pain on walking and ultimately gangrene.

Although strokes have been common for centuries (accounting for much of the 'apoplexy' of the past), heart attacks were not mentioned in most medical textbooks until after World War I. A sudden heart attack in a previously apparently healthy person was first reported in the USA only in the 1920s. Today, cardiovascular disease is the biggest single killer, causing 12 million deaths each year, one quarter of all deaths in the world. In rich countries it accounts for 40-50 percent of all deaths and, although there are little country-specific data available from Africa, the Middle East or Asia, it is estimated that cardiovascular diseases are the second leading cause of death (16 percent) in poor countries, after infectious and parasitic diseases (see **7. The Grim Reapers**).

The map shows that variations in cardiovascular diseases between countries are marked, due partly to differences in smoking and blood pressure and partly due to the influence of different diets. The rates in Eastern Europe and Russia are two to three times higher than those in France, Switzerland, Canada, Japan and China.

The heart symbols – 'Gender gap' – illustrate that men are more prone to cardiovascular disease than women – in general their risk is two to three times greater. Although still lower than men, women in Eastern Europe have the highest risk in the world. This risk is expected to rise further in many countries as more women enter their 50s and 60s as smokers.

Heart disease is avoidable. The inset graphic 'Change of heart' looks at deaths from heart disease in the USA only, which have fallen substantially since the 1960s. The fall in heart disease coincides with a reduction in smoking, changes in diet, control of blood pressure, and possibly changes in other risk factors. Heart disease also started to decline at about the same time in Australia, and shortly afterwards in England and Wales and some other rich countries. The largest decreases for women were in the USA and Australia. Conversely, in Central Europe in particular, deaths from heart disease are escalating. When people migrate, their risk of heart attack changes: when Japanese living in Japan (with a low rate) move to the USA (with a higher rate) their risk changes to approach that of their host country.

But even with recent reductions in the USA, cardiovascular diseases remain prevalent. About 67 million Americans currently have cardiovascular disease (mainly high blood pressure, but also heart disease and stroke). Almost one in two Americans die from cardiovascular disease – one every 32 seconds. In 1987 this amounted to about one million Americans, accounting for the loss of about five million years of potential life. Cardiovascular disease is estimated to cost the nation US$95 billion annually in health care costs and lost productivity. There are more than 1200 coronary care units in the USA and 332,000 coronary bypass operations are performed annually – three quarters on men, and more than half on people under 65 years of age. Research into cardiovascular diseases receives the third highest federal funding for health research in the USA, after cancer and AIDS (see note to **34. Training and Research**).

Sources:
World Health Organization (WHO), *WHO Features*, no 140, April 1990; Shepherd J., et al, 'Strategies for reducing coronary heart disease and desirable limits for blood lipid concentrations: guidelines of the British Hyperlipidaemia Association', *British Medical Journal*, vol 295, 1987; Oganov, R.G., et al, 'Preventing cardiovascular diseases in the USSR', *World Health Forum*, vol 6, Geneva: WHO, 1985; WHO MONICA Project: 'Assessing CHD mortality and morbidity',*International Journal of Epidemiology*, vol 18, no 3 (suppl 1) 1989; WHO, *Global Estimates for Health Situation Assessment and Projections*, Geneva: WHO, 1990; *World Health Statistics Quarterly*, 38, Geneva: WHO, 1985; Dwyer, Terry & Basil S. Hetzel, 'A comparison of trends in coronary heart disease in Australia, USA and England and Wales with reference to three major risk factors – hypertension, cigarette smoking and diet', *International Journal of Epidemiology*, vol 9, no 1; Goodwin, J.F. & I. Sharp, 'Preventing coronary heart disease', National Forum for Coronary Heart Disease Prevention, London, *British Medical Journal* vol 304, 1992; *1990 Heart and Stroke Facts, 1980*, American Heart Association, 'Age adjusted death rates for major cardiovascular diseases, US 1940-86: deaths per 100,000 population'; Sprafka, Michael J., et al, 'Continued decline in cardiovascular disease risk factors': (Minnesota Heart Survey, 1980-82 and 1985-87) *American Journal of Epidemiology*, vol 132, no 3, 1990.

Acknowledgements:
Dr Rory Collins, Clinical Trial Service Unit, University of Oxford; Professor Richard Peto, University of Oxford; Professor Bill Castleden, University Department of Surgery, Fremantle Hospital, Western Australia; Professor John W. Farquhar, Professor of Medicine, Stanford Center for Research in Disease Prevention, California.

19 CANCERS

Cancer is not a new disease, nor does it strike only humans – it has even been found in dinosaur skeletons, and there are ancient records of Egyptian doctors removing tumours with knives or red-hot irons.

The cancers referred to on the map exclude the benign tumours – the lumps, bumps and simple cysts, which do not spread and which cause few problems. This map shows deaths from 'malignant' tumours, when a normal body cell becomes altered and spins out of control, replicating itself to produce many millions of similar self-replicating cells, some of which may spread to other parts of the body, and eventually overwhelm it. There are dozens of different types of cancer, whose causes vary enormously. Cancer is thus a description of a group of diseases, in the same way that the term 'infectious diseases' describe illnesses as diverse as malaria and gonorrhoea.

Modern study of the causes of cancer date back more than 200 years with the observation that breast cancer occurred more often in nuns than in other women, and that chimney sweeps were particularly prone to cancer of the scrotum. Although both observations have been confirmed many times over, the reason for the first still remains elusive, while the combustion products of coal in contact with the skin are known to cause the second. Increased skin cancer in radiologists heavily exposed to X-rays, lung cancer in miners heavily exposed to radon and bladder cancer in aniline dye workers were all noticed in the early part of the 20th century, and habitual betel nut chewers were found to be at particular risk of oral cancer. After World War II, these rather casual observations were followed by meticulous studies conducted by the founders of scientific investigation into the causes of cancer, Doll and Hill in the UK, Wynder and Graham, and Hammond and Horn in the USA, first on the effects of smoking and then on the geographic differences and causes of many different types of cancer.

The best estimates for the proportion of cancer deaths attributable to various factors, in the USA for example, are dietary causes 35%; tobacco 30%; long-term infections 10%; reproductive and sexual behaviour 7%; occupation 4%; alcohol 3%; geophysical factors 3%; pollution 2%; medicine and medical procedures 1%; and food additives and industrial products, less than 1% each. This still leaves many completely unknown causes of cancer. As any one cancer may have more than one cause, the grand total will probably, when more knowledge is available, greatly exceed 200%.

Cancer is the third biggest killer in the world, causing five million deaths annually, divided almost equally between rich and poor countries (see **7. The Grim Reapers**). While cancer can occasionally affect children or young adults, about half the cases arise in middle age and half in old age. On the map, therefore, the risk of cancer will appear lower in countries with a younger population.

There has been a worldwide increase in the number of cancer deaths. This is mainly due to three things: the increasing size of the world's population, the reduction in other health problems leading to people living longer, and an increase in smoking. With the exception of smoking-induced cancers, the overall rates of cancer have not changed very much. Until recently, stomach cancer used to cause most cancer deaths worldwide, but it has now been overtaken by the lung cancer epidemic.

Because country-specific data are lacking from so many poor countries, 'Cancers by region' is used to give an overall global picture of cancer death rates. This also allows countries to compare their national rates with those of their region. This shows that death from cancer is much less common in poor countries, but again this principally reflects the younger age structure of the population.

'Cancers by site' contrasts the different cancers in men and women, and the differences in cancers between a rich and a poor country. In the USA, lung cancer is the most common cancer for both sexes, although the ratings of subsequent cancers differ for men and women. Although 99 percent of cancer deaths are in adult life, cancer still kills more children between one and 14 years than any other disease. What the graphic cannot show are the trends in cancer rates: deaths from lung cancer are increasing dramatically, deaths from breast, intestine (colon and rectum), prostate, pancreatic cancers and leukaemia are steady, while cancers of the stomach and womb are falling. Apart from lung cancer, the reasons for some of these changes are unclear.

Lung cancer rates in China are high, but liver, stomach and oesophageal cancers feature more prominently than in the USA. The two most important known causes of cancer in poor countries are smoking or chewing tobacco and the Hepatitis B virus, a major cause of liver cancer.

Some cancers have been known to disappear spontaneously, some have become more amenable to cure, and people with even wide-spread cancer may remain in apparent good health for months or years.

Currently, no single measure is known that would have as great an impact on the number of cancer deaths as a reduction in the use of tobacco. This is because even a small reduction in a major cause of cancer will have a far greater impact than a large reduction in a rare cancer.

Sources:

World Health Statistics Annual 1990, Geneva: WHO; Doll, R. & R. Peto, *The Causes of Cancer*, Oxford Medical Publications, 1981; Parkin, D.M., E. Laara & C. S. Muir, 'Estimates of the worldwide frequency of 16 major cancers in 1980', *International Journal of Cancer*, 41, 1988; Parkin, D.M., A J. Sasco & Dr P.H., *Lung Cancer: Worldwide variation in occurrence and proportion attributable to tobacco use*, International Agency for Research on Cancer, ob/686/660/18.12.1991; Weatherall, D.J., J.G.G. Ledingham, & D.A. Warrell, eds., *Oxford Textbook of Medicine.*, Oxford: Oxford University Press, 1983; Henderson, B.E., R.K. Ross, & M.C. Pike, 'Toward the primary prevention of cancer', *Science*, November 1991; *WHO Features*, no 140, Geneva: WHO, April 1990; *Cancer Facts and Figures, 1991*, American Cancer Society; Monfardini, S., U. Tirelli, D. Serraino &I. Fentiman, 'After 65, cancer has a different impact on life expectancy in men and women', *European Journal of Cancer,* vol 27, no 8, 1991; WHO, *Global Estimates for Health Situation Assessment and Projections*, Geneva: WHO, 1990;*World Health*, Geneva: WHO, March 1985.

Acknowledgements:

Dr Max Parkin, Chief, Descriptive Epidemiology Unit, International Agency for Research on Cancer (IARC), Lyon; Professor Richard Peto, University of Oxford. Data from *Cancer Facts and Figures, 1991* used with permission of the American Cancer Society.

20 SPITTING BLOOD

Almost two billion people alive today, one third of the world's inhabitants, are or have been infected by tuberculosis, spread mainly through an infected person coughing or breathing over another person. When someone has concentrated tuberculosis germs in their sputum they will, on average, infect at least a further ten people each year.

'Spitting blood' is a typical sign of active tuberculosis. But not everyone who spits blood has tuberculosis and not everyone with tuberculosis spits blood. The great majority of people who are infected remain well; only about one in ten develop symptoms and this depends on factors like age (the young and the old being the most vulnerable), whether tuberculosis is new to a community (when it affects people much more severely) and the general state of health and nutrition.

Statistics on tuberculosis, especially from poor countries, are frequently unreliable. They more often represent the standard of reporting rather than the true incidence of the disease, and this certainly accounts for some of the apparent differences between countries in Africa. A 646 percent increase in Uganda in 1990 relates not to a massive epidemic but to the expansion of the national tuberculosis programme. Major decreases in 1990 in Iraq, Kuwait and the Sudan are attributable to the deterioration of reporting systems due to war.

In an attempt to overcome some of the variability in annual statistics, data from five consecutive years have been pooled and then divided by five, to obtain average yearly numbers of new cases. The 'highest' figure for Djibouti is slightly misleading since it is partially attributable to the catchment area extending beyond its own borders.

Every year there are eight million new cases and three million deaths from tuberculosis. More than 95 percent of people infected live in poor countries, where nutrition and general health is poor, and which do not have the medical infrastructure for diagnosis, prevention and treatment. In such countries, tuberculosis tends to affect young and middle-aged adults, causing more than one quarter of avoidable deaths in this age group. On the other hand, tuberculosis in rich countries has become predominantly an illness of the elderly and infirm. The bar chart 'Declining deaths' shows the decrease in deaths from tuberculosis in England and Wales after peaking during the industrial revolution. The historical scale cannot adequately show the degree of improvement following the introduction of combination drug regimes to treat tuberculosis in 1947.

But the bar chart 'Rising cases' shows that in New York AIDS, by reducing the body's immune defence system and resistance, is having a major impact on the number of new cases of tuberculosis. New York is only one example. In the USA in general, AIDS is playing a leading role in the recent reversal of the long-term decline of tuberculosis. In the African countries with the AIDS virus symbol the number of notified tuberculosis cases has doubled in the last few years. This increase is clearly related to the AIDS epidemic. Already about three million people infected with HIV are also infected with tuberculosis, and the epidemics are moving in parallel. As HIV spreads to the more populated areas of Asia, where tuberculosis infection is widespread, a major increase in tuberculosis can be predicted (see **22. AIDS**).

On a more positive note, 90 percent of the world's surviving infants are now protected by immunization from childhood tuberculosis (see **35. Catching Them Young**).

Sources:
Sudre, P., G. ten Dam, C. Chan & A. Kochi, *Tuberculosis in the present time: A global overview of the tuberculosis situation*, WHO/TUB/91.158; *Expanded Programme on Immunization* (EPI), Information System, Summary for all the WHO regions, August 1991 (BCG updated January 1992). WHO/EPI/CESI/91.2; 'World tuberculosis toll on the rise', *Asian Medical News*, vol 13, no 8 1991; WHO, *Global Estimates for Health Situation Assessment and Projections*, Geneva; WHO, 1990.

Acknowledgements:
Dr F. Luelmo, Medical Officer, Tuberculosis Unit, Division of Communicable Diseases, WHO; Sir John Crofton; Ms Deborah McLellan, American Public Health Association.

21 FLU

Influenza is a humbling disease – even in modern times we are powerless to prevent it spreading around the globe. Nor has the standard treatment advice changed much over the centuries: to rest and take lots of fluids, although simple analgesics are now used for muscle aches. Anti-viral agents are being developed, but are as yet very expensive and thus their availability is extremely limited. Antibiotics are useless unless there is an additional, superimposed bacterial infection, as they have no effect whatsoever on viruses, including flu, the common cold, hepatitis, polio and AIDS.

Although influenza immunization early in an epidemic offers some protection (and is recommended for high risk groups – the very old, the very young, the debilitated), this protection does not last for long. The strains of flu viruses are perpetually changing, so that this year's immunization may not prevent next year's flu.

Although the flu virus was not identified until 1933, the symptoms of flu were described more than 2000 years ago, and few people escape an attack sometime during their lives. The 1989 Beijing A influenza virus, identified in Beijing in November 1989, circled the globe in less than two years, its spread probably hastened by modern travel.

Influenza A is the worst of the three strains of flu viruses: A, B and C. Mutant A forms cause pandemics about every 30 years, for example, 1989-92, 1957-58, 1918-19, 1889-92. The worst flu epidemic this century (1918-19) affected half the population in the world, and killed over 20 million worldwide. It was not the flu virus itself, but the superimposed streptococcus bacteria (attacking those already weakened by influenza) that caused most of these deaths. But far more people died than in World War I, and as a world killer it comes second only to the 14th century Black Death plague in the numbers killed by an infectious disease pandemic.

Acknowledgements:
Dr Nancy J. Cox, Chief, and Dr Lynnette Brammer, Public Health Scientist, both of the Influenza Branch, Centers for Disease Control, Department of Health and Human Services, Atlanta, USA (WHO Collaborating Centre for Reference and Research on Influenza); Dr J.J. Shekel, Director, National Institute for Medical Research, Medical Research Council, London (WHO Collaborating Centre for Reference and Research on Influenza); Ms Karin Esteves, Division of Communicable Diseases, WHO.

AIDS

The precise origin of AIDS is still obscure. To date, all that is certain is that the current epidemic began to spread across the world from Africa in the late 1970s.

Its mode of transmission is not obscure: it is spread by heterosexual and homosexual intercourse – anal, vaginal and oral; by needles, blood, semen and organ donation; and from mother-to-child. Worldwide 75 percent of people infected with AIDS acquired it heterosexually, and heterosexual transmission is on the rise.

There are three distinct stages to AIDS, although a person is infectious to others in all three stages. The incubation stage, when the virus has been irrevocably acquired but the usual blood tests are not yet positive, may last up to one year. The 'HIV positive' latent period, where the blood tests have become positive but there are no signs or symptoms of any disease, can last as long as ten or more years. The final phase is the 'AIDS syndrome', when the person becomes sick and usually lives for less than two more years.

The main map 'Reported AIDS' shows only the numbers with full-blown AIDS disease and only those that have been reported, a total of about 450,000 throughout the world by 1992. As the majority of cases are unreported, it is estimated that there are at least two million cases, as shown in the graphic 'The AIDS shadow'.

If people who are estimated to be HIV-positive (but who are still without symptoms) are included, the shadow lengthens to ten million infected by 1992. The inset cartogram 'AIDS in waiting' shows that two thirds of these ten million HIV-positive live in Africa, and only ten percent in Asia. But the AIDS shadow lengthens to 40 million HIV-positive by the year 2000 and the shadow symbolically falls across Asia. It is Asia that will bear the brunt of the AIDS epidemic in the future; even by the mid- to late-1990s, more Asians will become infected each year than Africans. Overall, more than 90 percent of those with AIDS will live in poor countries, and WHO predicts that 'the deaths of as many as one-fifth of young and middle-aged adults over a short period of time will lead to social turmoil, economic disruption and even political destabilization in many countries.'

Although the main map shows the combined numbers of AIDS for men and women, AIDS poses a special threat to women; by the year 2000 the annual number of new AIDS cases in women will begin to equal those of men. Women are substantially more likely to get AIDS from male sexual partners than men are from female partners. A woman is particularly vulnerable if firstly, the male partner has full-blown AIDS syndrome rather than being HIV-positive without symptoms; secondly, if she has had another sexually-transmitted disease during the previous five years; and thirdly, if the couple have anal intercourse. This is because other venereal infections, as well as the greater degree of trauma with anal intercourse, both damage the surface of the vagina or anus, with the result that the virus can enter more easily.

Children of AIDS mothers are particularly vulnerable. By the turn of the century, one third of AIDS cases will be children. Some 10-15 million children under ten years of age who escape infection from an AIDS-positive mother will be orphaned as a result of AIDS.

AIDS has thrown up more than the usual dilemmas of health care priorities. In some parts of Africa, up to half of hospital beds are filled with people with AIDS. AIDS mops up medical and health resources that could be used to treat curable diseases. In rich countries the proportion alive two years after being diagnosed as having full-blown AIDS has improved from 20 percent in 1984 to 50 percent in 1989. This is principally as a result of extremely expensive therapies, far beyond the pockets of most of those with AIDS in the world. But even in rich countries, there has been no improvement in survival in the last few years, indicating that the present therapies have produced their maximum effect, and further improvements will have to await new forms of treatment..

AIDS has also produced moral debate. Should health staff, surgical patients, engaged couples or prisoners be compulsorily tested for AIDS? Should a doctor break patient confidentiality and inform the partner of someone HIV-positive that they are at risk from AIDS? The whole question raises the dilemma between the privacy and freedoms of people with AIDS and the need for social responsibility in protecting those at risk. But in the words of John Stuart Mill, 'No one should have the freedom to harm others'.

Sources:
Update: AIDS cases reported to Surveillance, Forecasting and Impact Assessment Unit (SFI), Office of Research, Global Programme on AIDS, World Health Organization (WHO), January 1992; *Global Programme on AIDS: Current and Future Dimensions of the HIV/AIDS Pandemic*, A capsule summary, January 1992, WHO/GPA/RES/SFI/92.1; 'Thailand: by year 2000, 2-4 million may be HIV-infected', Centers for Disease Control, *CDC AIDS Weekly*, 28 October 1991; Dr Petros-Barvazian, Angele & Dr Michael H. Merson,'Women and AIDS: a challenge for humanity', *World Health*, November-December 1990, Geneva: WHO; '40 million HIV infections by the year 2000', *AIDS Weekly*, Geneva: WHO, May 1991; European Study Group, 'Risk factors for male to female transmission of HIV', *British Medical Journal*, vol 298, 1989; Coleman, D.G., et al, 'Changing disease patterns in AIDS', *British Medical Journal*, vol 304, March 1992; Mason, J.K., ed., 'Recording HIV status on police computers', *British Medical Journal*, vol 304, April 1992; Tanne, Janice Hopkins, ed., 'New York frees prisoners dying of AIDS', *British Medical Journal*, vol 304 April 1992; Goldman, Eleanore, Riva Miller, & Christine A. Lee. 'Counselling HIV positive haemophilic men who wish to have children', *British Medical Journal* vol 304, March 1992; Delamonthe, Tony, 'AIDS: rights versus responsibility', *British Medical Journal*, vol 303, September 1991.

Acknowledgements:
WHO Global Programme on AIDS, and in particular, Dr Paul Sato, Surveillance, Forecasting and Impact Assessment Unit, Office of Research.

23 TROPICAL DISEASES

There are 270 million people in the world infected with malaria, more than with any other tropical disease. Most live in parts of the world where health services are understaffed, underfunded and unevenly distributed, so that reporting of the disease is fragmentary. For example, countries in tropical Africa are estimated to have 80-90 percent of the world's malaria yet report less than six percent of the estimated global number. This would make a 'country specific' map on malaria highly misleading, so instead three broad 'risk bands' used by the World Health Organization are shown – areas where the risk of contracting malaria is high, where there is some risk, and where there is virtually no risk. Forty percent of the world's population, more than two billion people, remain exposed to high or moderate risk. Half of the remaining 60 percent live in areas where malaria never existed and half in areas where it has been eliminated. The symbol shows where plasmodium falciparum, the most severe type of malaria and the type that becomes drug-resistant, makes up a high proportion of all malaria cases. Drug-resistant malaria has increased from 15% of all cases in the early 1970s to 41% today.

In the early 1990s the world malaria problem is getting worse except in China and India. The conclusion of the Second Report of the Malaria Commission of the League of Nations in 1927 is still true today: 'The history of special antimalarial campaigns is chiefly a record of exaggerated expectations followed sooner or later by disappointment and the abandonment of work.'

Other tropical diseases in the bar chart 'Tropical torments' cause great pain and suffering, anaemia, sores, deformities, blindness, brain damage, internal damage and even death. Eradication of these diseases is extremely difficult for many reasons. Most are caused by parasites spread by moving targets (insects and snails), which can adapt and develop resistance to drugs; people move and carry disease to areas where there is no resistance; there is a lack of both public awareness and government funding; a whole range of measures is needed, including insecticides, traps, diagnostic tests and vaccines, as well as the infrastructure to use these efficiently.

There have been some successes. Drug treatment is helping to reduce the more serious effects of schistosomiasis, and the overall numbers of people infected are falling. Aerial spraying of breeding sites of disease-carrying blackflies in West Africa protects more than four million children from river blindness, and an effective new drug has been developed. Leprosy is now declining.

In addition to the diseases shown, two billion people have been infected with the Hepatitis B virus, and 300 million have become long-term infected carriers. Most live in poor tropical and sub-tropical countries; three quarters live in Asia. In poor countries transmission is usually from mother to child at birth whereas in rich countries it is usually from dirty needles, sex or, nowadays less commonly, blood transfusions. Two million people die from the effects of Hepatitis B each year: from primary liver cancer, chronic liver infection or liver cirrhosis. Over 20 countries in South East Asia, including China, have recently started preventive immunization programmes.

'Tropical diseases by region' shows that three quarters of people (460 million) with tropical diseases live in Africa, where the most rampant diseases are malaria, schistosomiasis, river blindness and African sleeping sickness. Some people have more than one disease. In Asia there are 110 million cases of tropical diseases; the most serious are malaria, schistosomiasis and filariasis. In Central and South America, more than 35 million people are infected with tropical diseases, in particular Chagas (trypanosomiasis), schistosomiasis and malaria. 'Progress' as well as poverty can contribute. The development of the Amazon basin is creating new breeding sites for malaria-carrying mosquitoes, leading to a substantial increase of malaria.

Europe and North America are not free from tropical diseases. Leishmaniasis is endemic in all countries around the Mediterranean and there is malaria in Turkey. Also, travellers can import tropical diseases, especially malaria (annually, almost 2000 cases to the UK, over 300 to Switzerland and about 1000 to the USA). 'Airport malaria', caused by mosquitoes carried into Europe on aeroplanes and infecting people living close to airports, has become a frequent phenomenon.

Sources:
World Malaria Situation in 1989, Geneva: WHO, June-July 1991; *World Report on Tropical Diseases*, Extracts from WHO Features, no 139, March 1990, Geneva: World Health Organization (WHO); WHO, *Global Estimates for Health Situation Assessment and Projections*, Geneva: WHO, 1990; '200 million may die prematurely in the 1990s', *WHO News*, Extracts from WHO Features, no 140, April 1990, Geneva: WHO; Najera-Morrondo, Jose, 'Malaria control: history shows it's possible', *World Health*, Geneva: WHO, September-October 1991, Geneva: WHO; Utroska, J.A., et al, *An Estimate of Global Needs for Praziquantel Within Shistosomiasis Control Programmes*, WHO/SCHISTO/89.102, Geneva: WHO; 'Eliminating hepatitis B', *Asian Medical News*, vol 13, no 10, August 1991.

Acknowledgements:
Jose Antonio Najera-Morrondo, Director, Dr Ken Mott, Chief, Shistosomiasis and other Trematode Infections, and Dr A.E.C. Rietveld, Malaria Unit: Division of Control of Tropical Diseases, WHO.

24 JAWS

The age of 12 years is used as the standard age for dental statistics by the World Health Organization, not because it has any medical significance but for very practical reasons. It enables information to be collected from a maximum number of children before they leave school and become less traceable. However, the information shown on the map is not only relevant to childhood, for although tooth decay (dental caries) occurs mainly in youth, dental care involving repair and replacement of initial treatment is needed for life.

The map shows that, in general, there are still more dental problems reported in rich countries than in poor countries but this is no comment on their dental health. In many poor countries, dental care is only available in the urban areas, or even confined to the capital city. For the majority, extraction is the only available treatment, and the 'filled' component of the 'Decayed, missing or filled teeth' key used on the main map is usually zero.

Three quarters of all oral health personnel live in rich countries serving one quarter of the world's population where oral diseases – dental and gum problems – are decreasing. The training of those working in poor countries is similar to training in dental schools in rich countries, training which may be quite inappropriate where there is only one oral care person for 50,000 or more people. There needs to be integration between the work of traditional healers and trained dentists to extend dental health care beyond the cities and more privileged. Paradoxically, there are more dentists than needed in many rich countries, with the tendency for more intervention and for more frequent replacements of fillings.

There is a sharp contrast between data for 1991 and 1969. In 1969 there was much less reported information on dental problems, whereas by 1991 there are data from most countries. This in part reflects a growing recognition of the importance of dental health and that problems with teeth are not just trivial complaints. The 1991 data also show that the incidence of caries has tended to fall in rich countries and rise in poor countries, albeit not to the level of the rich.

The decrease in caries in rich countries is partly due to preventive self-care, sound diet, dental services, and fluoridation of water supplies. Poor countries have few toothbrushes or dental services, and it is often impossible to fluoridate local water supplies like wells.

Removal of teeth is still the mainstay of treatment in poor countries. Astonishingly, as the graphic 'The empty mouth' shows, extraction of all teeth was still a frequent treatment for adults of some rich countries as late as the 1960s. Not so long before this, a coveted present for a young bride in the UK was to be paid to have all her teeth out before the wedding.

Sources:
World Health Organization (WHO), *Global Estimates for Health Situation Assessment and Projections*, Geneva: WHO, 1990; Leclercq, M.H., D.E. Barmes & J. Sardo Infirri, 'Oral health: global trends and projections', *World Health Statistics Quarterly*, no 40, 1987, Geneva: WHO; *World Health Statistics Annual, 1987*, Geneva: WHO; Thirty-first World Health Assembly, WHA 31.50. 24 May, 1978, *Fluorides and Prevention of Dental Caries*, Geneva: WHO; Eyitope Ogunbodede, 'Dental care: the role of the traditional healers', *World Health Forum*, vol 12, 1991, Geneva: WHO.

Acknowledgements:
Dr Jennifer Sardo Infirri, Oral Health Programme, WHO.

25 OF ONE MIND

In rich and poor countries alike the main mental and psychological problems are schizophrenia, depression, dementia, neuroses and psychosomatic disorders. People in poor countries have more psychological reactions associated with severe environmental stress, and suffer physical diseases of the brain caused by trauma, infections and parasitic diseases. The lifetime risk of getting a mental disorder is no less than 15 percent in most countries; at any point in time five percent of a population suffer from long-term mental illness or handicap.

The main map shows that, while specific data from individual countries are not available, severe mental problems – schizophrenia, severe depression and dementias – affect no less than two percent of most populations. The incidence of schizophrenia in particular is remarkably constant around the world, with between 2-4 new cases each year per 10,000 population between the risk ages of 15-54 years. There are no demonstrable differences in rates of schizophrenia between rich and poor countries.

In the world as a whole, there are more than 45 million people with severe schizophrenia or depression, and if the moderately severely mentally ill are included, the figure comes to over 200 million. In addition, between 5-8 percent of people over 65 years old are severely demented. Therefore dementia is found more frequently in rich countries because on average their populations are older.

The prevalence of milder neuroses – the difficulties of coping with life – differs, and is in part culturally conditioned. In some societies it is more acceptable for people to confide in their doctor that they feel depressed, whereas in poor countries people who are depressed will often somatize their distress and interpret their problems as tiredness and aches. These predominantly psychosocial problems are the largest single complaint category that takes people to consult health staff, comprising 30-35 percent of consultations in rich countries, and 15-20 percent in poor countries.

Most people at some time, and normally, experience symptoms – such as anxiety, depression, overactivity, elation, grief, guilt, anger, sleep difficulties, suspicion, flash thoughts of suicide (even murder), fears and fantasies – that, only when dominant and incapacitating, are labelled a 'mental disorder'.

Everyone is also subject to stress, which can be a stimulus or which can overwhelm, even causing mental and physical illness. Tables have been produced of stress factors, such as bereavement, divorce, giving up drugs/alcohol if dependent, illness or injury, losing a job, down to getting a parking ticket. Even theoretically happy events like marriage, pregnancy, financial changes for the better and holidays can contribute to stress.

There are between 90-130 million mentally retarded people in the world. Three to four in every 1000 below the age of 18 are moderately to severely retarded (having an IQ less than 50), and between 20-30 in every 1000 are mildly to moderately retarded (having an IQ 50-70). As less coping skills are needed to work in a field than to master the complexities of modern city life, they often function better in rural communities.

The pie charts on Scotland, which unlike most countries has good data on the subject, **115** shows the breakdown into the different types of mental problems requiring hospitalization, rather than general mental problems within the community. Thus, this inset represents the most serious end of the spectrum of those with mental difficulties, the majority having dementia, schizophrenia and other psychoses rather than milder neuroses.

The pie charts also highlight the different profile of mental illness between men and women. Here, but also generally, men have more schizophrenia and problems related to alcohol. Women suffer more from depression and senile dementia (because women live longer than men).

Treatment for mental patients has changed considerably since the time the mentally retarded or 'abnormal' were publicly humiliated at the stocks, burned at the stake or kept in chains. About 250 years ago the Frenchman Philippe Pinel and the English Quaker William Tuke introduced some humane treatment into mental institutions, which included gentleness, persuasion, a cheerful environment and visits from family and friends. But there the mentally different (and sometimes just the different) stayed until after World War II, in practice often offered little beyond custodial care. Since then more and more of the mentally disabled live within the community, but the debate continues as to how best this might be achieved.

Sources:
World Health Organization (WHO), *Global Estimates for Health Situation Assessment and Projections, 1990*, Geneva: WHO;*Prevention of mental, neurological and psychosocial disorders: Report by the Director-General*, Geneva: WHO, 1988; 'Evaluation of the strategy of HFA2000: seventh report on the world health situation', vol 1, *Global Review*, WHO, 1987; *World Health Statistics Annual, 1986*, Geneva: WHO; Sartorius, N., et al., eds. *Psychological disorders in general medical settings*, Toronto: Hogrefe & Huber on behalf of WHO, 1990; Sartorius N., et al., 'Early manifestations and first-contact incidence of schizophrenia in different cultures', *Psychological Medicine*, vol 16, 1986; 'Dementia in later life: research and action', WHO Technical Report Series no 730, 1986; *Initiative of support to people disabled by mental illness*, Geneva: WHO, Division of Mental Health 1988, WHO/MNH/MEP/88.6; *Global Medium-Term Programme*, Programme 10, Protection and prevention of mental health, 1990-1995, WHO, MNH/MTP/88.1.

Acknowledgements:
Dr W. Gulbinat, Senior Scientist, Division of Mental Health, WHO; Dr Edith Waldmann, The Richmond Fellowship International, London; Ms Margaret Haines, Head Librarian and Information Officer, King's Fund Centre, London.

26 ABILITY

We are all, to some extent, disabled, but the lives of seven to ten percent of the world's population are significantly altered by physical, mental or sensory problems. Mental and neurological disorders make up to 40 percent of this total in some countries, and over 42 million people have profound, severe or moderate hearing impairment.

Percentages of disabled vary from less than one percent to 21 percent, with rich countries in general reporting more disability than poor countries. Disability increases with age. In China, for example, 50 percent of people aged 80-85 years have limitations in contrast to five percent of 45-49 year olds.

Most countries do not report statistics on disability, and where they do, the data are often not comparable. Behind these figures lies variation in surveyed groups or ages, data collecting techniques (for example, only the most severe disability may be reported by poor countries) and the definition of disability itself. Even in a rich country like the USA, 'work disability' varies between eight and 17 percent of the population, depending on different methods of collecting information.

The terminology used for disabilities is confusing and controversial. The World Health Organization (WHO) has rejected the idea that disability is an illness, but there is still no single word to describe people with special needs that does not carry attitudinal, judgemental or preconceived bias. WHO defines disablement as the problems and issues faced by people who have experienced illness or injury resulting in long-term changes in appearance, or modification of functional abilities, daily activities, or life roles. The term disablement includes impairment, disability and handicap.

Impairment describes problems at the physical level, such as blindness, deafness, loss of sight in an eye, paralysis of a limb, amputation of a limb, mental retardation, partial sight, loss of speech, mutism. These may be caused by congenital and birth abnormalities, infectious and parasitic diseases (polio, tuberculosis, leprosy), heart and chest diseases, cancer and injury, for example, motor vehicle and other transport accidents, accidental poisoning, falls, fire, war, natural and environmental disasters. Disability describes difficulties at the personal level, such as difficulty seeing, speaking, hearing, moving, climbing stairs, grasping, reaching, bathing, eating, toileting. Handicap describes how people find themselves, such as bedridden, confined to home, unable to use public transport, not working, underemployed, socially isolated.

Not everyone is happy with these terms. Those working with children favour the terms 'children with special educational needs' and 'children with learning difficulties' in preference to 'mental handicap'. Using such terms shifts the emphasis away from negative labelling towards the practical help these children need to learn and cope.

'The young blind' shows that three quarters of the world's 1.5 million blind children live in Asia, seventeen percent in Africa and only a few in rich countries. Blindness in poor countries is mainly caused by measles and diarrhoea leading to vitamin A deficiency, traditional eye medicines, and gonorrhoea picked up from the mother at birth which affects the eyes of babies. Death rates among blind children in poor countries are high. In less poor countries, congenital eye disorders often associated with rubella (German measles) are the major causes. In rich countries, it is usually caused by inherited genetic diseases, or is due to extreme prematurity in very low birthweight babies who survive because of good intensive care.

The bar chart 'Canada' shows a breakdown into the different types of disability of those living in households, therefore excluding the minority who were unable to live in the community. thirteen percent of the general population were found to be disabled in this large, comprehensive survey.

The bar chart 'China' shows that hearing and speaking difficulties in China were mostly caused by old age, followed by ear infections. The data are taken from a large survey in 1987 on 1.25 million households which found that about five percent, or one in 20 people, were 'disabled'. Hearing and speaking difficulties were the commonest problem (39%), followed by reduced mental capacity (23%), disturbances of vision (18%), physical (16%) and psychological (4%) difficulties. The survey highlighted that only about half of the disabled had jobs, and 70 percent of the disabled remained illiterate; only six percent of disabled children who can hear and speak go to school (although this number is rapidly increasing) compared to 97 percent of the abled.

Facilities for the disabled vary enormously. An estimated 120 million disabled people living in poor countries could benefit from rehabilitation, but only 2-3 million of them are receiving services. Contrary to the belief that the most frequent special aid needed is a wheelchair, it is actually a hearing aid. Even among mobility aids, the greatest needs are for sticks and crutches.

While simple prevention and treatment at low cost is the cornerstone of management of disabilities, technological advances have released the potential of some disabled persons in more privileged circumstances. These include computers that can recognize voices or translate computer words into spoken words, and braille pads connected to terminals so that the blind can finger-read the screen.

Sources:
Disability Statistics Compendium, New York: United Nations (UN), Series Y, no 4, 1990; Marie, Chamie, 'Survey design strategies for the study of disability',*World Health Statistics Quarterly*, vol 42, no 3, 1989; Marie, Chamie, 'Aging, disability and gender', *Bold*, vol 2, no 1, 1991; World Health Organization (WHO), *Global Estimates for Health Situation Assessment and Projections*, Geneva: WHO, 1990; *World Health Statistics Annual 1990*, WHO, 1991; McLaren, D.S., 'Childhood blindness: a review and a caveat', *Medicine Digest Asia*, vol 9, no 7, July 1991; Ma, Zhiping, 'Welfare for disabled improving', *China Daily*, 16 April 1992.

Acknowledgements:
Dr Marie Chamie, Statistician, Demographic and Social Statistics Branch, UN Statistical Office.

27 YOUR MONEY OR YOUR LIFE

'Basic education and health for all are not just social expenditures but economic investments, not just indulgences which can only be afforded after countries have become prosperous but the foundations without which widespread prosperity will not be achieved.' UNICEF.

Lack of necessary finance remains a major stumbling block to improving global health. As the main map shows, a government target of spending as little as five percent of its income on health remains out of reach for most countries.

The symbols show that some countries have more than doubled their health spending since 1960, while in others it has fallen. In poor countries overall, it has increased from 1.0% to 1.4% of GNP, although in the poorest only from 0.7 % to 1.0 %.

The bar chart 'Kill or cure' contrasts the proportion spent by some of the highest military-spending governments on health and the military. Globally, there are only a minority of governments that spend more on health than on the military, and these are mainly the rich countries. In general, 40 percent of government spending in poor countries is devoted to the military and servicing of debt, twice as much as is spent on health and education combined. Nothing less than massive demilitarization would enable poor countries to redirect government funds towards improving health and welfare.

Globally, military expenditure shows no sign of abating; in fact, it is rising fast, at between 3-4 percent annually. Over US$1000 billion is spent on the military each year – US$860 billion in rich countries and US$170 billion in poor countries. No wonder then that in poor countries there are eight times as many soldiers as there are doctors, and health services remain under-funded.

Figures from only a few countries are available for the inset map 'State support' which shows what proportion of a nation's health bills are met by government. It is estimated that, overall, governments in rich countries provide 58 percent of health expenditure compared with a mere 40 percent in poor countries.

In an attempt to offset rising health care costs and increasing demand, governments are looking at other ways of financing health care. These include a fee-for-service, compulsory work insurance for work-related accidents and illness, private health insurance, employer subsidies, and subvented health facilities run by non-governmental organizations. Many poor countries are experimenting with private health insurance, which in Brazil and Mexico now covers almost the whole population. The governments of Rwanda, Zambia and Zimbabwe subsidize mission health services. Most poor countries now have fee-for-service health care, especially in urban areas. Such schemes are important in countries which cannot raise taxes to fund medical costs. In Africa about five percent of operating costs have been recouped by introducing charges, useful in financial terms, but a long way from solving the whole problem.

Charges present difficulties. For one thing, how can they be made for preventive health care, which often brings no immediate benefit to either government or individual, yet remains essential to long-term improvement in a community's health? Should those that can afford it pay more? Should a flat fee be applied to all services, or just a fee for drugs? Should there be any exemption for people who need more expensive drugs? In practice it is the poor for whom access becomes harder when charges are introduced. To identify the poor fairly or correctly is easier in theory than in practice as willingness to pay is not the same as ability to pay.

Medical costs are rising relentlessly everywhere in countries as diverse as China and the USA. China provides free medical care to all employees of government and state-run enterprises. The number of people covered has grown from four million 40 years ago to over 130 million today (ten percent of the population), and is increasing at one million a year. The costs to the state of this free medical treatment rose by 550 percent between 1978 and 1989 compared to a 100 percent rise in national income (GNP) – likened in the Chinese press to an 'out of control snowball'. At present, 16 percent of health care in Chinese cities is funded by the government in contrast to only three percent in rural areas.

In the USA, medical costs are rising twice as fast as the national income (GNP). In 1990, over 12% of GNP was spent on health, up from 9% in 1980, 7% in 1970, and 5% in 1960. Half of the increase in the 1980s was due to general inflation, 25 percent was due to medical care inflation and 25 percent was due to increases in the volume and intensity of medical services. Hospital care takes 38% of funds, 19% is spent on doctors' services, 8% on nursing home care, and 35% on other spending. Fewer and fewer people in the USA have health insurance. There are now 40 million people uninsured – the largest number in 25 years – mainly because of the costs of insurance. Over 20 percent of people in New Mexico and Texas have no health insurance. The newest class of uninsured are white, working age adults, many with middle and even high incomes.

There are large segments of health care that receive almost no funding from government. With some exceptions, government health spending is limited to 'Western' medical services. People themselves have to pay to consult the herbalist, bone-setter, acupuncturist or a holistic healer.

Sources:
United Nations Children's Fund (UNICEF), *The State of the World's Children 1992*, New York and Oxford: Oxford University Press for UNICEF, 1992; World Health Organization (WHO), *Global Estimates for Health Situation Assessment and Projections*, Geneva: WHO, 1990; World Bank, *World Development Report 1991*, Oxford: Oxford University Press, 1991; United Nations Development Programme (UNDP), *Human Development Report 1992*, New York and Oxford: Oxford University Press, 1992; 'Reporting on survey by Center for National Health Program Studies, the Cambridge Hospital', *The Nation's Health*, American Public Health Association, February 1992; 'Medical costs rising twice as fast as the economy's average', *The Nation's Health*, American Public Health Association, November 1991; Yang Pei-lin & James S. Lawson, 'Health care for a thousand million', *World Health Forum*, vol 12, 1991, Geneva: WHO; 'Costs of free medical care are out of control', *China Daily*, 25 January 1992; 'Dead end for free medical treatment', *China Daily*, 25 July 1991; Abel-Smith, Brian, 'Health economics, financing health for all', *World Health Forum*, vol 12, 1991, Geneva: WHO; 'Medical and health services and medical education in China today', Report of HKMA delegation to China, October 1987, Hong Kong Medical Association, February 1988.

Acknowledgements:
Dr Bernard Hausner, Senior Information Officer, UNDP, Dr Stacye Brown, Consultant, Population, Health and Nutrition Division, Population and Human Resources Department, The World Bank; Dr Beverley Carlson, Senior Adviser, Monitoring and Statistics, Programme Division, UNICEF.

28 A DOCTOR IN THE HOUSE?

This map portrays provision of 'doctors' and 'nurses' mainly within 'Western' medicine. The term 'doctor' usually includes registered practitioners and medical assistants: people who have had only partial training, but who perform many of the functions of a doctor, including simple operations. A 'nurse' usually includes all graduate, practical, assistant and auxiliary nurses, as well as para-professional health workers, first aid workers, traditional birth attendants and so on. Definitions vary a great deal between countries, so that comparisons should be treated with caution.

There are over 5 million doctors in the world, half a million dentists, almost 9 million nurses and 4 million other health personnel. They are distributed very unequally: almost half live in Europe which has less than 20 percent of the global population. South East Asia, which accounts for quarter of the world's population, has fewer than 8 percent of the world's doctors. The distribution is even more uneven looked at country by country. In rich countries there is one doctor for every few hundred people. In the poorest, more than 20,000 people have to share one doctor.

What the map cannot show are the inequalities within a country. These can also be extreme. In poor countries as many as 80 percent of the doctors may work in urban areas while 80 percent of the population lives in the countryside, often without any medical care whatsoever. The cost of training one doctor for an urban teaching hospital could train thousands of paramedics to work in rural health care.

There is on average one nurse for every 150 people in rich countries in contrast to only one for every 5000 people in the poorest countries. The job of nurse varies considerably throughout the world. In rich countries nurses may be highly specialized and work with extremely complicated technological equipment, for example, in intensive care units. In rural areas in poor countries, often in the absence of any doctor, they may take total responsibility for basic health care and for referring the sick to the next level of care.

Because this map is concerned only with 'Western' medicine, most of the world's health care workers do not actually appear. It excludes the village elder who dispenses valuable advice to the young, the untrained nurse who cares for the elderly, the acupuncturist, the holistic healer, the bone-setters, the spiritual healing counsellors, the parents and family who look after sick children and each other.

Sources:

The World Bank, *World Development Report 1991*, Oxford University Press, 1991; United Nations Development Programme (UNDP), *Human Development Report 1992*, New York and Oxford: Oxford University Press, 1992; Health Manpower Data Base of the Centre de Sociologie et de Demographie Medicales, personal communication, March 1992; *World Health Statistics Annual 1988*, Geneva: WHO; *Global Estimates for Health Situations Assessment and Projections*, Geneva: WHO, 1990.

Acknowledgements:

Dr Bui Dang Ha Doan, Director, Centre de Sociologie et de Demographie Medicales, Paris; Dr Stacye Brown, Consultant, Population, Health and Nutrition Division, Population and Human Resources Department, The World Bank: Dr Beverley Carlson, Senior Adviser, Monitoring and Statistics, Programme Division, UNICEF; Dr Bernard Hausner, Senior Information Officer, UNDP.

29 STITCH IN TIME

As stated on the map, 'access' to health services is defined by the World Health Organization as the proportion of the population that can reach appropriate local health services on foot or by the local means of transport in no more than one hour. This definition does not relate to whether people could afford the health care if they were to get there but simply to whether such facilities exist. Nor does it include, as this is not known, access to traditional forms of health care.

In many poor countries, less than half the people have access to health care. The symbol shows, not surprisingly, that rural people in poor countries are particularly disadvantaged. For example, in most of South America, 80-90 percent of the urban population has access to health care in contrast to less than 40 percent of the rural population. A large differential also exists in much of Africa.

China is the remarkable exception. The three-tier health system in China, incorporating traditional doctors as well as 'Western-trained' doctors, was designed to take health care to the people. By committing funding and personnel to the rural health clinics, China has become the model for other poor countries. Eighty percent of China's rural population have access to health care, and 94% of women are attended in childbirth by a trained attendant, in contrast to between 30-50% in most other poor countries (see **3. Perils of Pregnancy**; inset map 'You're on your own').

Other countries are following this example. Since it became independent in 1972, Bangladesh has raised government expenditure on the rural health clinics which serve the great majority of the people from 10 percent to 60 percent. But in general the 80% of people who live in rural areas in poor countries remain neglected by the central government. It is not uncommon for 75% of a government's public health spending to serve the richest 25% of the population. Most resources go to expensive trained doctors and elite hospitals in urban areas.

The inset 'Back to basics' shows that in 1987 only a minority of health funding was spent on primary health care. Since then, the total percentage of national income spent on health as a whole has not increased, but the proportion devoted to primary health care is progressively increasing.

Sources:

United Nations Children's Fund (UNICEF), *The State of the World's Children, 1992*, New York and Oxford: Oxford University Press for UNICEF, 1992; World Health Organization (WHO), *Global Estimates for Health Situation Assessment and Projections*, Geneva: WHO, 1990; *World Health Statistics Annual, 1989*, Geneva: WHO.

Acknowledgements:

Dr Beverley Carlson, Senior Adviser, Monitoring and Statistics, Programme Division, UNICEF; Dr Bernard Hausner, Senior Information Officer, UNDP.

30 HEALTH AID

Aid is there; it is floating around – billions of dollars of it. But little is being spent on the fundamental essentials for improving the economy of poor countries – primary health, primary education and population programmes. In addition, the global share of aid earmarked for health projects has fallen over the last decade.

This map shows who gives and who receives aid. The donors' contribution represents Official Development Assistance (ODA). This is the net distribution of loans and grants made on concessional financial terms by official agencies of the 18 high income members of the Organisation for Economic Co-operation and Development (OECD) and the Organization of Petroleum Exporting Countries (OPEC), to promote economic development and welfare. The definition is meant to exclude purely military assistance, but the borderline is sometimes blurred.

The recipients' portion represents ODA received from all sources, not only the OECD and OPEC. But as 85 percent of total aid comes from the 18 high-income members of the OECD alone (not including OPEC countries) the figures give a fair comparison.

Worldwide ODA totals about US$55 billion a year. The donors of the largest total sums are Japan, the USA and then France. But the map shows the amount of aid given as a percentage share of the donor country's own national income (GNP) in which case the USA gives less than half the OECD average of 0.33 percent of GNP donated by all OECD countries. Countries that give the highest percentage of their own GNP are Norway, Sweden, Denmark and the Netherlands. Most OPEC countries contribute much less, although Saudi Arabia is a major donor, giving 1.46 percent of GNP.

Only about 5% of this aid is given to health and population programmes. A mere 1% of all international aid goes to primary health care systems which could prevent or treat 80% of the disease, malnutrition and early deaths in poor countries; another 1% goes to family planning services and 3% goes to all other health care.

Of additional funding, not shown on the map, from international agencies such as the UN agencies, the World Bank and the European Community, 8% is allocated for health and population programmes. World Bank aid for population, health and nutrition programmes has grown rapidly in recent years, increasing to 7% of all World Bank aid in 1991, up from 4.5% in 1990 and 0.3% in 1987.

The inset 'Wide of the mark?' shows that some countries earmark aid more wisely than others. The proportion of total aid allocated to 'basic needs' – defined as primary health care, primary and secondary education, family planning, rural water supply and sanitation – varies widely. Some aid is spent wisely: the pie chart shows that China is a good example of appropriate use of health aid, using the money principally for primary health care and preventive care, rather than funding projects which primarily benefit urban elites.

The value of aid from rich to poor countries is more than negated by capital flow in the opposite direction. Each year, repayment of capital and interest on loans costs poor countries three times more than they receive in aid, and this net financial transfer from poor to rich countries is increasing, an issue highlighted at the 1992 Earth Summit held in Rio de Janeiro.

Poor countries owe the banks and governments of rich countries as much as US$1,320 billion, half their collective national income (GNP). The most severely indebted countries now owe the equivalent of their combined GNP. Further debt and servicing restructurings and reductions will be necessary if these countries are to have any hope of financing improved health care. Countries with the greatest total external debt are Brazil, Mexico, Argentina, India and Indonesia.

A further problem is that arms imports by poor countries absorb the equivalent of 75 percent of all aid received by poor countries as a whole. The total developing country debt in the early 1990s has been estimated to be about the same as the annual military budget of the world. The total debt of poor countries could be written off in only a few years by an annual 20 percent cut in military spending.

Sources:
United Nations Children's Fund (UNICEF), *The State of the World's Children 1992*, New York and Oxford: Oxford University Press for UNICEF, 1992; World Health Organization (WHO), *Global Estimates for Health Situation Assessment and Projections*, Geneva: WHO, 1990; The World Bank, *World Development Report, 1991*, Oxford: Oxford University Press, 1991; WHO, *Investors in Health: Health as a Determinant of Sustainable Development*, Geneva: Office of External Coordination Planning, Coordination and Cooperation, Geneva: WHO, 1991; Vaillancourt, Denise, Janet Nassim, Stacye Brown, *Population, Health, and Nutrition: Fiscal 1991 Sector Review*, Population and Human Resources, The World Bank.

Acknowledgements:
Dr Stacye Brown, Consultant, Population, Health and Nutrition Division, Population and Human Resources Department,

The World Bank; Dr Beverley Carlson, Senior Adviser, Monitoring and Statistics, Programme Division, UNICEF; Foreign Loan Office, Ministry of Public Health, People's Republic of China; Dr Jean-Pierre Poullier, Chief, Statistics Section; Mr Bevan B. Stein, Head, Reporting Systems Division; Yasmin Ahmad, Creditor Reporting System, OECD.

31 COMPLEMENTARY MEDICINE

The term 'complementary' medicine refers to a wide range of medical systems other than 'Western' medicine. Practitioners of complementary medicine include village healers, acupuncturists, homeopaths, naturopaths, practitioners of traditional medicine and spiritual healers.

Only scanty information exists for either traditional medicine or the new holistic approach to health. There are no global data on the numbers practising complementary medicine. WHO estimates that 80 percent of people in the world rely chiefly on traditional medicine for their primary health care needs.

The only 'complementary' health system for which worldwide data are available is chiropractic, which claims recognition as the third largest primary health care system in the Western world after medicine and dentistry. Chiropractic (Greek: 'treatment by hand') emerged as a separate profession in the USA one hundred years ago, and the main map shows that its 54,000 qualified practitioners are now located in 50 countries, with 25 training colleges in seven countries.

Treatment emphasizes joint adjustment, other manual techniques, lifestyle modification and exercises. Chiropracters make no use of drugs or surgery, but will refer patients for medical care when those interventions are necessary. Their principle interest is the relationship between impaired movement of the spinal vertebrae and the nervous system, and the effect of this on health. Information from Canada, New Zealand, the UK and the USA shows that 80 percent of the work of chiropractors relates to musculoskeletal pain, 10 percent to headaches and migraine, and the remaining 10 percent to a variety of other problems.

Homeopathy was developed in Germany by Dr Samuel Hahnemann in 1807 as a reaction against the bloodletting and harsh pharmacy of the day. Observing that taking the cinchona bark reproduced symptoms of malaria, he developed a theory that 'like cures like'. He also believed that to bring about healing the smallest possible dose of medicine should be used in order to stimulate the body's own life force. The inset map 'Spread of homeopathy' shows its spread across the world during the 19th century.

Official recognition still varies country by country but the inset 'Homeopathy in India' illustrates its popularity there. There are reported to be 14,000 practitioners of homeopathy in Pakistan, 1500 in Nepal, 300 in the former USSR and 93 in the Netherlands (where a further thousand Western-trained doctors occasionally prescribe homeopathic medicines).

Traditional medicine refers to the therapeutic practices that have been in existence long before the development and spread of 'scientific' medicine, and which have succeeded over the centuries through a process of trial and error. Given the limited access of many poor countries to 'Western' health care and given the shortage of pharmaceutical drugs and products (see notes to **33. The Medicine Cabinet**), the World Health Organization adopted a resolution in 1977 urging governments to evaluate and utilize traditional forms of healing.

Only a few countries, most notably China, have integrated traditional medicine into their national health system. The rural clinics, the pharmacies, and even the Chinese Pharmacopoeia on medicines and drugs have 'Western' and traditional sections side by side. Other countries, like Bangladesh, India, Nepal, the Philippines, Sri Lanka and the Sudan, have strengthened the role of traditional medicine in their health systems. This integration has not met with much success in Africa, where in most countries it remains a form of private practice outside the formal health system. WHO encourages greater investigation and recognition of traditional medicine. There are now 27 WHO Collaborating Centres for Traditional Medicine throughout the world – 5 in Africa, 3 in the Americas, 1 in the Eastern Mediterranean, 3 in Europe, and 15 in Asia. But in general the relationship between Western medicine and other health systems has been an uneasy one, sometimes hostile.

People in rich countries who are turning to holistic health (and again no comprehensive data exist) are often critical of the bias of 'Western' medicine towards technology. They believe that treatment by the knife and by pills often masks, and leaves unresolved, an underlying problem. They are asking 'Why did I get sick? Has some germ singled me out or is my immune system below par and not functioning properly enough to ward off illness? Is my nutrition poor? Am I over-worked? What is the real cause of my problem?' They are searching for more natural and conservative methods of maintaining and improving health rather than simply treating disease, such as better nutrition, fitness, and the adoption of a positive outlook, inward and outward on the world.

Many of us would like to believe in these modalities, but there is as yet little scientific, documented proof of their usefulness. Is such evaluation appropriate? Perhaps some aspects of healthy living cannot be evaluated – how can a massage, a walk in the woods or spiritual healing be subject to a randomized, double-blind trial?

The ideal would be for 'Western', traditional and 'alternative' medicine to complement each other. There is a need for the ambulance at the bottom of the cliff to care for the people who fall off, but an equal need for other health practitioners to be at the top of the cliff, finding out why they did it and how it could have been prevented.

Sources:
Farnsworth, Norman R., et al, 'Medicinal plants in therapy', *Bulletin of WHO*, 63 (6), 1985; Chapman Smith, David, ed., *The Chiropractic Report*, vol 2, no 3, March 1988; 'Alternative therapy', British Medical Association, Report of the Board of Science and Education, May 1986; 44th World Health Assembly, *Traditional medicine and modern health care*, A44/10, 22 March 1991, Geneva: WHO; 'Hanuman and the healing herb', *World Health*, June 1983, Geneva: WHO; *Traditional Medicine*, Global Medium-Term Programme, Programme, 12. 4, 1990-1995, December 1987, TRM/HTP/87.1, Geneva: WHO; Akerele, Olayiwola, 'Traditional medicine and primary health care: a time for re-assessment and re-direction', *Curare*, vol 13, 1990. Dr J.P. Puri, Homeopathic Association of India, personal communication.

Acknowledgements:
Dr David Chapman-Smith, World Federation of Chiropractic, Toronto; Dr Donald Petersen, *Dynamic Chiropractic*, Toronto; Dr Barry Decker, Vital Life Centre, Hong Kong; Dr J.P. Puri, Homeopathic Association of India, Dr Olayiwola Akerele, Programme Manager, Traditional Medicine Programme, WHO.

32 CONTRASTING FORTUNES

X-ray services aid in the diagnosis of illness. The distribution of the 440,000 X-ray units in the world roughly correlates with the distribution in numbers of physicians and with the wealth of a country. For instance in the Ivory Coast there are nearly 200,000 people per X-ray machine compared to less than 2000 in the USA. The map shows how much the numbers of X-ray examinations per 1000 population vary, even in rich countries. For example there are almost double the numbers of X-rays taken in the USA than in the UK. There are little data from poor countries, but 70 percent of the world's population has either no or only limited access to X-ray services.

This is not to suggest, however, that all countries should aspire to having a high number of X-ray examinations per person. In rich countries, X-ray services account for 6-10 percent of all health care expenditure, but it would be far more appropriate for poor countries to concentrate on immunization programmes or simple primary health care in the rural areas than to spend scarce resources on expensive technology and machinery for urban elites.

While the data on the main map combine all types of X-ray diagnosis, the inset 'On screen' shows that the frequency of diagnostic X-ray examinations of specific parts of the body also varies considerably. To a degree this reflects the different diagnostic techniques available in different countries, but it also reflects the differing patterns of disease throughout the world. Mammography (X-ray examination of the breast) is shown as being performed between four to eight times more commonly in the UK, Holland, France, Italy and the USA than it is in Japan; this is entirely appropriate as breast cancer in Japan is very rare. Conversely, the Japanese carry out a very large number of X-ray investigations on the stomach (nearly nine times the UK frequency), but stomach cancer is the top cause of can- **123** cer deaths in Japan, with rates more than double those in the UK.

Some countries use 'mass chest screening' for diagnosing tuberculosis. 'On screen' also shows that the Japanese carry out chest X-ray examinations nearly four times as frequently as most European countries. But Japan has about 55,000 new cases of tuberculosis each year compared to 10,000 in France and 6000 in the UK. The rates per 100,000 population are 46 in Japan, 19 in France and 11 in the UK. China, not shown, performs double the number of chest screening X-rays as Japan, but China has over two million new cases of tuberculosis a year, an incidence rate of 191 per 100,000 people (see **20. Spitting Blood**).

New diagnostic tools such as CT scans (computerized tomography) and magnetic resonance imaging (NMRI) are now widely used in rich countries. The more powerful X-rays used for cancer radiotherapy treatment are only available in 70 percent of countries, and the modern, more sophisticated, nuclear medicine services in 50 percent. Where these facilities exist in poor countries they are mainly in the capital or major cities; they are often used by untrained personnel; and they often lack facilities for upkeep and repair.

Although diagnostic X-ray examinations give undoubted benefits, they need to be weighed against a certain risk. All exposure to ionizing radiation (of which X-rays are part) convey some risk, such as a slightly increased risk of contracting cancer. The risk from a single X-ray examination or even several X-rays is quite small, but it is not zero. While the benefit normally far outweighs this, X-rays and X-ray doses should clearly be kept to an absolute minimum. In the UK, surveys have shown that patient doses for the same X-ray examination can vary by factors of 10 or more at different hospitals. As poor X-ray machine design and inadequate maintenance contribute to patient dose, this risk will be borne disproportionately by poorer countries.

The inset 'Radiation' shows that most radiation comes from natural sources, and only 12-15 percent comes from medical X-rays. But among artificial sources of radiation, the average European will receive at least ten times more radiation in his or her lifetime from diagnostic medical procedures than from all other sources of manufactured radiation combined (including Chernobyl). The use of radiography will increase as populations age, especially in rich countries, as older people tend to require more diagnostic and radionuclide investigations.

Sources:
United Nations Scientific Committee on the Effects of Atomic Radiation (UNSCEAR), 1958, 1962, 1972, 1977, 1982, 1988; Bennett, B.G., 'Exposures from medical radiation worldwide', *Radiation Protection Dosimetry*, vol 36, 1991; Mettler, F.A., et al., 'Analytical modelling of world-wide medical radiation use', *Health Physics*, 52, 1987; Contento, G. et al., 'A comparison of diagnostic radiology practice and patient exposure in Britain, France and Italy', *British Journal of Radiology*, 61, 1988; Wall, B.F., 'British medical X-ray statistics and their relevance for radiation protection policies', (*Statistics of Human Exposure to Ionising Radiation) Radiation Protection Dosimetry*, 36, nos 2-4, 1991; *Global Estimates for Health Situation Assessment and Projections, 1990*, Geneva: WHO.

Acknowledgements:
For data for the map and other information: Dr Barrie Lambert, St Bartholomew's Hospital, London.

33 THE MEDICINE CABINET

The quarter of the world's population living in rich countries consume more than three quarters of the world's pharmaceutical drugs. In some countries of Europe and North America, nearly US$300 is spent per person per year on pharmaceuticals, in contrast to US$5 in poor countries; in some parts of sub-Saharan Africa the figure is only US$1.

High expenditure on pharmaceuticals does not necessarily give optimum value. In the USA, which is a heavy spender, life expectancy is shorter and other health indices are poorer than in countries spending much less on drugs – for example, Hong Kong, Spain, Sweden, the Netherlands and Norway. Conversely, while the map shows that low spending on pharmaceuticals is generally confined to poor countries whose health is also poor, China has demonstrated that health can be improved without heavy reliance on expensive drugs.

Approximately half the world's population still lacks regular access to the most basic

drugs. About 80 percent of countries have no proper system of procurement and distribution, and the latter is often far from fair. Too often scant resources are spent on expensive drugs for the privileged few while people in the countryside go without.

The inset 'New drugs' shows the World Health Organization's guidelines on the less than 300 'essential drugs' needed by countries with limited resources. WHO suggests that village health posts need only 10-15 drugs, district hospitals about 100, and teaching hospitals 200 drugs. The cost of medicines per person in primary health care (health centre level, two visits per year) should be approximately US$1. Thus, countries with limited finances are advised to put their drug resources into immunization and essential drugs (which include contraceptive drugs and devices such as condoms), and to make these available for the whole population. This modest essential drugs list is in contrast to the 1500 new pharmaceutical products – virtually all researched and introduced by the pharmaceutical companies – that are launched onto the market each year. However, closer inspection reveals these include only about 50 new chemical entities; most 'new' medicines are reformulations of old products.

There is no doubt that pharmaceutical products (including immunizations: see **35. Catching Them Young**) have had a major impact on the relief of pain, disablement and distress. Modern products enable women to plan their families more reliably than ever before; analgesics play an important role in enabling people with terminal pain to die more comfortably or in relieving the intense pain of shingles; anti-epileptic drugs and antidepressants (properly used) have reduced invalidism and enabled those affected to function socially; nowadays children in Western countries rarely develop brain abscesses following a middle ear infection, because the ear infection is promptly treated with an antibiotic; medicines for duodenal ulcers substantially reduce the need for surgery; insulin sustains the lives of young diabetics; anaesthetics enable surgery to be performed without awareness of pain, which has revolutionized the treatment of injuries and accidents. Few people would choose to have a broken bone set, an amputation or a stomach operation without anaesthesia.

But there is no medicine known that is without some potential side effect. In general, between one to three in every 100 hospital admissions are due to drug reactions, which may range from skin eruptions to, in the extreme, death. In spite of the thousands of medicines prescribed, drug reactions usually result from very few drugs: antibiotics, aspirin, digoxin, diuretics, heparin, insulin, prednisolone and warfarin. Those most at risk are the very young and the very old, those with previous drug reactions, babies in the womb, and those who are taking several medicines together. The risk of side effects in poor countries is higher, because instructions on taking the medicines may not be included or, if they are, are often not in the local language or are insufficiently comprehensive.

A further problem, and not a new one, is the misuse of legal medicines by both the medical profession and by the consumer. Historically, herbal, mineral and metal-based medicines have all been misused. Energetic purging, for example used for many complaints, often left the sufferer worse off than before. In the early 1990s, pharmaceutical products are sometimes aggressively promoted to doctors, who as a result may prescribe needlessly expensive or inappropriate drugs, giving antibiotics for the common cold, for example. This can lead to the emergence of resistant strains of bacteria. Many people medicalize their lives, relying on a pill to start and end their day. But this may mean one fails to address the underlying cause of malaise.

Legal drugs that affect feelings, like tranquillizers and sleeping tablets, have been seriously abused for centuries. In 1987-88 there were over 22 million reported cases of abuse of legal drugs, often in combination with alcohol and other substances.

It is an erroneous belief that herbal drugs are without problems. There is less difference between herbal and manufactured pharmaceutical medicines than many people realize. Most 'Western' medicines were extracted from plants until very recently, when technology enabled herbal extracts to be produced synthetically in the laboratory, which subsequently led to the manufacture of additional chemical compounds. However, remedies from nature are still sought and used in 'Western' medicine, such as the new cancer treatment drug extracted from the bark of the Pacific yew tree, and refined by research and pharmaceutical organizations.

It is not possible to guess at the wealth of medicinal plants used by people in poor countries; only a fraction have been studied. The WHO Collaborating Centre for Traditional

Medicine in the University of Illinois has established a computerized database on medicinal uses of natural products. The US National Institutes of Health are currently investigating 4500 plant specimens from Africa, South America and Asia, from which it is estimated that between three and thirty wholly new drugs will be discovered. A search for a treatment for AIDS has added new impetus to this task, and the Illinois Centre together with another WHO Collaborating Centre in Stockholm, are coordinating the task of scanning herbal remedies for anti-AIDS potential.

Exactly who will benefit financially – and this could be measured in millions if not billions of dollars – from any successful discoveries of new medicinal compounds from plant sources in poor countries is an intriguing question. Environmental treaties protecting plant resources and rain forests are forcing into the open the question as to whether the poor country has 'ownership' over these resources, or whether the biotechnical industries in the rich countries have unlimited rights of access, development, marketing, patents and profits. Rich countries should be concerned that the global destruction of forests will cause the loss of healing medicines. Poor countries are equally concerned, as they cannot afford to buy 'Western' pharmaceutical products to replace the missing herbal remedies.

Sources:
World Health Statistics Annual 1990, Geneva: WHO; World Health Organization (WHO) *Global Estimates for Health Situation Assessment and Projections*, 1990, Geneva: WHO; *Action Programme on Essential Drugs*, Report for the Biennium 1990-1991, WHO DAP/MAC(4)/92.4, Geneva: WHO, February 1992; 'The use of essential drugs', WHO, (Sixth List). *Technical Report Series* 796, Geneva: WHO, 1990; 44th World Health Assembly, *Traditional Medicine and Modern Health Care*, A44/10. 22 March 1991, Geneva: WHO; Akerele, O., 'Medicinal plants and primary health care: an agenda for action', *Fitoterapia.*, vol LIX, no 5, 1988; 'Hanuman and the healing herb', *World Health*, June 1983, Geneva: WHO.

Acknowledgements:
Dr F.S. Antezana, Director, and Dr German Velasquez, Drug Action Programme, WHO; Addiction Research Foundation, Toronto; Dr Jane Ferguson, Technical Officer, Adolescent Health Programme, WHO; Dr Olayiwola Akerele, Programme Manager, Traditional Medicine Programme, WHO; Mr Cheng Siang Pang, Singapore.

34 TRAINING AND RESEARCH

The map shows the location of 1351 medical schools for the training of doctors in 'Western' medicine in 127 countries. The size of these medical schools varies, both in terms of student numbers, and in numbers of hospital beds available for teaching. Some countries have a large number of small schools, for example: India has 106 medical schools, mostly with under 1000 beds; similarly Japan's 80 schools average just over 900 beds. However, the opposite situation exists in Albania, which has just one medical school of over 18,000 beds. Most countries have a range of different sized schools, and generally student numbers are roughly related to the numbers of beds.

Some of Europe's medical schools were established centuries ago: for example St Bartholomew's in London (1123), Montpelier (1180), Bologna and Oxford (13th century), Prague (1348), Krakow (1364), Vienna (1365) and Heidelberg (1390). However, most medical schools date from the middle of the 20th century.

The symbol on the map and all three insets relate to medical research – the countries of origin of scientific papers, the principal topics researched, health and pharmaceutical patents, the amount of money given to research. By medical research is meant research into the causes, patterns and prevention of diseases; testing and usefulness of diagnostic investigations; evaluation of the effectiveness of treatments, for example, surgical and medical procedures, pharmaceutical drugs; and economic analysis of cost-effectiveness of different procedures and treatment.

In general it has been 'Western' medicine that has embraced the need for scientific research. Traditional health systems have established themselves by the tests of time rather than by laboratory testing or statistical investigation. However, traditional herbal remedies are currently being scientifically investigated (see notes to **31. Complementary Medicine**; **33. The Medicine Cabinet**).

The 'book' symbol utilizes a large database (CHI) with international coverage of 3100 scientific publications to obtain comparisons of published medical research in two main categories: those with direct clinical relevance, and those of a more basic biological nature. In 1988 the USA accounted for 40% of the world's 175,731 research publications for clinical medicine, the next highest share of 11% belonged to the UK. For biomedical research the situation was similar, with the USA accounting for 38% of the world's 75,219 publications and the UK 8%. The database is biased, however, towards journals in the English language.

The inset 'Research priorities' lists the numbers of papers on medical topics published in 3700 of the world's most influential journals. The largest numbers of papers are on general clinical medicine, followed by basic biology, brain and behaviour, medical drugs, immunology and heart and lung diseases. What is not shown is that 1981-90 output has increased most in anaesthesia, intensive care, and heart and lung medicine, reflecting the growing importance of these areas.

Research is not only carried out within universities but also in many other research centres within public and private agencies and foundations. The inset 'Patents' is an indirect indication of research carried out principally in the commercial sector. In 1988 the category 'health, agriculture, food' accounted for 6527 out of a total of 52,720 European Community (EC) patents and 11,491 out of a total of 85,413 US patents. As shown, the majority were from the USA and EC countries, but Germany and Japan are taking an increasing share of both. Similarly, almost half of the 1950 pharmaceutical patents in the USA were from the home country, other countries strong in this field being Japan, Germany and the UK.

Research priorities can also be assessed by the amount of funding they receive. In 1992, the US Congress approved US$9 billion for the National Institutes of Health and US$3 billion for the Alcohol, Drug Abuse & Mental Health Administration, money beyond the wildest dreams of most other countries. The stalwarts of research funding are cancer and heart disease, but AIDS funding has now put heart disease into third place. 'The ratings' inset shows that while these three illnesses receive the most in dollar terms, the amount spent for each death varies greatly.

This US research money is not confined to the USA: the National Institutes of Health, often dubbed the flagship research enterprise of the USA, spend over US $100 million, or 1.5 percent of their total budget, on international activities, more than many national governments allocate to their own country. Canada receives most, followed by Japan, the UK, Israel and China. In contrast, many research agencies, for example, in the UK and France (and other health organizations in the USA), get little research funding from their governments. They are driven to raise money by donations, from street shops selling used clothes, bequests, direct mail and television appeals.

Money spent on drug research by all the pharmaceutical companies worldwide has been estimated at US$18 billion per year and is constantly rising, far outstripping even the US government's contribution.

Overall, rich countries spend US$30 per person per year (US$30 billion) on health-related research, a hundred times more than the US$0.30 per capita spent by the poor countries. In Africa, research has declined by 35 percent in the last 20 years and *Science* reports that 'faculty salaries are so low that most teachers have to supplement their wages by driving taxis or raising chickens'. Only five percent of the world's scientists work in poor countries, and they are part of a constant 'brain drain'.

Sources:
World Health Organization Medical Schools Directory, 6th ed, 1988; *Science et Technologie Indicateurs 1992*, Paris: Observatoire des Sciences et des Techniques; World Health Organization (WHO), *Global Estimates for Health Situation Assessment and Projections, 1990*, Geneva: WHO; 'Funding focus: cancer, Alzheimer's top research priorities', *Medical Research Funding News*, 13 November 1991; *Science*, vol 253, 1991, *British Medical Journal*, vol 303, September 1991; *The Hong Kong Association of the Pharmaceutical Industry Bulletin*, no 35, December 1991; Norman, Colin, et al 'Science budget: selective growth', *Science*, 7 February 1992; Stout, Hilary, 'Grim debate: adequacy of spending on AIDS is an issue not easily resolved', *Wall Street Journal*, April 1992; Anderson, Alun, 'Funding in Europe: how the big three cope', *Science*, November 1991; 'Top 10 NIH international research & training award recipients', NIH *Annual Report of International Activities*, fiscal year 1990; 'Biotechnology, critical care, computing top list of fast-growth fields in science', *Science Watch*, October 1991; *Science Indicators Database*, ISI, 1981-90; Cozzens, Susan, 'Literature-based data in research evaluation: a manager's guide to bibliometrics', SPSG concept paper no 11, 1990.

Acknowledgements:
For data for the map and other information: Harriet Muir Moxham and Lesley A. Rogers, The Wellcome Trust, London, who wish to thank Joe Anderson, The Wellcome Trust and Remi Barre, of the Observatoire des Sciences et des Techniques, Paris.

35 CATCHING THEM YOUNG

It is difficult to comprehend the global success of the immunization of infants. In 1974, when the WHO Expanded Programme on Immunization (EPI) programme was launched, immunization services were virtually non-existent in poor countries and less than five percent of infants were immunized. Now, in less than twenty years, 80 percent of all infants in the world are immunized against the major diseases of diphtheria, whooping cough, tetanus, measles, polio and tuberculosis.

This immunization programme has provided a major breakthrough not only in protecting children, but also in training half a million health workers and initiating regular contact between health services and the family.

A wide range of organizations have collaborated in an unprecedented manner, including the World Health Organization (WHO), the United Nations Children's Fund (UNICEF), the World Bank, the United Nations Development Programme (UNDP) and Rotary International. UNICEF is the largest supplier of the vaccines used. Rotary International has mobilized hundreds of thousands of members in almost all countries to provide volunteers and raise well over US$200 million in support of immunization against polio – the largest fund-raising effort ever undertaken by a voluntary service organization in support of a specific cause. The World Health Organization has commented that this coalition reflects a remarkable consensus in a world when so many things go wrong: children should be immunized, children can be immunized, children will be immunized.

While the lives of over three million infants a year are now being saved by immunization, this still represents less than one third of immunization's potential contribution to world health. Two million children still die because they are not immunized with currently available vaccines (at an average cost of US $13 per head). A further five to six million die from diseases which could be prevented by the development of new vaccines, such as AIDS, Japanese encephalitis, influenza B and hepatitis A.

It is sombre to reflect that all the children born in all the poor countries of the world could each year be immunized for less than the amount spent annually on cigarette advertising in the USA.

Sources:
United Nations Children's Fund (UNICEF), *The State of the World's Children 1992*, New York and Oxford: Oxford University Press for UNICEF, 1992; World Health Organization (WHO), *Global Estimates for Health Situation Assessment and Projections*, *1990*, Geneva: WHO; The World Bank, *World Development Report 1991*, Oxford: Oxford University Press, 1991; Foege, William H. & Donald A. Henderson, 'Management priorities in primary health care', Walsh, Julia A., & Kenneth S. Warren, *Strategies for Primary Health Care*, Chicago and London: The University of Chicago Press, 1986; *World Health Statistics Annuals, 1988 and 1990*, Geneva: WHO.

Acknowledgements:
Dr Beverley Carlson, Senior Adviser, Monitoring and Statistics, Programme Division, UNICEF; Mrs Carole Torel, Technical Officer, Expanded Programme on Immunization, WHO.